The Parks and Mountains of Colorado

The Parks and Mountains of Colorado

A Summer Vacation in the Switzerland of America, 1868

By SAMUEL BOWLES

With an Introduction and Notes
by James H. Pickering

UNIVERSITY OF OKLAHOMA PRESS
NORMAN AND LONDON

Other Books Written or Edited by James H. Pickering

James Fenimore Cooper, *The Spy: A Tale of the Neutral Ground* (New Haven, Conn., 1971)

Fiction 100: An Anthology of Short Stories (New York, 1974, 1978, 1985, 1988, and 1992)

The World Turned Upside Down: The Prose and Poetry of the American Revolution (New York, 1975)

The City in American Literature (New York, 1977)

Literature: An Anthology (Jeffrey D. Hoeper, coed.) (New York, 1982, 1986, and 1990)

Enos A. Mills, *Wildlife on the Rockies* (Lincoln, Nebr., 1988)

Library of Congress Cataloging-in-Publication Data

Bowles, Samuel, 1826–1878.
[Switzerland of America]
The parks and mountains of Colorado : a summer vacation in the Switzerland of America, 1868 / by Samuel Bowles ; with an introduction and notes by James H. Pickering.
p. cm.
Originally published: The Switzerland of America. Springfield, Mass.: Bowles & Co., 1869.
Includes bibliographical references (p.) and index.
ISBN 0-8061-2408-3
1. Colorado—Description and travel—To 1876. 2. Bowles, Samuel, 1826–1878—Journeys—Colorado. I. Pickering, James H. II. Title.
F780.B77 1992
917.8804'2—dc20 91-28589
CIP

The paper in this book meets the guidelines for permanence and durability of the Committee on Production Guidelines for Book Longevity of the Council on Library Resources, Inc.∞

CONTENTS

ILLUSTRATIONS

EDITOR'S ACKNOWLEDGMENTS

IN recovering the history of Colorado as it was in 1868, I have benefited from the help of many people, and I would like to acknowledge them here: the staff of the Colorado Historical Society; William R. Baldwin, University of Houston; Director Robin Downes and the members of the Interlibrary Loan Department of the University of Houston's M. D. Anderson Library; Alexander Drummond, Ward, Colorado; Lynne K. Fonteneau, Williams College Library; Nancy Leonard, New-York Historical Society; Valerie McQuillan, Connecticut Valley Historical Museum; Thomas J. Noel, University of Colorado at Denver; David Null, General Library, University of New Mexico; Katherine Phillips, Boston Public Library; Duane A. Smith, Fort Lewis College, Durango, Colorado; Monica Vigil, *Rocky Mountain News* library; Cassandra M. Volpe, University Libraries, University of Colorado at Boulder; Stephen G. Weisner, Springfield Technical Community College, Springfield, Massachusetts; and the staff of the Western History Department, Denver Public Library. I am particularly indebted to Jim Benedict of Ward, Colorado, a student of Colorado in his own right, who one quiet May evening not so long ago took down a copy of Bowles's *Switzerland* from his study shelf, handed it to me, and said that here was "a little gem" that ought to be back in print.

JAMES H. PICKERING

Houston, Texas

The Parks and Mountains of Colorado

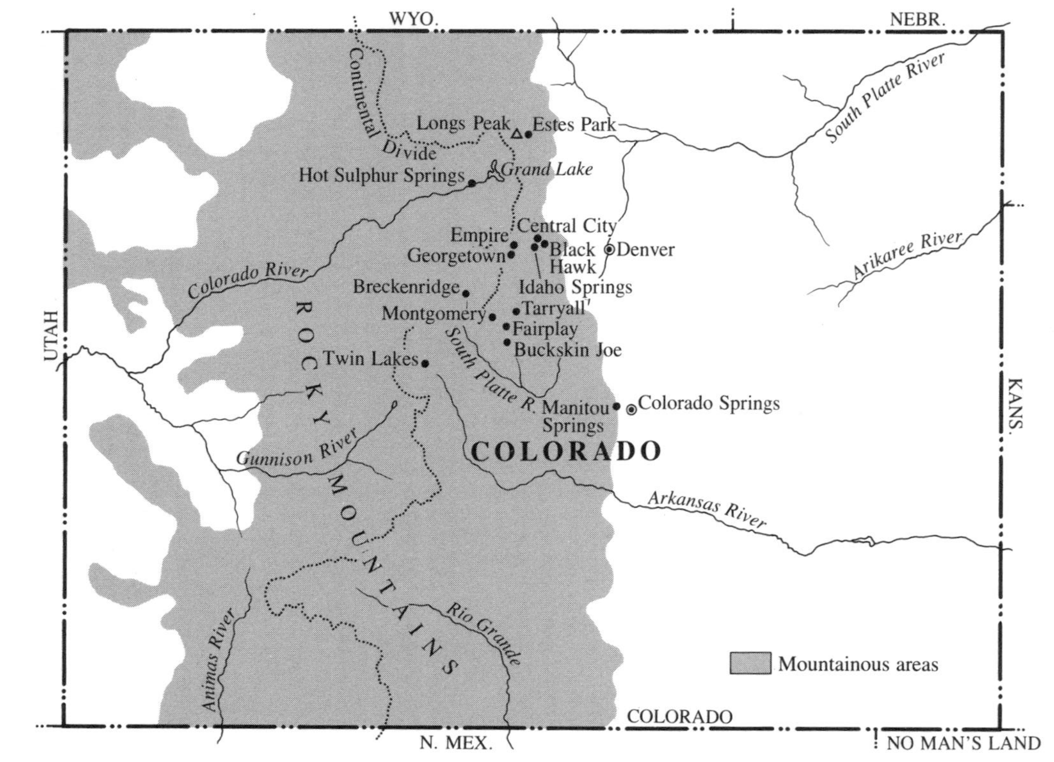
WYO.
NEBR.
UTAH
KANS.
N. MEX.
COLORADO
NO MAN'S LAND
Continental Divide
Longs Peak
Estes Park
South Platte River
Hot Sulphur Springs
Grand Lake
Arikaree River
Empire
Central City
Black Hawk
Denver
Georgetown
Colorado River
Breckenridge
Idaho Springs
Montgomery
Tarryall
Fairplay
Buckskin Joe
Twin Lakes
ROCKY MOUNTAINS
South Platte R.
Manitou Springs
Colorado Springs
COLORADO
Gunnison River
Arkansas River
Rio Grande
Animas River
Mountainous areas

EDITOR'S INTRODUCTION

As Samuel Bowles and his party so often noted in crossing the plains to Cheyenne, Wyoming, in the summer of 1868, the West was changing. Signs of that change were everywhere. Perhaps the most obvious were the modern and luxurious Pullman cars of the Union Pacific that the travelers boarded in Chicago. Three years earlier it had taken more than a week to reach Cheyenne by stagecoach; now, thanks to the railroad, it took just a day and a half. The end of the line was Creston Station, 737 miles west of Omaha; in early August, prior to returning to Cheyenne to begin the trip south to Denver, Bowles and his entourage arrived there in time to participate in the ceremony laying the last rail on the Atlantic slope of the Continental Divide. Nine months later, on Monday, May 10, 1869, the driving of a gold spike at Promontory, Utah, completed the "wedding of the rails," linking the nation in one continuous span of wood and iron. The news "Done!" flashed by telegraph east and west, set off widespread, often spontaneous celebrations in the form of parades, military salutes, steam whistles, wild ringing of bells, services of thanksgiving, and elaborate displays of fireworks. "There will speedily be other railroads across our Continent," Bowles wrote later that same year. "But this, the first, will forever remain the one of history; the one of romance. Its construction in so short a time was the greatest triumph of modern civilization, of all civilization, indeed."[1]

Bowles, Schuyler Colfax, and William Bross, the three senior members of what the Colorado press would refer to as "the Colfax party," were friends of long standing. All three had contributed to the founding of the Republican party in 1854, and their friendship was cemented by loyalty to party ideals and fortunes— Bowles and Bross as partisan newspaper editors, and Colfax, a former editor, as Speaker of the United States House of Representatives and recently nominated candidate for vice president. What brought them to Colorado in 1868 was the prospect of enjoying in each other's company the fellowship of "camp and saddle," while exploring and taking in mountain scenery.

There were, of course, personal agendas as well. Bowles, the editor-in-chief of the *Springfield* (Massachusetts) *Republican,* was an attentive observer of the national scene. He came west on a kind of working vacation, intent on surveying the Colorado Territory for his readers back home while showing his eighteen-year-old daughter, Sarah Augusta (Sallie), something of life in the newly opened West. For Bross and Colfax, however, the trip had other purposes. Both were decidedly political animals, and their very presence invariably had the effect of transforming all such journeys into "affairs of politics and government."[2] As editor of the *Chicago Tribune,* William Bross shared Bowles's journalistic interest in the West. But while "no temptation, however seductive," could induce Bowles to make a speech,[3] Bross, who was up to his ears in politics as Illinois lieutenant governor, could not resist the opportunity to address an audience. Colfax, of course, had politics very much on his mind as well.

Schuyler Colfax, William Bross, and Samuel Bowles. (FROM SAMUEL BOWLES, *OUR NEW WEST: RECORDS OF TRAVEL BETWEEN THE MISSISSIPPI RIVER AND THE PACIFIC OCEAN* [HARTFORD, CONN., 1869])

And in Bross he found the perfect companion to lend a hand with some unofficial campaigning among the citizens of Denver and in Colorado's mining towns.

Schuyler Colfax had the widest agenda of all. For him "vacationing, visiting relatives, courting, and talking politics were mixed in fairly equal proportions."[4] The courtship involved his traveling companion Ellen (Nellie) Wade, the niece of Ohio Republican senator Benjamin Wade, whom he had met in Washington sometime earlier. Though according to tradition Colfax proposed to Nellie Wade on the summit of Mount Lincoln that summer, the truth is that the couple's secret had already been shared with their companions. In fact, in delivering a speech at Omaha, where the party had to cross the Missouri and change trains, Colfax had made the news public. Although Grant, the soldier, never surrendered, Colfax told the crowd, "I did; and I appear before you rather as a prisoner of war than otherwise."[5]

Their visit of 1868, moreover, represented a much-anticipated reunion and return engagement. Three years earlier, in May 1865, taking advantage of Colfax's position as chairman of the House Committee on Post Offices and Post Roads,[6] the three had rendezvoused at the border town of Atchison, Kansas, then the western terminus of the railroad. There they had joined Albert D. Richardson (1833–69), a correspondent for the *New York Tribune,* to begin an ambitious and memorable journey of inspection across the continent to the Pacific. On their fifteen-week trip, the foursome traveled some twelve thousand miles—half by sea, a full third by stage. They crossed Kansas and Nebraska to visit the mines of Colorado, Nevada, and California; inspected (with a critical eye) Brigham Young's Mormon experiment beside the Great Salt Lake;

explored the Big Tree groves at Calaveras and Mariposa, the Yosemite, and other scenic wonders of California; and passed overland north through the Oregon and Washington territories to Puget Sound and Vancouver Island, returning home by way of the Isthmus of Panama.[7]

Bowles, Bross, and Richardson were veteran newspapermen interested in seeing the West, and for them the trip could not have been better timed. Leaving home almost before the sounds of Civil War guns had died away at Appomattox, they had the good fortune to anticipate—in some instances by only a matter of weeks—the westward rush of reporters, editors, artists, and politicians eager to interpret in word or picture the vast and little-known area beyond the hundredth meridian. There was considerable truth, as well as pride, in Bowles's subsequent assertion to Speaker Colfax that "our party were almost the first that ever had traveled Across the Continent simply to see the country, to study its resources, to learn its people and their wants, and to acquit ourselves more intelligently, thereby, each in our duties to the public,—you in the government, and we as journalists."[8]

No one profited more from that experience than Samuel Bowles. The most immediate result was the series of letters written home to the *Springfield Republican,* in which he shared with his readers his impressions and expanded knowledge of the West. These thirty-two letters, together with eight "Supplementary Papers," were collected and published at Springfield in "substantially their original shape" the following year as *Across the Continent: A Summer's Journey to the Rocky Mountains, the Mormons, and the Pacific States, with Speaker Colfax.*

As a summary account of the state of the West in the final years before the completion of the transcontinental railroad, *Across the Continent* was a significant achievement. In his lengthy "Introductory Letter," addressed to Schuyler Colfax, Bowles was careful to make his purposes clear. This was not, he explained, "a Diary of a personal journey; nor a Guide-Book; nor a Hand-Book of statistics," though, in fact, it represented something of all three. Rather the letters "aim to give, with compactness and comprehensiveness, the distinctive experiences of the Overland Journey; to describe, as vividly as I may, the various original scenery that the route and the country offer; to portray the social and material developments of the several States and Territories we visited,—their present and their future, their realization and their capacity." Though Bowles took special care in describing for his eastern readers the West's topography, climate, and scenery, as well as the customs and peculiarities of its inhabitants—most notably the Indians, Mormons, and Chinese— his real message was Manifest Destiny: the American West as a source of untapped wealth and economic promise, whose key to development was the Pacific railroad. Though it had not as yet laid a single rail beyond the Missouri, Bowles did not hesitate to pronounce the railroad "the great work of the day; the great want, the great revealer, the great creator of this Empire of ours west of the Mississippi."[9] The railroad, he insisted, was the "great theme" that "presses itself upon us more deeply, more solemnly, than any other offered by our journey and its observations" and must be supported by everyone who believes in America's "progress and civilization and national unity" as a transcontinental empire. "Men of the East! Men at Washington!" Bowles concluded in peroration, "here is payment for your great debt; here is wealth unbounded; here is the commerce of the world; here the complement of a Republic that is continental; but you must come and take them with the Locomotive!"[10] Events in the three years that followed did little to diminish Bowles's faith.

The trip to Colorado in 1868, by contrast, was a far more modest undertaking. Bowles and his companions arrived in Denver on Saturday, August 8. Less than four weeks later, having completed an extended and exciting expedition into South Park, they were again heading east. By September 11, in fact, Schuyler Colfax was back home in South Bend, preparing to surrender his status as widower and readying himself for the fall campaign, which would elevate him to the vice presidency. However short the time, Bowles made use of the occasion to pen a new series of letters to his readers back in Springfield on the state of Colorado and the West. These letters, slightly rearranged and edited, were published in book form in 1869 as *The Switzerland of America: A Summer Vacation in the Parks and Mountains of Colorado,* a work that soon came to occupy an important place in the developing literature promoting the scenic wonders of Colorado and the Rocky Mountain West.

Contemporary interest in Bowles's Colorado letters and book doubtless owed almost as much to the reputation and prominence of their author and his two traveling companions as it did to the subject itself. Among those knowledgeable about the journalism and politics of the day, Samuel Bowles, Schuyler Colfax, and William Bross were familiar names. Samuel Bowles (1826–78), the party's self-appointed chronicler and the youngest of the three, stood at the very height of his journalistic career. Bowles had entered on that career early. In 1844, at the age of eighteen, he had taken over the editorial manage-

Samuel Bowles of the *Springfield Republican*.

ment of the *Springfield Republican* from his father, shifted the paper's focus from local to national news, and gradually transformed a small, rather provincial country weekly into one of the nation's most respected small-city daily newspapers.[11] In so doing, Bowles established his own credentials as a journalist whose authoritative views and endorsements on the great public issues of the day—from the annexation of Texas in 1844 down through Reconstruction and the scandals of the Grant era—were widely sought. Though his assessments of men occasionally missed the mark (he once characterized Abraham Lincoln as a "simple Susan"),[12] Bowles's judgments on most matters were well informed and sound. He was known, as one contemporary journalist put it, as "a close observer; [and] a pointed, suggestive, 'meaty' writer."[13]

The Connecticut Valley town of Springfield was by no means the world, and much of Bowles's cosmopolitanism and breadth of knowledge came as a result of his travels. Beginning about 1862, when he made the first of four trips to Europe, Bowles traveled just as widely as time and circumstances would permit, to the point it could be said that he "traveled more than any other of the great journalists of his time." Bowles's formal education had ended by the time he was seventeen, and in a very real sense travel became a substitute for the maturing effect of college, expanding his reach of experience in a way that books alone could never do. Wherever he went, Bowles developed the habit of "taking notes, writing letters to the paper, or filling his mind with facts and impressions about men, women, and public affairs to be drawn on later,"[14] a habit that, in turn, directly contributed to his success as newspaper editor in chief.

Travel also served Bowles as relaxation and as a form

of badly needed therapy. Throughout his life Bowles suffered from a series of debilitating physical ailments,[15] which he compounded by a self-imposed demand for perfection and chronic overwork. In the words of his grandson, Richard Hooker, Bowles "lacked the capacity for repose"; as a consequence, "travel and change, the chance to see new sights, and to talk with men and women unhampered by office demands, came nearest to yielding rest."[16]

Schuyler Colfax (1823–85) also believed in the virtues of travel, particularly when it could be conveniently combined with politics. Colfax, understandably, was the central figure of the journey, as he had been three years before, when "on every conceivable and inconceivable occasion" he was "welcomed by officials and citizens, with processions, banners, and artillery salute."[17] A short, slender widower (he stood five feet six and weighed 145 pounds), what Colfax may have lacked in physical stature he more than made up for in popularity as one of the country's "best and most promising statesman." Following his transplantation from New York to Indiana, the rise in Colfax's political fortunes had been meteoric. Elected to Congress at thirty-two and selected as Speaker of the House nine years later, Colfax was the "idol of South Bend"[18] and the celebrated darling of the Republican party. It had been widely rumored that Colfax would succeed Lincoln, and his presence with Ulysses S. Grant on the ticket in the fall of 1868, most astute onlookers believed, was but a prelude to the presidency itself. "Colfax has got the White House on the brain," Bowles had candidly confided to a friend in September 1867. "Too bad. He is too good a fellow to go daft on that subject."[19]

Samuel Bowles's great admiration for Colfax, however

judiciously framed, was unmistakable. "There are no rough points about him," Bowles wrote in 1865:

He is not of brilliant or commanding intellect, not a genius, as we ordinarily apply these words; but the absence of this is more than compensated by these other qualities I have mentioned,—his great good sense, his quick, intuitive perception of truth, and his flexible adherence to it, his high personal integrity, and his long and valuable training in the government. Without being, in the ordinary sense, one of the greatest of our public men, he is certainly one of the most useful, reliable and valuable; and in any capacity, even the highest, he is sure to serve the country faithfully and well. He is one of the men to be tenaciously kept in public life; and I have no doubt he will be. Some people talk of him for president; Mr. Lincoln used to tell him he would be his successor; but his own ambition is wisely tempered by the purpose to perform his present duties well.[20]

Colfax was everything that Bowles was not—sure of himself in every situation; easy, affable, and outgoing (to the point of being nicknamed "Smiler Colfax"); an able speech-maker—and the editor from Springfield was content to live in his shadow. Colfax accommodated himself to the world easily, and it was this accommodation that ultimately proved fatal to their friendship. Bowles, like his Puritan ancestors, was a confirmed moralist in matters having to do with public conduct and personal rectitude. When in 1872 the widespread rascality and greed of the Grant era reached even Colfax, implicating him in the Crédit Mobilier scandals, Bowles's response was immediate, judgmental, and unforgiving; and their once-warm relationship became strained to the point of dissolution.[21]

William Bross (1813-90), lieutenant governor of Illinois and editor of the *Chicago Tribune,* was the senior member of the group. Pronounced by Bowles "our paterfamilias, our 'governor,' " Bross was a robust and healthy-looking man of fifty-five, formidable in appearance and manner behind his bushy beard and thick beetling eyebrows. Born in New Jersey (a fact, he joked, that disqualified him from the presidency, "as the Constitution requires that officer to be a native of the nation"),[22] Bross attended Williams College and spent a decade as a schoolmaster before moving to Chicago in 1848, where he quickly emerged as "one of the country's most remarkable talents, as a businessman, a journalist, and a Chicago booster."[23]

Like his friends Bowles and Colfax, Bross was an early and ardent supporter of the Republican party; in fact, Bross's *Tribune* had been the first paper to propose the candidacy of Lincoln. In traveling together, Bross and Colfax worked the political circuit to perfection. Noted for his "fluency of delivery" and "his full, sympathetic, and natural tones" as "a ready and most popular stump speaker,"[24] Bross played the partisan heavy to Colfax's statesmanlike pose whenever the two were prevailed upon to address a public gathering, which was virtually everywhere they went. This strategy had delighted those who turned out along their route to the Pacific in 1865, and it would work just as effectively in the mountains of Colorado in 1868. Though Colfax had let it be known in advance that he was coming to Colorado as a private citizen, not as a candidate for the office of vice president (because, it was said, for a candidate for so high an office to politic on his own behalf "did not comport with his ideas of propriety"),[25] opportunities to advance the cause of Republicanism were not to be neglected. In fact, as Colfax explained to W. E. Chandler, secretary of the Republican National Committee, in a letter of August 10,

1868, he had arranged, in advance, through his Denver brother-in-law Daniel Witter, "to make our visit a speaking tour. Lt. Gov. Bross is along who is an effective stumper & who enjoys it. I have agreed to make non-political talks, but, as you saw I did at S. Bend etc[.] I can work in 'Let us have peace' & the glorious history of the Rep. party, while Bross can walk into the Dem. party, platform etc. So it will make a fair division of labor without trespassing on the proprieties by me."[26]

The party that Bowles, Colfax, and Bross brought with them to Colorado was a fairly large one and would become even larger as their vacation in the mountains progressed. Where the journey of 1865 had been a strictly masculine affair, this one was literally dominated by ladies and as such had a gay and festive holiday look. Accompanying the three principals were Colfax's mother and stepfather, Hannah and George Matthews, and his half sister, Carrie Matthews; Sue Matthews, Carrie's Michigan cousin; Sallie Bowles; Ellen ("Nellie") Wade, Colfax's fiancée, who was included when the Speaker told Carrie Matthews to invite a friend; and William Todd, Colfax's twenty-two-year-old private secretary.

In contrast to the luxury of their private car on the Union Pacific, the overnight, twenty-four-hour ride by stage from Cheyenne to Denver was tedious, tiring, and thoroughly uncomfortable. Horse teams were changed every ten miles, with the company reserving its finest team, six perfectly matched dapple grays, for the last relay coming into Denver. Once in the city, the party temporarily split up. The members of the Colfax family, Sue Matthews, and Ellen Wade went off to stay with the Speaker's sister Clara Witter and her husband, Daniel, at their house at the corner of Seventh and Larimer streets.

Bowles and his daughter Sallie were the guests of John Pierce, Colorado's former surveyor general, whom Bowles had apparently met on his earlier visit to Colorado. Bross was made welcome by the family of John Evans, Colorado's territorial governor between 1862 and 1865, who was then engaged in constructing the Denver Pacific Railroad north to Cheyenne. The Evanses lived in a red-brick mansion at Fourteenth and Arapaho, whose stylishness "set the pattern for merchants, promoters, and land speculators."[27]

The arrival of the Colfax party in Denver on the morning of August 8 was warmly announced in that day's edition of the *Rocky Mountain News*. For much of the journey, Bowles had not been feeling well, a fact that the *News* did not disguise from its readers.[28] The *News* would continue to show great interest in the doings of Colfax and his companions throughout their visit to Colorado, noting their various itineraries and activities and making certain, whenever possible, that a reporter went along to send stories back to Denver.

On Monday evening, August 10, after a day of rest, Colfax and Bross made the first of their public appearances to deliver a set of speeches from the stage of the Denver Theater. True to the script they would follow among the mining towns, Colfax began with a relatively brief and flattering speech extolling Coloradans for the obvious changes and improvements that had taken place since their visit of three years before, following which Bross talked on things political for "nearly an hour." Bowles did not attend, partly because of ill health and partly (characteristically) to avoid having to speak. The next morning the whole party started for Georgetown and Central City along Clear Creek, "from which point," the

Rocky Mountain News informed its readers, "the ladies will return here and the gentlemen go on into Middle Park. After returning from there, they will go to the South Park, where they will stay a week or two, or as long as they can afford to."[29]

Though both Bowles and Colfax, optimists by temperament, would attempt to put the best face on everything they saw, the fact was that the Colorado they visited in 1868 was grappling with the latter stages of severe economic recession. The boom, begun in 1859 with the discovery of gold along Clear Creek, in South Park, and across the Mosquito Range along the Arkansas River, ended once the easily recoverable pockets of placer (surface) gold ran out. Beginning in the spring of 1864, Colorado's prosperity began to decline dramatically, and the four years that followed were, as Territorial Secretary Frank Hall later recalled, "undoubtedly the darkest in our history."[30]

The problem faced by Colorado's mining industry, as Bowles correctly reported, was basically one of technology. The technology of placer mining could be easily learned by anyone able to wield a pick and shovel or a pan, or to manipulate a sluice box, as the thousands of "Fifty-niners," the vast majority of whom had been raised on farms, readily proved. Hard-rock mining, on the other hand, required a much more sophisticated technology and remained stymied until the late 1860s by the lack of satisfactory refractory techniques to separate the gold efficiently from its surrounding granite and quartz. Stamp mills, which had proven fairly effective in California and Nevada, were only marginally so in Colorado and failed to save any but a fraction of the available gold. Also lacking was adequate equipment and capital for underground mining and adequate access to railroad transportation. As a result, Colorado's mining industry languished. Diggings were abandoned as miners left for other parts, and once-busy mining towns such as Hamilton, Tarryall, Fairplay, Montgomery, and Buckskin Joe were left deserted or half-empty, their wooden stores and houses in decay.[31] Other factors contributed to Colorado's economic hardship as well: rampant speculation in mining claims; the Civil War, which syphoned off young, able-bodied men for the army, cut western immigration and raised the cost of labor; and the continuing high cost of food, caused by the slower-than-expected development of the territory's agriculture and several seasons of grasshopper infestation.

Denver, sitting on the treeless and exposed eastern slopes of the Rockies, had functioned as little more than a supply depot for the mines during the early sixties and as a result felt the full brunt of the downturn. The town's population dwindled to three thousand, causing major distress among Denver's merchants and a widespread decline in property values. As if to underscore the end of boom times, tragedy struck on the night of May 19, 1864. Following several days of rain, a fifteen-foot-high wall of water roared down the dry bed of Cherry Creek, submerging west Denver, tearing buildings—including the Methodist Church, the offices of the *Rocky Mountain News*, and City Hall—from their foundations and creating widespread desolation and ruin. Nevertheless, the city quickly rebuilt. Two- and three-story fire-resistant brick structures of the sort Bowles admired as giving a "permanent and prosperous air to the town" replaced earlier wooden buildings, and the completion of an irrigation system in 1865 brought green trees and lawns to the parched prairie. By the time the Colfax party arrived, Denver was listless, quiet, and "dull," but doing better. "Things look less brisk, but more substantial," Bowles noted. "The town 'feels its oats' less and its dignity more." In fact, 1868 was a year of revival: some three hundred new buildings were constructed, and the population, buoyed by prospects of the railroad and the end of Civil War, recovered to about four thousand. Though Bowles predicted for Denver "a gratifying future of growth" as it moved through what he called its "kernal years,"[32] the town would remain for another decade very much a new town. The 1870 census revealed that of the 4,759 Denverites counted, only 10 percent had lived there as long as five years. The remainder, recent historians have noted, "were newcomers who had replaced disappointed earlier residents."[33]

Adding to Denver's and Colorado's distress during the summer of 1868, as Bowles, Colfax, and their fellow vacationers were to learn firsthand, was the very real threat of a full-scale Indian war. A depressed economy, in fact, was perhaps the last thing on anyone's mind that August, for the Indians of the plains—the Arapahos, Cheyennes, Sioux, Kiowas, and Comanches—had embarked on a series of depredations that soon posed a direct threat to the citizens of Colorado.

During its first years of territorial status after 1861, Colorado had largely escaped serious problems with the Indians. For their part, the local tribes had been content to watch the influx of Fifty-niners with interest bordering on amazement, and there was surprisingly little conflict between them. Moreover, under the terms of the Fort Wise treaty of 1861, the Cheyennes and Arapahos, the two tribes occupying Colorado's plains, had ceded their lands east of the mountains in exchange for a small reservation along the Arkansas, leaving that area relatively quiet. By 1863, however, the situation had begun to deteriorate. The traditional hunting grounds, with the herds of buffalo, antelope, and deer upon which the Plains Indians so much depended, lay directly across the emigrant routes. This encroachment was exacerbated by the coming of the railroad, first by the advance of the Union Pacific across the plains from Omaha, and later by the Union Pacific's Eastern Division (later the Kansas Pacific), building northwest from Kansas City. The result was the ongoing series of violent incidents known as the Indian wars. In the absence of news about the Civil War, these episodes created a more or less constant refrain in newspapers like the *Rocky Mountain News*, where they appeared during the period of Bowles's visit under such lurid and inflammatory headlines as "Indians, Murders and Depredations," "Indian Outrages," or "More Indian Murders," further heightening the sense of tension and alarm.[34]

Violence begot violence. The early attitudes of moderation and accommodation on the part of whites became transformed into highly emotional calls for extermination, making almost inevitable tragic events like the slaughter of Black Kettle's Southern Cheyennes in November 1864 at Sand Creek in southeastern Colorado. Acts of revenge followed, initiating a full-blown, if sporadic, war that extended from Missouri across the plains into Wyoming and westward toward Nevada. Isolated farms were pillaged and burned, not infrequently with loss of life and tales of survivors led into captivity by the "hostiles," livestock run off, and stagecoaches and wagons attacked.

By the fall of 1867, following an attack by General W. S. Hancock that destroyed a Cheyenne village containing three hundred lodges, the Indian uprising reached Colorado's borders. It fell to Territorial Governor Alexander Hunt, who had taken office earlier in the year, to deal with a situation in which the territory seemed beset on both its eastern and western borders by marauding Indians.[35]

Hunt had to contend, simultaneously, with the seven tribes of Utes that made their homes in the mountains and parks of central Colorado. Traditionally the Utes had gotten along fairly well with whites, but in time they too became a target for removal. In fact, at the very time Hunt was worrying about the Arapahos and Cheyennes, he was called to Washington to help negotiate a treaty removing the Utes to a reservation in southwestern Colorado.

The treaty, approved by all parties in Washington on March 2, 1868, was a fair one by the standards of the day. Nevertheless, the Senate insisted upon modifications prior to ratification, with the result that during the period of Colfax's visit Hunt was forced to return to the mountains in an effort to persuade the various Ute tribes to acquiesce to the changes. To complicate matters still further, at this very moment news arrived in Denver that a band of Arapahos, numbering about two hundred, were raiding the length of the eastern Rockies. Thus began the episode known as the Indian War of 1868, or Hall's War, after Territorial Secretary Frank Hall, who, in the absence of Governor Hunt and an organized militia to call upon, was forced to meet the threat as best he could. In addition to firing off a series of telegrams demanding the intervention of the army, Hall dispatched a messenger to the Colfax party warning them not to return to Denver by way of Colorado City (Colorado Springs) as planned, setting the stage for the dramatic conclusion of their visit to South Park and to Colorado.[36]

It was against such a background that Bowles, Colfax, Bross, and the other members of their party began a series of trips through the parks and towns of mountain Colorado. Their itineraries were varied and well planned, thanks to advance arrangements made by Governor Hunt and Schuyler Colfax's brother-in-law, Daniel Witter. Following the visit to Idaho Springs, Georgetown, Empire, and Central City, camping out almost all the way, the ladies returned to Denver, while Bowles, Colfax, and Bross attempted to recapture some of the masculine camaraderie of 1865 by taking a brief trip into Middle Park over the Berthoud Pass. There they not only met up with two of Colorado's great historic figures—William Byers, the editor of the *Rocky Mountain News*, and Major John Wesley Powell and the members of the Colorado Scientific Exploring Expedition—but found themselves encamped next to a large body of Utes who had moved down to the banks of the Grand River to negotiate a new treaty with a delegation that included Governor Hunt, Major Daniel Oakes, and Charley Utter. The irrepressible Byers, who, in the words of Wallace Stegner, "was a pioneer, an opener, a pass-crosser of a pure American breed" and one of the greatest promoters and entrepreneurs in Colorado history,[37] had come into Middle Park over Berthoud Pass with the Powell expedition on August 7 for several reasons.[38] Among these were his plans to develop the hot sulphur springs of Middle Park into a health spa and resort.[39] The other and more immediate reason had to do with his determination to make the first recorded ascent of Longs Peak—a feat he accomplished on August 23, 1868, as a member of the small party led by the one-armed Major Powell.[40]

Bowles, Colfax, and Bross spent three days in Middle Park, exiting on August 17 by way of Boulder Pass. From there they moved down through the mountains toward their appointed rendezvous in South Park with Governor Hunt and the ladies, which took place at Hamilton on August 25. For several days they traveled both together and apart, with Colfax and Bross periodically detaching themselves to fulfill previously arranged speaking engagements at Breckenridge, Granite, Oro City, and other places. Bowles visited the mining towns of Breckenridge, Tarryall, Fairplay, and Hamilton and climbed Grays Peak before joining the entire Colfax entourage for their trip with saddle horses, carriages, wagons, and elaborate camping equipage over the Mosquito Range to the valley of the Arkansas River.

While they were camped near the Twin Lakes, a messenger arrived from acting governor Hall, announcing the Arapaho incursion on the eastern plains and touching off an Indian scare. Though the episode was not, finally, without its lighter side, at the time it was serious business indeed. "It was a night to remember, with a shiver—," Bowles recalled,

> lying down in that far-off wilderness with the reasonable belief that before morning there was an even chance of an attack of hostile Indians upon our camp, more than half of whose members were women and children,—after an evening spent in discussing the tender ways Indians had with their captives, illustrated from the personal knowledge of many present; aroused after the first hour's feverish rest by a new messenger from another quarter, galloping into camp, and shouting, as if we were likely to forget, that "the Indians were loose, and hell

> was to pay;" followed by the coming of furious storm of rain and hail and thunder and lightning, sucking under our tents, beating through them, to wet pillows and blankets,—at any other time a dire grievance, now hardly an added trial; every ear stretched for unaccustomed sound, every heart beating anxiously, but every lip silent; all eagerly awaiting the slow-coming morning to bring renewal of life and the opportunity to go farther on and to safer retreats.

The night ended without further interruption, and as Bowles confessed with customary wryness: "This deponent had the soundest, sweetest night's sleep he had had in the mountains. Some natures will be perverse, and if one must be nervous, it is a great help to be conscious of it."[41]

Nonetheless, Bowles, Colfax, and party broke camp at dawn and recrossed the Mosquito Range to South Park with a mounted escort of "about twenty gallant young gold miners" who had come down from Oro City. There, heeding Hall's warning, they turned north to Hamilton, which intersected the road to Denver. "All together," Bowles writes, "there were [in this "grand 'outfit' "] from seventy-five to one hundred persons, and as many animals, as it moved back over the mountains into South Park again."[42] Near Hamilton, to everyone's surprise, they were encircled by a party of friendly Utes, who insisted on accompanying them on their homeward journey. Together, a mile beyond Fairplay, they spent the memorable night at "Camp Ute," an occasion complete with speeches, singing, and the passing of peace pipes, to which a much-relieved Governor Hunt contributed a steer in honor of his guests. The remainder of the return trip to Denver by way of Bailey and Turkey Creek marked a prosaic and uneventful end to an unforgettable journey.

"Just back from the mountains, weary, but well," Bowles wrote his wife from Denver on September 6, two days following their return, "with all sorts of rare experiences, joy, pain, comfort, discomfort, each in rich variety; I riding muleback all the time—twenty to thirty miles a day; no time or strength to write; every day full of fatigue with riding and camp-work—too full—and no post-office to mail letters at, if written; an Indian scare, and a change of route, and a hurried journey back to town, to escape chance of danger; all vivid, enlivening, and strengthening."[43]

As his letter suggests, much of the charm of Bowles's subsequent book, reissued here as *The Parks and Mountains of Colorado: A Summer Vacation in the Switzerland of America, 1868,* unmistakably lies "in its open-air quality" and in its contagious "sense of the exhilarating gallop, the healthy fatigue, the joviality beside the camp-fire."[44] But it offers a great deal more as well. Despite the short time at his disposal, Bowles managed to cover considerable ground, and the composite portrait that emerges in the retelling provides a fascinating and accurate rendering of the condition of the Colorado Territory during one of the most eventful periods in its history.

Bowles presumably worked from notes or journal entries made at the scene or jotted down at the end of the day, which he periodically composed into single letters. His commitment to the fidelity of fact and place is everywhere apparent. Though he wrote a decade before the Hayden surveys of the 1870s provided the first full account of Colorado's physiographic features, Bowles's own sense of topography is amazingly correct in terms of direction, size, contour, and distance, making it fairly easy, even now, to retrace his journey. Difficult geography did not faze him, not even the Platte River, which, as he discovered in South Park, "divides, subdivides, and redivides almost indefinitely." "I wish the Coloradians would abolish the sinuosities and multiplications, and put the Plattes into numerals, as Platte 1, 2, 3, 4, 5, and so on," Bowles observed. "As between learning the Plattes and conjugating a Greek verb, where's the choice for hardness?"[45]

Bowles had a special talent for capturing objective detail, together with the journalist's ability to measure, synthesize, and summarize for the reader the significance of what he had seen. Bowles missed very little, and there is no indication that he tried to embellish or falsify what he saw and reported. His descriptions of the appearance, as well as the economic, social, and political conditions, of Denver and the small mining towns he visited are of particular interest and value to the modern historian. Bowles faithfully captures the desolate and depleted mood of these once-busy mining villages, with their miles of empty, scarred ravines, their deserted mills, and their abandoned and rusting equipment. The mining towns that Bowles visited, as contemporary photographs reveal, were "rough and ragged" places, ugly beyond belief even in boom times, their surrounding mountain slopes denuded by mining, erosion, indiscriminate timbering, and fires (sometimes deliberately set and often allowed to burn out of control).[46] It would take another generation of Coloradans to understand fully the long-term implications of such profligacy, carelessness, and waste.

Bowles's book is enlivened by its author's zest for life and adventure, his wry sense of humor, and his gift for the terse and well-turned phrase. Particularly entertaining and valuable as well are the glimpses Bowles provides into the somewhat more prosaic events of everyday life in Colorado's backcountry settlements, which he intersperses with sketches of such colorful mountain characters as Commodore Stephen Decatur (who, reportedly, was none other than the brother of William Bross) and Charley Utter. One of the important features of Bowles's book, in fact, is the gallery of historic individuals introduced to the reader— figures such as William Byers, Major John Powell, Alexander Hunt, John Evans, General John Pierce, Daniel Oakes, Charley Utter, Uriah Curtis, General Lord, Stephen Decatur, Ashley Franklin, and Marshall Silverthorn, who were then in the process of leaving their distinctive marks upon the unfolding history of Colorado.

There are, to be sure, some minor errors of fact, omission, and imbalance. For example, Bowles uses the occasion of the Ute Indian encampment in Middle Park to engage in a well-informed discussion of the government's vacillating Indian policy with its "mixed state of war and bargaining" and its humbuggery of treaty making ("the direct parent of all our Indian woes and theirs too. Neither party keeps the bargain").[47] Yet, at the same time, Bowles seems imperfectly aware of the critical importance of Governor Hunt's presence in Middle Park and later in South Park, where he was attempting to gain acquiescence to the Senate-amended treaty of March, thereby preventing another Indian uprising, this time on Colorado's exposed western flank.[48]

The other imbalances in Bowles's book are, for the most part, caused by the author's penchant for overoptimism in portraying the future prospects of Colorado and the West. This is particularly true in the case of his prediction that "under the new order of things," Colorado's agriculture would soon assume, as in California, "the place of the first interest, the great wealth."[49] In reality, such a state of self-sufficiency would not be achieved for another decade or more.[50] Bowles's enthusiasm was perfectly understandable. To promote the West it was necessary to replace the myth of the Great American Desert (the widely reported existence of which had been thought to inhibit the expansion of the agricultural frontier) with the image of a self-sustaining garden able to serve as a foundation for the expansion of commerce and trade. In his discussion of Colorado's mining industry, Bowles fared much better. Thanks to Nathaniel Hill's Swansea refractory process, which, as Bowles notes, was even then being put into operation at Hill's new Boston and Colorado Smelting Works at Black Hawk, his prediction about the imminent revival of Colorado's mining fortunes proved to be more accurate.

Bowles's book is greatly enhanced by its pictorial quality and by its author's taste for the romantic and picturesque— characteristics that are fully in keeping with the genre of travel literature to which the book belongs. Bowles had a gift for isolating diffuse impressions, especially those involving light and color, and the skill to translate them, by means of verbal sketches, into compelling pictures for his readers. This is particularly true of some of Bowles's most memorable descriptions: the snowstorm that overtakes him at the top of Boulder Pass; the field of flowers along Boulder Creek, where "the greenest of grass, the bluest of harebells, the reddest of painter's brush, [and] the yellowest of sunflowers and buttercups" conspire with the "bluest" of Colorado skies; and, above all, the awe-inspiring views from the crests of Grays Peak and Mount Lincoln. "It was not beauty,"

Bowles writes of the scene from Grays Peak, "it was sublimity; it was not power, nor order, nor color, it was majesty; it was not a part, it was the whole; it was not man but God, that was about, before, in us." Counterbalancing his enthusiasm for such scenic descriptions, and as a way of reinforcing them, Bowles upon occasion admits that he is at a loss for words. "I believe I have exhausted my adjectives and every known variety of picture frame," he confesses in gazing across the expanse of South Park, "in trying to set the . . . landscapes in the mind's eye of the reader. . . . Only seeing can be feeling and believing."[51]

Like most well-remembered journeys, this one, too, left its mark. Many of the relationships formed or reconfirmed during that brief August trip turned out to be lasting ones, and the scenes visited made a deep and lasting impression upon the various members of the Colfax party. Three romances and subsequent weddings were an outgrowth of the Colorado trip, Schuyler Colfax's marriage to Ellen Wade the following November being but the most famous.[52] Moreover, the trio of Bowles, Colfax, and Bross (together with Mary Bowles, the new Mrs. Colfax, and William Bross's daughter Jessie) would return to Colorado the very next summer on their way to Oregon and Washington to celebrate the opening of the Pacific railroad. Written recollections of this trip are few, though Bowles did write his daughter Sallie from Fall River, Colorado, on July 27, 1869, recounting the party's return from Georgetown, where they ascended an unnamed mountain near Grays Peak. We "saw all the grand-panorama of snow-mountains," Bowles told her, "equal to what you and I saw from Lincoln."[53]

William Bross was sufficiently taken with the scenery

and future prospects of Colorado in 1870 to become treasurer of the Chicago-Colorado Colony, a planned agricultural community modeled upon the Union Colony at Greeley, which later became the town of Longmont.[54] Bross's love of travel and the outdoors remained with him until the end of his life. Though suffering from diabetes, which ultimately caused his death in 1890, Bross made three return trips to the West in 1879, in 1883, and in 1887. During the second of these, which took him to Estes Park, Colorado, Helena, Montana, and Yellowstone, he also returned to Twin Lakes, first visited with the Colfax party fifteen years before. A surviving photograph shows an aging and white-haired Bross sitting on the rock-strewn shore, fishing pole in hand, pensively looking out into the lake.

The future was less kind to Schuyler Colfax, who in 1868 had been so much at the center of things. Though he claimed to have been fully exonerated by the congressional investigations into the Crédit Mobilier scandal of 1872–73 and was given a hero's welcome upon his return to South Bend, Colfax's political standing was ruined. And the subsequent revelation that in 1868, as chairman of the House Committee on Post Offices and Post Roads, he had accepted a four-thousand-dollar campaign contribution from a contractor who supplied envelopes to the government so eroded his reputation that Samuel Bowles became publically critical, bringing their relationship to a sad and premature conclusion. When Colfax traveled to Springfield in 1874 to speak, he refused Bowles's invitation to stay at his home, rebuking Bowles for excoriating him "over and over again, with base crimes" of which Bowles should have known him to be "absolutely incapable."[55]

It is commonplace to observe that mountains do not change. Books about mountains have much the same kind of staying power. Modern readers of Bowles's account of the "Switzerland of America," particularly those who are familiar with the scenes that the author describes so well, will find that Samuel Bowles's book remains as fresh, fun, and informative in our day as in his own. The distinctive charm of Colorado, Bowles writes, "is the atmosphere, so clear and pure and dry all the while, as to be a perpetual feeling, rather than vision, of beauty; invigorating every sense, softly soothing every pain, lending a glory to landscape and life alike, clothing every feature of nature with beauty, and giving the eye of every spectator the power to see it."[56] So it very much still seems.

The Parks and Mountains of Colorado

A Summer Vacation in the Switzerland of America, 1868

AUTHOR'S PREFACE

THESE letters of a Summer Vacation,[1] in saddle and camp, among the great Central Parks and Mountains of America in Colorado, are gathered into this volume in order both to satisfy and stimulate the public interest in a region of our New West designed to a peculiar place in the future of America. We saw enough of it in our stage ride across the Continent in 1865 to suggest that it would become the Switzerland of America;[2] Bayard Taylor, a wider traveler and closer observer, made a more familiar tour in 1866, and more formally pronounced the same judgment;[3] and now, after a new visit, and an intimate acquaintance with all its details, we find our original enthusiasm more than rekindled, our original thought confirmed.

The distinctive physical feature of Colorado is her wide elevated Parks,[4] lying among her double and treble folds of the continental range of mountains—great plains, like counties in Illinois and Iowa, or states in New England, six thousand to nine thousand feet above the sea-level, surrounded by mountains that rise from three to five thousand feet higher; plains, green with grass, dark with groves, bright with flowers; mountains, dreary with rocks, white with snow. The distinctive charm is the atmosphere, so clear and pure and dry all the while, as to be a perpetual feeling, rather than vision, of beauty; invigorating every sense, softly soothing every pain, lending a glory to landscape and life alike, clothing every feature of nature with beauty, and giving the eye of every spectator the power to see it—this is the indescribable thing that lifts Colorado out of other lackings, and more than compensates, in the comparison, for what is peculiar to Switzerland.[5]

Here, where the great backbone of the Continent rears and rests itself; here, where nature sets the patterns of plain and mountain, of valley and hill, for all America; here, where spring the waters that wash two-thirds the western Continent and feed both its oceans; here, where mountains are fat with gold and silver, and prairies glory in the glad certainty of future harvests of corn and wheat—here, indeed, is the center and the central life of America,—fountain of its wealth and health and beauty. Switzerland is pleasure and health; Colorado is these and use besides—the use of beauty, and the use of profitable work united. I beg every traveler by the Pacific Railroad not to "pass it by on the other side;"[6] for, in so doing, he would offend the best that is in him.

Springfield, Mass. SAMUEL BOWLES
February, 1869

I.

THE PACIFIC RAILROAD

The Contrast of 1865 and 1868—Vice-President Colfax, Governor Bross and their Summer Vacation Party—Chicago and the Ride thither—The Pullman Cars of the West—From New York to San Francisco without Leaving the Car—West from Chicago—Council Bluffs and Omaha—Across the Plains by Railroad—Cheyenne—Up the Mountain—The Charms of Scenery and Atmosphere—Railroad Cities, their Rise and Fall—How the Railroad is built—Back to Cheyenne.

ON THE DIVIDE OF THE ATLANTIC AND PACIFIC OCEANS, AUGUST, 1868

TO-DAY the Pacific Railroad climbs over the line that separates the waters of the oceans.[1] We sit astride the crest of the continental mountains, and see the last rail on the Atlantic slope and the first on the Pacific fastened down. It is an era in our lives,—it is an era in our national life. Three years ago, the Pacific Railroad was hardly commenced,—not a rail was laid this side of the Missouri River; now there are eight hundred miles of iron track from that river west;[2] on the other side from the Pacific Ocean east, six hundred miles are laid; and early in 1869,—while you are reading these pages, my friend,—the Continent will be spanned, and the cars will run from ocean to ocean.[3] Only the energy of a Republic could perform such a work in so brief a time.

Three summers ago, our little party of four persons

were ten days and nights in stages in reaching this point from the Missouri River;[4] now our larger party of a dozen have been swept up hither in a day and a half from Omaha, and two days and a half from Chicago.[5] Another year the journey from Boston to San Francisco, that then occupied a full month, will be compassed in a single week. Dividing the across-the-continent trip into thirds, this crest of the mountains is two-thirds the way from the Atlantic to the Pacific. Chicago is twelve hundred miles from Boston; here we are twelve hundred miles from Chicago; and about the same distance from San Francisco in the other direction.

Our summer vacation party to these central mountains of our New West is the outgrowth of the excursion that Speaker Colfax led across the Continent in 1865.[6] Now as then he is the central figure. Governor Bross of Illinois comes next, now as then the favorite of the crowds that gather at every stopping place for a speech, and the leader in all our enjoyments.[7] We miss one of the original four;[8] but new recruits and the ladies, then denied us, carry up our numbers to near a dozen. Chicago is the gathering-point; there the Old West culminates, and the New West begins. Soon she must cast her lot with the East,—for westward, indeed, the star of empire takes its way; but for the season, she sits in the center of railway commerce, East and West, and, motherly and queenly both, broods benignantly over the Continent.

Whether you come west to Chicago by Erie or New York Central, by Pittsburgh and Fort Wayne, by Michigan Southern or Michigan Central, leaving at the same hour, you are swept into Chicago at the very same moment. The thousand mile journey is run on either route to one schedule of time. Passengers, who part at the supper table at Rochester, bow to each other out of the rival car windows twenty-four hours later at the junction of the two Michigan roads in the outer suburbs of Chicago; while those, who bade each other good-bye in New York twelve hours earlier, race along side by side on the Fort Wayne and Michigan Southern roads, through the slaughter-house and bone-boiling adjacencies of the great city of the North-west, to their neighboring station-houses.

It seems strange that in this new and rough West of ours, where the fight is fresh with all the elements of nature, and ease and luxury, if not despised, at least are generally postponed, there should be more comfortable and luxurious accommodations for railway travel than anywhere else in the world. Yet it is so. Europe and the Atlantic states provide on none of their railways as yet so elegant and ease-giving carriages as the saloon and sleeping and refreshment cars that are offered to travelers on the long routes of the West. They are the invention of Mr. George W. Pullman,[9] who has thus associated his name forever with one of the greatest improvements in railway travel. Some are provided with kitchen and larder, and will furnish at any hour a meal that rivals Delmonico;[10] and the traveler can leisurely eat breakfast or dinner from his own little private table, as the train sweeps along at the rate of twenty or thirty miles an hour. Their broad, luxurious seats or sofas by day are turned at night into generous beds with clean linen and close curtains if you would have them. The ventilation is perfect; the freedom from dust and cinders only tolerably so; but the chief limitation is in the way of toilette accommodations. One disposed to abandon himself or herself to privacy and much water in this respect chafes somewhat at the common corner and wash-bowl and single looking-glass, however elegant and cleanly; but when a dozen to forty people undertake to keep house for three days or a week in a single car, there must be some sacrifices of fastidiousness to the spirit of travel. That the Pullman car demands so few is the wonder.

These cars are owned by companies distant from the railroads, and added to the trains of the latter by special arrangements. Additional charges are made to passengers who occupy them, varying with the amount of room and service taken, but about on a par with the prices of first-class hotels for lodgings and meals. To enjoy their comforts to the full, a party of a dozen or twenty should charter the exclusive use of one; and when the continental pleasure travel to the Pacific sets in next year, this will be a very common fashion. Starting from Boston, New York, Niagara, or Chicago, in your Pullman parlor, dining-room and bed-room, with servants to attend to all wants, the journey to San Francisco may be made with a degree of comfort and luxury, unequalled heretofore in all the dreams of travel, and without necessarily leaving the car from the beginning to the end of the three thousand mile ride. Such a company and such a car were ours from Chicago to the present end of the Railroad and back, and four days of more comfortable and enjoyable travel—while half a continent of plain and mountain and river was unrolled before us—can hardly be imagined. A little house organ was built into the side of our car, and by its aid we kept time to the music of nature as we rolled over the prairie and up the hills to the crest of the continental mountains.

From Chicago to Omaha, where is the beginning of the Pacific Railroad proper,[11] is five hundred miles, across Northern Illinois and through Central Iowa, by the Chicago and North-western Railway, and crossing the Mississippi River midway. Two more roads, lower down in Illinois and Iowa, will be done next year—those by Rock Island and Burlington—and give Chicago and Omaha three connecting lines, and all nearly direct. St. Louis, also, has a railroad connection with Omaha by the road down the Missouri River to St. Joseph and Kansas City, meeting at both points lines across Missouri to its commercial city. In fact, this puts Omaha and the Pacific Road one hundred and twenty-five miles nearer to St. Louis than to Chicago; but Chicago is more than that farther east.

Though but a new country, for most of our way, from Chicago to Omaha, we were rarely out of sight of the golden stubble of wheat or the rich green of waving cornfields. The wonder is constant alike at the richness of the soil, the beauty of the rolling prairie, the abundance of the harvests, the rapid settlement and cultivation of the country,—where all the people came from, and where all the grain and hay they grow goes to.

Council Bluffs in Iowa and Omaha in Nebraska are one in inspiration and growth; but the muddy Missouri rolls between, and makes them nominal rivals. Both are having a rapid development, and must be great towns. The roads from the North, South and East, to connect with the Pacific Road, must all center at Council Bluffs. The wide meadow—three to five miles wide—between the bluffs and the river will be intersected with their tracks, and thickly planted with their depots, and peopled with their dependents. Three roads—north to Sioux City, south to St. Joseph and St. Louis, east to Chicago—are already here; two more will come next year; and in ten years as many lines will center at this point. Already Council

Bluffs has eight thousand inhabitants, and she added thirteen hundred buildings last year. The older and more attractive parts of the town lie back on the bluffs and in the wooded ravines among them—a winning location, where healthfulness and beauty appear combined, and where will gather the real resident population of Council Bluffs.

Omaha rises more directly and symmetrically from the opposite bank; its bluffs or plateaus sweep us sharply from the water, and circle around in a grand amphitheatrical form,—somewhat as Springfield lies to the Connecticut River; you see its majesty of location and its wide-spreading improvements at a glance; the operations of the Pacific Road, of which it is the beginning and the headquarters, have given it almost feverish development; and it already holds a population of fifteen thousand to seventeen thousand. But with such rich conjunction of water and railway communication; with the river at its feet, navigable to the Rocky Mountains, north and west, and to the Gulf of Mexico, south—two thousand miles in either direction; with the workshops and head-quarters of the great Railroad of the Continent within its territory, and all the lines from the East and North and South centering before and around it, to make their connections and transhipments; with a State back of it certainly as large and as rich in agricultural wealth as any in the great West,—Omaha surely need feel no misgiving as to the future, but may proudly accept her destiny as one of the great interior cities of the nation. Directly, a bridge will be raised over the river to Council Bluffs,[12] and then passengers and merchandise can go back and forth in the same cars that they came in from New York or Sacramento.

Now out upon the grand continental Railroad into the

ocean of the Plains. It is five hundred miles to the base of the central mountains; up an imperceptible but steadily ascending grade of ten feet to the mile; and for nearly the whole distance along by the wide but shallow, fierce but fallow Platte River, which, gathering in the melted snows of all this slope of the Rocky Mountains, sweeps across the wide plains,—that, one day, by dams and ditches, it is destined to fertilize for miles on each side and make its wilderness to blossom as the rose,—and carries the grand tide in the Missouri below Omaha. For two hundred miles, Nebraska is slashed by cross rivers, tributaries of Platte or Missouri; the land lies in long, beautiful rolls; timber is in tolerably good supply; and the soil is as fertile as any in the West. The climate is well-balanced; oats, corn and wheat yield as richly and as of fine quality as in any state in the Union; and the rapid growth and great wealth of Nebraska are the surest things in our future. Hardly any state in the Mississippi and Missouri valleys has larger capacities. The settlement of her first two hundred miles west from the Missouri is surprisingly rapid; well-cultivated farms are rarely out of sight; and the population has certainly trebled in this three years' interval of our visits.

This limit passed, the prairie roll ceases; timber and side-streams are no more seen; the dead level of the Plains fills the eye; relieved only, twenty to thirty miles north and south, by the faint line of low bluffs, and a scant, irregular growth of cotton-woods along the line of the Platte itself. But the grass is strong and green; the soil laughs at the old nickname of the great American desert;[13] here, at least, is pasturage unbounded,—wheat, too, I believe, without irrigation, and with irrigation everything. But the first results of the Railroad are to kill what settlement and cultivation these plains had reached under the patronage of slow-moving emigration, stage-travel, and prairie-schooner freightage. The ranches which these supported are now deserted; the rails carry everybody and everything; the old roads are substantially abandoned; the old settlers, losing all their improvements and opportunities, gather in at the railway stations, or move backwards or forwards to greater local developments. They are the victims, in turn, of a higher civilization; they drove out the Indian, the wolf, and the buffalo; the locomotive whistles their occupation away; and invites back for the time the original occupants.

The day's ride grows monotonous. The road is as straight as an arrow. Every dozen or fifteen miles is a station,—two or three sheds and a water-spout and woodpile; every one hundred miles or so a home or division depot,[14] with shops, eating-house, "saloons" uncounted, a store or two, a few cultivated acres, and the invariable half a dozen seedy, staring loafers, that are a sort of fungi indigenous to American railways. The meals are abundant and good,—breakfast, dinner and supper each the same as the other, and only apt to be uncertain in bread and butter. We yawn over the unchanging landscape and the unvarying model of the stations, and lounge and read by day, and go to bed early at night. But the clear, dry air charms; the half dozen soldiers hurriedly marshalled into line at each station as the train comes up, suggest the Indians; we catch a glimpse of antelopes in the distance; and we watch the holes of the prairie dogs for their piquant little owners and their traditional companions of owls and snakes,—but never see the snakes.

Fremont (46 miles from Omaha) and Columbus (91) are the most considerable and promising settlements of Nebraska on the line of the road. The latter disputed the political capital with Omaha, but Lincoln, little more than a paper town as yet, and off the railway line, has won it from both. Old Fort Kearney, 200 miles out, a representative of the old-time life of the Plains, is fading away.[15] The chief stations of the Railroad, so far, are Grand Island (153 miles), North Platte (291), Sidney (414), Cheyenne (516), and Laramie (572). Julesburg, last year so lively a settlement, and at one time before an important military post, is now abandoned altogether,—a few log and board shanties and turf huts are all that remain of its former high uncivilization.[16] Cheyenne alone takes on the air of permanency and feels the hopes of promise. After "Hell," as the end town of the Railroad has been appropriately called, moved on, it was a serious question with her whether to be or not to be,—whether she was anything or nothing. The problem seems to be solved in her favor. She stands at the end of the Plains, at the beginning of the Mountains; the Railroad must have important shops here; it is the point of divergence for Colorado to the South, and the Railroad to Denver connects with the main line here,—ultimately the Kansas or St. Louis Pacific Railroad will, as Congress has ordered,[17] make its connection by this branch; a fine agricultural country surrounds, feeding the mountains beyond,—altogether material enough to make a permanency of Cheyenne. She has now three or four thousand inhabitants, who are settling down into reasonable soberness and serious work; three daily papers struggle for support; several good church buildings are erected or erecting; brick and stone are supplanting canvass and rough boards as building materials; and taverns and restaurants and stores will respond to all human appetites and needs and tastes. Though the town is six thousand feet above the level of the sea, it lies on an open prairie country, and the mountains are only dimly discernible in the distance. It is the principal settlement of the new territory of Wyoming,[18] but so near Colorado, that the latter territory covets and half claims it.

Now the road grows more interesting. We do not enter mountains, except in fancy,—they have been levelled for our track; but the plain ascends rapidly; the debris of the old mountains stand around in fantastic shapes; the forms of the remaining mountains rise vast and majestic, blue and white and black, in the far distance, north and south; in thirty-two miles the track ascends over two thousand feet, but so uniformly is the rise distributed that at no point is the grade above eighty feet to the mile; and at Sherman or Evans's Pass,[19] we are eight thousand two hundred and sixty-two feet above the sea level—the highest point in the whole line of the Pacific Railroad, yet the crest, not of the main or continental range of mountains, but of its eastern line of "Black Hills," so called. Out of narrower plain, free from these ruins of the old mountains, down a thousand feet or so, the road next enters upon and crosses the wide Laramie Plains; a trifle sheltered, yet open to sharp suns and long, piercing breezes, and selected for their various attractions for the summer homes of the railroad officials. These were famous hunting-grounds of the Indians; agreeable resting-places for the emigrant caravans of old; and long the chief outpost of the army in the mountain region.[20]

All this section of the road for one hundred and fifty miles west of Cheyenne possesses the greatest novelty and charm for the traveler. The senses all dilate with what is spread before and around him; rich black mountains bound the horizon north and south; a dash of snow on peak or side occasionally enlivens the view and deepens the coloring; along your pathway are fine valleys or broader plains, rich in grass and flowers; nature has fashioned it for a railroad; scattered around in valley or plain, as the track approaches the summit, are monuments of rock, grotesquely or symmetrically arranged; here a wall as if for a bulwark, there the ruin of cathedral or fort, again a half-finished building, anon the fashion of a huge, dismasted screw steamer, with paddle astern and pilot-boat ahead; over all an atmosphere so pure that the eye seems to take in all space, and so dry and exhilarating that life titillates at every avenue, and we mount as if on angel's wings. Here would seem to be the fountain of health; and among these hills and plains is surely to be many a summer resort for the invalid and the pleasure-seeker in the by no means distant future. The hills have timber, though the plains are bare of it, and the water runs pure and bright, and carries trout in abundance, as plains and mountains give deer, mountain sheep, antelope and grouse. This whole wide pathway up and over the mountains seems to have been fashioning for its present use for ages. The hills have wasted into plain; those solid walls of fieldspar and granite disintegrated and dissipated into a fine gravel, that is the very perfection of a railway bed; where these "buttes" or monuments of remaining rock, that lie scattered about with such picturesque effect, are all that are left, the very kernel, so to speak of what was once but a close succession of real rocky mountains—a Pelion upon Ossa[21] that forbade passage to wheel of wagon or car.

But the next section of one hundred and fifty miles is a sad contrast. The charms of atmosphere and of distant mountains remain; but the green grass, the flowers, the pure water, the oases of trees, all depart, and we have a dreary waste of sage bush, a barren, alkali, dusty soil, little water, and that bitter and poisonous. This is the Bitter Creek country,[22] so horrible to slow emigrant travel, so painful to stage passengers. The eye has no joy, the lips no comfort through it; the sun burns by day, the cold chills at night; the fine, impalpable, poisonous dust chokes and chafes and chaps you everywhere. It is within this region that my letter is dated, and that the track crosses the continental divide. Rolling hills abound, but no mountains. The track winds easily along; but a water train has to be added to the usual supply trains, and the expense of construction is greatly increased by the distance which all material and all food and drink have to be drawn. Deep wells will in the future relieve the poverty and poisonousness of the surface water, whose alkali elements not only render it unfit for drink but impossible of use in the boilers of the engines.

Spite of the obstacles, however, the track marches on with magic rapidity. Ten to fifteen thousand men are at work on the grading of the three hundred miles between this point and Salt Lake valley. Following the completion of their work come the gangs of track layers with their supply trains. First the ties or sleepers, brought up from below or out of the neighboring hills, and carried several miles ahead of the train by innumerable mule teams. Then rails and spikes are transferred to platform cars and pushed up to the end of the track; and by help of horse and a dozen practiced men, working like automatons with brains, the iron lengths are dropped in place, spiked down, the car rolled over them, the work repeated, and again and again, at the rate of from *three* to *eight* miles a day,—the only limit yet found being the power of the completed road to bring up sleepers and rails to the supply trains of the contractors. The gangs of track-layers number in all from four hundred to five hundred; are picked men; live on the train or in tents which the train brings along as the track progresses; and are fed by the contractors in so good a style that no apologies were necessary in inviting our party of ladies and gentlemen to dine with them, and no hesitation felt on our part in accepting, nor any repentance at having accepted. It was one of the "squarest" meals of our whole trip so far.

For a few weeks now, Benton,[24] in this Bitter Creek country, is the end of the open road, and here passengers and freight going west are transhipped, and here are temporarily gathered that motley crew of desperadoes, outcasts and reckless speculators, that are following the road's progress, and rioting in the license and coarseness of unorganized society. It is a most aggravated specimen of the border town of America, not inaptly called "Hell on Wheels," and unknown to all other civilizations or barbarisms. One to two thousand men, and a dozen or two women, are camped on the alkali plain in tents and board shanties; not a tree, not a shrub, not a blade of grass visible; the dust ankle deep as you walk through it, and so fine and volatile that the slightest breeze loads the air with it, irritating every sense and poisoning half of them; a village of a few variety stores and shops, and many restaurants and grog-shops; by day disgusting, by night dangerous; almost everybody dirty, most filthy, and with the marks of lowest vice; averaging a murder a day; gambling and drinking, hurdy-gurdy dancing and the vilest of sexual commerce, the chief business and pastime of the hours,—this is Benton. Like its predecessors on the track, it fairly festers in corruption, disorder and death, and would rot, even in this dry air, should it outlast a brief sixty-day life. In a few weeks, its tents will be struck, its shanties razed, and with their dwellers will move on fifty or a hundred miles farther to repeat their life for another brief day. Where these people came from originally; where they will go to when the road is finished, and their occupation is over, are both puzzles too intricate for me. Hell would appear to have been raked to furnish them; and to it they will naturally return after graduating here, fitted for its highest seats and its most diabolical service.

Beyond this one hundred and fifty mile section of desert country, that marks the divide between the waters of the two oceans, the road crosses Green River and enters upon the descent into the Salt Lake basin.[25] The country here changes rapidly; it is broken by mountain ranges, and coursed by fresh rivers; and every way becomes most interesting to the traveler, and most difficult for the railroad constructor. The section from Green River to the Salt Lake valley is the hardest part of the whole line of the Union Pacific Road to build; heavy rock cuttings and embankments, sharp curves, and tunnels are necessitated; yet there is nothing in it all so serious and expensive as the work on the line of the railroads through and over the Allegheny Mountains, or worse than that the Boston and Albany Railroad encountered west of Springfield. The traveler will find pleasure, however, where the contractors met labor; the wonderful Church Butte,[26] the charming high valley region about Fort Bridger,[27] the narrow, rock-embraced canyons or gorges of Echo and Weber,[28] the white-capped Wasatch Mountains,[29]—all will awaken his enthusiasm and wonder, and lead him down to the settlements and civilization of the Mormon saints[30] in a frame of pleasurable and curious excitement.[31] He will need all its stimulus, however, to carry him contented over the new and wider desert country that the road will yet take him, along and beyond the Humboldt valley,[32] through northern Nevada, and on to the now double-welcome glories of the Sierra Nevadas.[33] And here upon the threshold of California, we leave him to find his own way.

Everybody inquires how the Pacific Railroad is built? Well or ill—as faithful as fast—befitting or betraying the royal endowment of the American people? A monosyllable will not answer the question. Well, with a qualification; ill, with a qualification. As well, certainly, as new roads are generally built in America—better surely than the North-western Road is built across Iowa. As well, too, as is consistent with such speed. The ties are plenty, a third thicker at least than is usual in the East; the rails as good as the Pennsylvania iron consciences and poverty will permit; and the adjustments all faithfully made and by competent workmen. I could wish the bed had been thrown up a foot higher across the Plains, to escape the flood of possible heavy rains and the drift of snows; long sections are certainly imperfectly ballasted, or not at all; wooden bridges and culverts need to be rebuilt with stone; tressle-work should be replaced by embankments; and embankments need widening; many curves and circles should be cut across, the line straightened and shortened; and grades lowered or evened up. But the builders agree as to all this, except perhaps the height of the bed across the Plains, and are proceeding with the improvements and reconstructions as fast as the greater necessity for pushing on to the end will permit them. The only dispute there can be is as to the degree or extent which these completions and reconstructions are necessary or should be required.

The road has been and will be such a mine of wealth to its owners, they should be held by public and government to a strict performance of all their obligations,—they should give us in return for our gifts of money and land and privilege a thoroughly first-class road in every respect. But, on the other hand, exacting security for the perfection, they should be allowed generous time to do it in. The materials, stone, ballasting and timber, for all the work required, are upon the line; and when the rush of progress is over, and the road opened through, then the work of bringing up every part and every detail to perfection should be insisted upon by the one party, and cheerfully executed by the other. Self-interest invites the managers to this fidelity; they have found the road most profitable to build; they are likely to find it as profitable to own and run; and dependent as they must largely be upon the favor of public opinion and the protection and care of the government, aside from the necessity of having the road in thorough condition for its safe and profitable use, they will see how desirable it is they should leave no cause for complaint in the condition and management of the property.

No internal improvement was ever so generously endowed,—none was ever so wonderfully built. The government bounty was voted in ignorance of the difficulties and cost of the work.[34] They have proven much less than was expected. The entire road from the Missouri River to the Pacific Ocean is about one thousand seven hundred miles long. The California company builds six hundred miles, the New York company about one thousand one hundred, and their junction is near Salt Lake, Congress voted sixteen thousand dollars government bonds per mile of plain country; thirty-two thousand dollars per mile of more difficult territory; and forty-eight thousand dollars per mile of the higher and rougher mountains passed over; and it also authorized the companies to issue mortgage bonds of their own to equal amounts, which should take precedence in security of the government bonds. From one-half to two-thirds of the entire line is probably through "plain" country, yet, from a mixture of deception and ignorance, only about one-third was so counted. The average government grant was thirty thousand dollars a mile, and the companies' first bonds, which have found ready sale, just doubled this sum as the cash provision for the construction of the road, or sixty thousand dollars per mile. But the actual cost has not probably been over half this, or not far in excess of the government grant alone,—certainly, with equipment, it will not average over forty thousand dollars per mile. This would leave a net cash profit on the building and opening of the road of thirty-four million dollars. But, back of all this, the companies have the capital stock of the road, and own half the lands for a width of twenty miles along their tracks. There never was such a gigantic speculation on the American continent at least;[35] and it is safe to predict that no other railroad will ever win such largess from the government as this has.

To show how deceived or mistaken the government agents were in the character of the work to be done, the traveler only need to look at the one hundred and fifty miles of road west from Cheyenne, and remember that this is the section for which they allowed the highest price of forty-eight thousand dollars a mile as heavy mountain work. In fact, it is about as fine a country to build a railroad through as lies on the face of the globe. It is one long, inclined plane, with a fine, disintegrated granite for its soil, worked by plow and scraper, and affording the solidest and most permanent road bed that exists in America. Only a few hills had to be cut through, or embankments made, or streams crossed. The California company had no such rich streak of luck as this; their forty-eight thousand dollars a mile section was grievously heavy mountain work, over the rough and broken Sierra Nevadas, requiring heavy rock cuttings and many tunnels. But they had, to make up for it, no "plain" or sixteen thousand dollars a mile track at all; it was all forty-eight thousand dollars and thirty-two thousand dollars a mile, while many of their miles were as easy to build as the line across the Plains of the eastern section.

But no matter now! Only by such appeal to cupidity have we got this continental roadway opened so soon,—a gift to our nationality, to our commerce, to our wealth, that is worth in five years more than it all cost. And now if the gigantic corporations that own and use it will but let our politics alone, give the country faithful service and at a fair price, and spend some of their profits in opening branch lines to Montana, Idaho, and Oregon, we will gladly give them welcome to their fortunes, and cry quits.

The path and the profits of the Pacific Railroad are likely to be for some time from fresh subjects in our American lives, and so justify this long letter about them. We turn back the track to Cheyenne, and thence follow the mountains down to Denver to begin our real Summer Vacation in Colorado.

II.

TO DENVER AND THERE

Where the Mountains Lie—The Stage Ride from Cheyenne to Denver—Scenes in the Stage-Coach at Night—Meals on the Road—How Denver Looks—Its Growth, Attainments, and Prospects—The Mountain View from the Town—Denver and Salt Lake City Rivals in Beauty of Location and Attraction for Travelers.

DENVER, COLORADO, AUGUST, 1868

IT is the old story over again—the railroads do not show you the best of the country. Their tracks run through the back yards in towns, and away from the hills and among the barren wastes of the interior. You no more see the Rocky Mountains in riding over the Pacific Railroad than you do New York in going through the Fourth Avenue tunnels, or Springfield in steaming by the mechanic shops and restaurants of Railroad Row. Nature graded a grand pathway for the locomotive across our Continent; the mountains fall back to the right of us and to the left of us,—so far away that we catch only the dim outline of their greatness,—leaving but here and there a quaint ruin of or majestic monument to her mighty labor, that civilization may go by steam from ocean to ocean. The great mountain center of the Continent lies below the present railroad line; it looms up in the distance at Cheyenne; it marches along the southern horizon as you sweep up and across the magnificent Laramie Plains; it cheers you through the rolling alkali dust of the Bitter Creek country; and it shoots its spurs in beauty and in power before you, as you seek, more slowly, a descending path into the Salt Lake basin. But would you behold it in all its majestic grandeur, its multiplied folds of hight, with fields of ice and snow and rock, its beauty of infinite form and color, its wealth of flora and its wealth of gold and silver,—all the grand landscape and the hidden promise of the finest mountain region that the world holds,—then you must switch off from the main road, and come into the heart of Colorado, which is the very heart of our western Continent.

Bear in mind, too, that the great Pacific Railroad does not touch Colorado. It goes a few miles above the northern border. A branch road is now building from the main track at Cheyenne down to Denver, the capital and focal point of the state.[1] While waiting for that to be finished, next year, we travel this one hundred miles in a six-horse coach. If we could do it all by daylight, nothing could be more pleasant. The road lies across the last fifty miles of the Plains,—through high rolling green prairies, cut every fifteen or twenty miles by a vigorous river, with border of rich and cultivated intervale, and line of trees marking its progress from mountain debouch to the slow-sinking, wide-reaching horizon,—to the right the grim mountains with towering tops of rock and snow,—to the left the unending prairie ocean, with only an occasional cabin and scattered herd of cattle to break its majestic solitude and indicate human settlement; there is such magnificent outdoorness in the continuous scene as no narrower or differently combined landscape can offer, and so long as the day lasts it is a thing of beauty and of joy. But it is a twenty hours' ride, and the stage arrangements make a night of it. And in stage-riding it is peculiarly true that it is the first night that costs. It is more intolerable than the combination of the succeeding half-dozen, were the journey prolonged for a week; the breaking-in is fearful,—the prolongation is bearable. The air gets cold, the road grows dusty and chokes, or rough and alarms you; the legs become stiff and numb, the temper edges; everybody is overcome with sleep, but can't stay asleep,—the struggle of contending nature racks every nerve, fires every feeling; everybody flounders and knocks about against everybody else in helpless despair; perhaps the biggest man in the stage will really get asleep, which doing he involuntarily and with irresistible momentum spreads himself, legs, boots, arms and head, over the whole inside of the coach; the girls screech, the profane swear; some lady wants a smelling bottle out of her bag and her bag is somewhere on the floor,—nobody knows where,—but found it must be; everybody's back hair comes down, and what is nature and what is art in costume and character is revealed,—and then, hardest trial of all, morning breaks upon the scene and the feelings,—everybody dirty, grimy, faint, "all to pieces," cross,—such a disenchanting exhibition! The girl that is lovely then, the man who is gallant and serene,—let them be catalogued for posterity, and translated at once,—heaven cannot spare such ornaments; and they are too aggravating for earth.

Every ten miles we stop to change horses, and the driver, night or day, signalizes the approach to a station by a miniature war-whoop, that, as the Bostonians say of their great organ, "must be heard to be appreciated,"—it is certainly rather startling to new ears. Every thirty miles or so, a "home" station and a "square meal." Dinner, supper and breakfast are all alike, and invariably generous and good, more uniformly so, indeed, than those along the railroad line from Chicago to the mountains, We missed willingly some of one sort of "home" stations, that we encountered out here three years ago in the "Across the Continent" ride,—single-roomed turf cabins, bare dirt floors, milkless coffee, rancid bacon, stale beans, and green bread, and "if you don't like these help yourself to mustard;" but we welcomed heartily, at the Laporte station,[2] where is the most of a village on the road, our old host and hostess, with whom the Indians then prevailed on us, in their charming fashion, to pass a sweet and silent Sunday in their little retreat of Virginia Dale park in the mountain on the old road,[3]—lady and gentleman now as then by diviner gifts than those of milliner or tailor. It was pleasant to see they had prospered, and got out among neighbors, where Indian raids, of which they had survived no fewer than eight in their solitary Dale station, now abandoned, were less threatening; pleasant to have the ladies confirm the picture in "Across the Continent" on comparison with the original; pleasantest of all, perhaps, to find *she* had not forgotten our weakness for good victual. Those sup well who sup with our heroine of Virginia Dale, and if they would have especial grace and greeting, let them prove acquaintance with the "Colfax party."

The Vice-President often dwells on "the two kinds of welcome," and it was the other kind that we met at the next eating-place. Our stage was an "extra," and "ran wild," and so came along unawareness. It was a trifle rough, therefore, to rouse a lone woman, at one o'clock in the night, to get us some supper or breakfast,—whichever you choose to call it. She could do it, she said, but she didn't quite like to. But who could resist the gallant Vice-President whether pleading for ballot or breakfast; or the offers of help from the ladies; or the final suggestion of the driver? She wavered at the first; the second operated as a challenge to her capacity; and the third was irresistable.[4] There is no king on his route like a stage driver,— he has a "dreadful winning way" with him, both for horses and women. The philosophy of it I do not understand, but the fact is universal and stubborn; he is the successful diplomat of the road; no meal can be begun till he is in place; and there are no vacant seats where he drives,— even the cold night air would not send our girls off his box, and inside, during this long ride. So, at two o'clock in the morning, we sat down to beef and ham and potatoes, tea and coffee, bread and butter, pies, cakes and canned fruits,— not even the edges of the "squareness" of the meal rubbed off, and good humor everywhere.

We cross the rivers Cache-a-la Poudre,[5]—which indicates that some Frenchman deposited his powder here aforetime,—St. Vrains,[6] Big Thompson,[7] Little Thompson,[8] Boulder,[9] Clear Creek,[10] and finally the South Platte, to which all the others are tributary; and, having left Cheyenne at ten o'clock in the forenoon, gay and aggressive, we are tumbled out of the stage at Denver at eight the next morning,[11] feeble and flabby, hungry and humble, with a dreadful "morning after" feeling and appearance and movement about us.

But the air of Denver,[12] both inside and outside the houses, is very recuperating; we were soon toned up, and began to look about us. The town has spread out and settled down a good deal within three years. Things look less brisk, but more substantial and assured.[13] The town "feels its oats" less and its dignity more. It has passed its hot and fickle days, when gamblers reigned, and "to be or not to be" was the everlasting question that fretted everybody who owned real estate, and with which they, in a sort of your money-or-your-life manner, assaulted every stranger the moment he got out of the stage. Now, though trade is dull, and I have seen but one fight since I came to town, the Denverites all wear a fixed fact sort of air, and most of them are able to tell you, in a low and confidential chuckle, calling for envy rather than sympathy, that they own a quarter section just out there on the bluff, to which the town is rapidly spreading, and where the capitol buildings and the fine residences will all be located,[14] or a few corner lots down near the river, where the mills and the factories are destined to rise in the near future. Long lines of brick stores already give permanent and prosperous air to the town; its dry and its wet rivers are both newly bridged;[15] irrigating ditches scatter water freely through streets, lawns and gardens, and now flowers and fruits, trees and vegetables lend their civilizing influences and their permanent attractions to the place; national banks emit their greenbacks and will "do" your little note most graciously at from one to two per cent a month and "a grab mortgage" behind it; Episcopal Bishop Randall from Boston has established an excellent school for girls;[16] the Catholics have a larger educational establishment; the Methodists have the handsomest church and wear the best clothes;[17] the Baptists and Congregationalists are lively and aggressive; the stores are closed Sundays; the nights are quiet and the police have a sinecure; free schools are organized;[18] and three daily papers and two independent weeklies are published in the town.[19] Kitchen girls are scarce and a dear luxury, with pay at fifty dollars to seventy-five dollars a month; but the consequences is that the cooking is excellent, and people live "first rate." The dwelling-houses are mostly small, a single story or a story and a half, but within are comforts and luxuries in abundance, and one house boasts a true

Van Dyke.[20] The emigrant and the traveler must "move on" by Denver if he would get beyond the organization of the best American social and intellectual life.

I see I have spoken of Denver's "dry river," which calls for a parenthetical paragraph in explanation. The South Platte sweeps around the lower part of the town, broad and turbulent, of certain volume but uncertain track, useless for navigation but excellent for irrigation; but more sharply through the center of the business section lies Cherry Creek,[21] now a broad bottom of dry sand, and only occasionally enlivened with any water. For years after the founding of the town, none appeared in its bed, and supposing it to have been deserted altogether, the people builded and lived in the bottom. Stores, shops and dwellings, streets and blocks appeared there; it was the heart of the town; the printing office was there, also the city records; but of a sudden, after a heavy rain, there came a flood pouring down the old river bed, not gradually and in rivulets, to warn, but a full-blown stream marched abreast with torrent force and almost lightning speed, reclaimed its own, and swept everything that had usurped its place into destruction.[22] Since then, the people have paid respect to Cherry Creek; at some seasons of the year there is still a little water in its sands, but for the most part it is dry through the town; but nobody builds in the bed, and bridges over its path pay tribute to what it has been and may be again. Farther up its line, there is water in it now; but the sands consume and an irrigating ditch seduces it all away before it reaches the limits of the city.

Her central location, under the mountains, in the Plains section of the state, gives Denver a fine climate the year through; is favorable for trade to all parts of the state; secures to her the outgo and the income of the mining districts; makes her also the chief market for all the productions of the farming counties, and the focal point for all travel to and from the mountains, as well as north to the Railroad, and south to New Mexico; and endows her with a scene of mountain panoramic beauty, one hundred miles long, now touched with clouds, now radiant with sunshine, then dark with rocks and trees, again white with snow, now cold, now warm, but always inspiring in grandeur, and ever unmatched by the possession of any other city of Europe or America. The finest views of these mountains are obtained farther out in the Plains, where the more distant peaks come into sight, and the depth and variety, as well as the height and beauty of the range, are realized; and wider and older travelers than I,—who have seen the Cordilleras of South America from the sea, as well the Alps from Berne,[23] join in the judgment that no grand mountain view exists, that surpasses this, as seen from the high roll of the prairie just out of Denver, and over which the town is fast spreading, and so on from twenty to forty miles farther east. The one point of grandest view is located at the last "home station" on the Smoky Hill road,[24] about thirty-five miles east from Denver, and along which the St. Louis Pacific Road will probably be built another year.

With these charms of climate and landscape, with a settled and intelligent and prosperous population already of four thousand to five thousand,[25] with business connections and facilities, social order and attractions, religious and educational institutions, all well organized, and fed by their own interior force,—growing from within out, and not simply by fresh importations of eastern material,—and holding the conceded position of the social, political and commercial capital of the state, Denver has a gratifying future of growth before it. Another year will bring through it the Pacific Railroad on the St. Louis route,[26] connecting here with the branch of the main or central road that drops down from Cheyenne; a railroad is already commenced, also, towards the mining centers of the mountains by the Clear Creek valley;[27] and it cannot be long before a southern road will be demanded, down from Denver along the base of the Mountains to southern Colorado and Santa Fe. Not unlikely, indeed, it will prove wiser to carry the first southern Pacific Railroad around this way, rather than to strike diagonally across to Santa Fe from the present terminus of the St. Louis Road, as is proposed, for this route is through a rich and already partly developed agricultural country, while that goes by half or wholly barren table-lands, not likely to be at all occupied for many years, and never capable like this of holding a large population.

Coal and iron and clay are found in the neighborhood; the hills give timber; the valleys every grain and vegetable and many fruits; and Denver cannot well escape a steady and healthy growth, and the destiny of becoming one of the most permanently prosperous, as it will be certainly one of the most beautiful of our great western interior cities. I rank it along with Salt Lake City. Both are off the main line of the continental railroad; but both have locations amid developed natural wealth and conceded natural beauty, that must command their future, and make it one of power and prosperity. Six hundred miles apart, with the continental range of mountains separating them, there can be no rivalry between them, save in social graces and pleasure attractions, and here the Mormon supremacy in Salt Lake will give Denver great advantages.

III.

THE GEOGRAPHY OF COLORADO

The Back-bone of the Continent—The Mother Mountains of America—The Three Great Divisions of Colorado—Her Plains, Her Folds of High Mountain Ranges, Her Great Natural, Elevated Parks—North, Middle and South Parks; their Surroundings and their Beauties—The Unknown West of Colorado.

IN THE MOUNTAINS, COLORADO,
AUGUST, 1868

As Pennsylvania is the key-stone in the Atlantic belt or arch of states, so is Colorado the key-stone in the grand continental formation. She holds the back-bone, the stiffening of the Republic. Lying a huge square block in the very center of the vast region bounded by the Mississippi valley on the east, the Pacific Ocean on the west, and British America and Mexico north and south, the continental mountain chain here dwells in finest proportions, exaggerates, puffs itself up and spreads itself around with a perfect wantonness and luxuriance of power,—great fountains of gold and silver, and lead and copper, and zinc and iron,—great fountains of water that pours itself in all directions through the whole interior of the Continent, feeding a wealth of agriculture that is little developed and never yet dreamed of even,—great fountains of health in pure, dry and stimulating air,—great fountains of natural beauty; she may proudly bid the nation come to her for strength, for wealth, for vigor,—for rest and restoration,—and may well call her mountains the Sierra Madre, the Mother Mountains of the Continent.

Her geographical prominence and parentage are but type and promise of her future relations to the developed and developing life of the nation. Stretching two hundred and sixty miles north and south, and three hundred and seventy-five miles east and west, her territory has three natural subdivisions. The eastern third is of the Plains, and forms their western section,—a high rolling plateau from four thousand to five thousand feet above the sea level, richly watered by streams from the mountains, the strips along the rivers ripe for abundant harvests of grain and fruits and vegetables, the whole already the finest pasture land of the Continent, and with irrigation, for which the streams afford ready facility, capable of most successful cultivation,—beautiful in its wide, treeless sea of green and gray, with waves of land to break the monotony and lift the eye on to the great panorama of mountains, snow-slashed and snow-capped, that hangs over its western line through all its length of two hundred and sixty miles, and marks the second or middle division of the state. This is of about equal width,—mountains one hundred, one hundred and fifty, two hundred miles deep,—on, on to the west, till even this pure air tires of carrying the eye over peak on peak, over range on range,—you think you must look over into Brigham Young's fertile valleys, and trace the Colorado River out of its grand mystery, even if the outer and faintest rim does not shadow forth the Sierra Nevada of California.

Starting from an elevation at the end of the Plains of five thousand to five thousand five hundred feet, these mountains rapidly carry you up to eight thousand, ten thousand, thirteen thousand, near to fifteen thousand feet above the sea level.[1] Nine, ten, and twelve thousand feet peaks are scattered everywhere,—they are the mountains,—while those that mount to thirteen or fourteen thousand are plenty enough to be familiar, and are indeed rarely out of sight. They do not form a simple line, ascending from one and descending to another plain or valley, but are a dozen lines folded on, and mingled among each other, in admirable confusion; opening to let their superfluous waters flow out; closing to hold their treasures and defy the approach of man; gathering up all their strength, as it were, to make a peak or two of extra massive proportions, cold with snow and dreary with rock; and shading down into comparatively tender hills, that woo the forests and the flowers to their very summits. The line of peaks that divide the waters that flow to the Atlantic from those coursing into the Pacific,—"the divide," par excellence,—twists and turns through the territory, very much in the style of a long and double-backed bow, making an almost entire circle sometimes, and then coming back to its mission as a north and south line. Within its huge folds are other "divides," separating the feeders to rival rivers of the same continental side, or rival feeders of the same river, and other ranges with peaks as high as the parent range; and within and among them all the hills, as if tired of height and perpendicularity, give way to wide plains or prairies, with all the beauties and characteristics of plains and prairies outside the mountain region, and the added charm of holding little baby mountains of their own to diversify the landscape and feed forest and stream, while up and around them grow, through woods and grassy openings, the grand parent ranges that guard and enfold what are well called NATURAL PARKS.

These Parks are a distinctive and remarkable feature of this mountain center or belt of Colorado. They open upon the traveler at frequent intervals in charming unexpectedness; rich with grass and water, with trees and flowers, with soft beauty of outline and warm beauty of color, in most admirable contrast to the rough rocks and white snow of the high ranges around. Most of these Parks are of course, petite,—little wide valleys around the heads of single streams, or the conjunctions of several, or the homes of sweet lakes; but there are four great ones that mark the phenomenon and give the name. These are North Park,[2] Middle Park, South Park and San Luis Park,[3] varying in size from twenty by fifty miles to one hundred by two hundred, or say from Rhode Island to Massachusetts,—little episodes and interjections among these mountains, by whose size, as thus stated, you may take in some sense of the extent and majesty of the region, of which they are a sub-feature, as a whole.

The North Park extends up to the northern line of the territory and within thirty or forty miles of the Pacific Railroad; through and out of it flow the head waters of the North Platte; its streams are thicker with trout, and its sage brush and buffalo grass and wooded hill-sides offer more deer and wolves and antelopes and bears than are found in the lower and more frequented Parks, but its soil is colder as its elevation is higher, and its charms of color and vegetation more stinted. Middle Park lies next below, and separated by a single but high sub-range of the main mountains. This is fifty miles wide by seventy miles long, and as the continental divide sweeps around on its eastern side, all its waters flow into the Colorado of the West and so into the Pacific. But it embraces within itself several high ranges of hills and two or three different valleys.

The great peaks of the territory lie marshaled around it,—Long's Peak, Gray's Peaks, and Mount Lincoln,[4] north-east, south-east and south-west, each from thirteen thousand to fourteen thousand five hundred feet high; and snow-topped mountains circle its whole area. Milder and more beautiful in landscape than the North, it yet falls behind its neighbor on the other side, the South Park, which is thirty miles wide and sixty long, and, fellowshiping with the North Park, comes into the inner tail of the bow, carries the continental divide on its west, and furnishes the waters of the Arkansas and the South Platte.

This (the South) is the more beautiful of the Parks and the better known. Mining discoveries within and around it have opened roads through it, and bordered it with settlements.[5] It offers a remarkable combination of the beauties of the Plains and those of the Mountains. They mingle and mix in charming association. Wide areas of rich prairie open out before the level eye; upraise it or turn one side, and grand snowy mountains carry the sight up among the clouds; and between these types of natural beauty are plentiful shadings in gently rolling hills, long level banks, thick and diversified forests, bright and bountiful streams,—all the grand panorama of natural beauty that hill and valley, mountain and plain, winter and summer, snow and verdure, trees and rocks, water and waste can produce in combination and comparison, is here spread before the spectator, not from a single spot or in a single hour of his travel, but from mile to mile, from day's journey to day's journey, ever the same various scene, yet ever shifting in its kaleidoscopic alliances and changes.

The San Luis Park lies along and around the Arkansas and its tributaries in Southern Colorado and Northern New

Mexico, is the largest and perhaps the most varied of the series of great Parks, centers about a grand lake, and is rich alike in agricultural and mineral promise. The Indians have robbed us of our promised peep into its lines,[6] and we know it only by its kinship to those we have visited, and the enthusiastic descriptions of those to whom it is familiar. But the South Park as yet takes the palm among the Coloradians, perhaps only, however, because it is the more accessible, and its beauties more thoroughly explored. Certainly it lies more closely in the lap of the great mountains; and Mount Lincoln and Pike's Peak,[7] perhaps the most noted and remarkable of all the high peaks of the territory, sentinel it north and south, feed it from their snows, protect it from the rough winds, shadow it from the sharp suns.

In spite of these great elevations, the traveler carries summer skies as he keeps summer scenes with him at this season in most of his excursions among the mountains and their parks in Colorado. We borrow our ideas of mountain travel and mountain heights from Switzerland and the White Mountains of New Hampshire. Among them both, vegetation ceases at about five thousand feet above the sea level, and perpetual snow reigns among the Alps at seven thousand to eight thousand feet, and would in the White Mountains if they went as high. But here in these vaster mountain regions than either of Western America, the hills themselves only begin to rise from the Plains at an elevation of five thousand five hundred feet. And at that height, though the nights are always deliciously cool, the summer's days are as warm as if not warmer than they ever are in the valleys of the New England States, and snow enough for sleighing or to force the cattle to shelter or other food than the prairie is only a rare chance,—a memory of the oldest, or a dream of the youngest inhabitant. At six thousand or seven thousand feet, in the valleys of the mountains, the small grains and the tenderer vegetables are successfully cultivated, and at seven thousand five hundred and eight thousand five hundred feet, potatoes, turnips and cabbages thrive. The Middle Park ranges from seven thousand seven hundred to nine thousand feet high in its level sections, and the South from six thousand five hundred to seven thousand five hundred, while the higher plains and embraced hills of both run up to ten thousand and even eleven thousand feet. Yet grass grows richly and abundantly through both; hay is a great natural crop, and is cured already for all the wants that can be reached; and in the lower parts of the South Park, cattle winter out of doors, and the smaller grains and hardier vegetables are grown with great success and profit. Flowers are beautiful and abundant up to ten thousand or eleven thousand feet,—so beautiful and abundant that I must reserve them for special description,—the largest and best timber grows at nine thousand to eleven thousand feet, and trees do not cease till you pass above eleven thousand five hundred feet, while the real, absolute and perpetual snow line,—such snow and ice as are found universally in Switzerland at eight thousand feet,—is not reached at all in these mountains. At twelve thousand feet, it begins to lie in great patches on the shaded sides of the hills, or in deep ravines, and goes on to multiply in such form as the mountains rise to their greatest height at fourteen thousand to fourteen thousand five hundred feet. But it absolutely covers no mountain peak; the tops of Gray's Peaks and Mount Lincoln, the highest points in the whole region, are dry and bare, at least at midday, through August, though in reaching them you may go over snow fields twenty or thirty feet deep and miles long, though nearly every morning's sun may glance brilliantly off the freshly whitened peaks of all the high mountains in sight, and though it makes everywhere and at all times a significant feature in all the landscape visions of the country. The full mountains of snow and the vast rivers of ice that belong to Switzerland are not here, and are certainly missed by the experienced mountain traveler; but for their absence we have many compensations,—a more varied and richer verdure, a wider range of mountains, with greater variety of form and color, these elevated Parks, that have no parallel anywhere for curious combinations of landscape feature and beauty and practical use, a climate in summer that fosters comfort and makes high mountain travel both much more possible and agreeable, and an atmosphere that, in purity and dryness, in inspiring influence upon body and mind, can find no match in any part of Europe, nor elsewhere in America.

The third or western great division of Colorado is comparatively unknown.[8] Explorers have crossed it here and there; adventurous miners have penetrated into this and that of its valleys; but it holds no real population, and its character is known only in a general way. The great mountain ranges shade down irregularly through it into the vast interior basin of the West, instead of breaking off almost abruptly, as they do on their eastern side, into the level plains; the Grand,[9] the White,[10] the Green and the Gunnison,[11] the great feeders of the Colorado of the West, slash freely through it, often by narrow and unapproachable gorges, often too through wide and rich valleys; many a high park, with rough sage brush and tall grass, spreads itself out, cold and dreary in the north, warmer and more fertile in the south. Many a fable of rich mines, of beautiful valleys, of broken and ruined mountains,—the debris of great conflicts of nature,—many a deep faith in untold wealth and unnumbered beauties do I hear of and about this section of the territory; but the fact remains that it has but few settlers and no especial history,—and I gather the conclusion that it is in every way less interesting to traveler, less enticing to speculator or settler, than the middle and eastern divisions. New and thorough explorations are in progress through its lines;[12] another year will add something to our knowledge of its valleys and mountains; but for the present it is perhaps as much unknown land as any section of equal size in the United States.

IV.

TRAVEL AMONG THE MOUNTAINS

From Denver up into the Mountains—How the Honest Miners Travel, and Colorado Families Make Summer Excursions—The Clear Creek Valleys—The Scene of Bierstadt's Storm in the Rocky Mountains—The Outfit for a Trip to Middle Park—We Celebrate the Mule—The Upper Valley of Clear Creek, and up the Mountain Side—The Flowers, the Shrubs, and the Trees of the Higher Regions.

Top of Berthoud Pass, August, 1868

Going into the mountains from Denver,[1] the traveler has choice of several roads. To the north he passes up Boulder Creek to Boulder City and its sub-villages and mining camps;[2] more directly west are the Clear Creek valley routes,[3] one by Golden City,[4] and on to North Clear Creek, with Black Hawk and Central City,[5] that run into each other and form the chief mining town of the territory, and passing from here over to South Clear Creek, with Idaho,[6] Fall River,[7] Mill City,[8] Empire[9] and Georgetown[10] on its line,—this being the daily stage route, and the other, farther south, going up the Mount Vernon road,[11] and striking down into the South Clear Creek valley below Idaho; while still farther south, where Bear Creek and Turkey Creek come out of the mountain range,[12] is the road that leads up and through the South Park country. At this season all these roads are good,—for mountain roads; in most part quite excellent and much traveled, and kept in repair by tolls collected under territorial charters.[13] Fifty miles is the end of the stage line and wagon road at Georgetown; and a like distance on either road takes you into the midst of the high mountains, and to the foot of the continental range. The Boulder and both the Clear Creek roads all connect by cross-roads in the mountains; but there is no direct connection between the South Park and the upper Clear Creek valleys save by trails. A tri-weekly stage-wagon goes direct from Denver into the South Park region to supply its villages with mails and carry passengers.

All these roads introduce one delightfully to close companionship with the mountain scenery,—first through the long, wide prairie; then into narrow valleys; occasionally a bold gorge or canyon and a broken mountain; up and among and over high hills, commanding majestic views of higher summits beyond; through little wooded parks or open fields, where grain grows and flocks feed, and somebody keeps "a ranch;" by lively streams with tangles of willows and hops and clematis, and fruity shrubs up the drier and higher banks; among flowers everywhere, growing finer and plentier the higher you climb; out and in forests of various species of cotton-wood and evergreen, often brown and dead through wasting fires that have swept the hill-sides, or half cleared for the consuming rage of the gold and silver furnaces, but still a rich possession of beauty and wealth for the country; under a sun always searching with heat, but through an atmosphere growing rarer and rarer and drier and drier, and ever fresh and cool,—the day's ride is thus a perpetual pleasure and surprise to the newcomer.

We scattered in disorder on our first trip to the mountains. The Vice-President and the Governor took the stage and fulfilled several appointments to make speeches.[14] Governor Hunt of the Territory made up a camping excursion for the young ladies,[15] with carriage, saddle-horses and outfit of tents, blankets, cooking-stove and "grub" in bulk, and moved leisurely up by the Mount Vernon road,—reckless of time or taverns, and stopping wherever hunger or night overtook them.[16] That patriarch of the country, General Pierce,[17] and myself, drove "a one-horse shay" by the same route; and when we grew hungry, we picked out a brook and a choice lot of grass, turned the horse loose for an hour, and lay among the flowers and disposed of huge piles of bread and butter and meat, that we had brought with us, after the fashion of the country. This independent camping habit is almost the rule with home travelers here. It grew up with the necessities of the early settlements and the roving, straggling ways of the miners. The taverns are not now frequent or good; the climate favors the outdoor life at this season; and with provision in abundance, blankets, a coffee-pot, a frying-pan, and a sack of flour and a side of bacon, either in a wagon, or packed on an extra horse, if you are journeying in the saddle, even pleasure-travelers find it much the more comfortable and decidedly the more independent mode, while to the old settler, and especially to a miner, it is altogether a matter of course. One of these hangs his blanket and his coffee-pot and frying-pan, with a joint of meat and a bit of bread, around his saddle, and without extra animal or companion, is good for a week's journey among the mountains. What he lacks for food he finds in the streams or woods, or buys at the occasional ranch, and at night a deserted cabin, which is nearly always at hand, where miners have been and are not, or a roadside tree and an open camp fire furnish him shelter and warmth.

He sleeps the sleep of the tired, and if it rains and he gets wet, the renewed fire dries him, and the climate never encourages colds. So with the multiple of our single traveler; with companions conveniences and comforts increase, but the fashion is the same; and whole families,—mothers and babies included,—will, with covered wagon and a saddle-horse or two, make a pleasure visit to the mountains, after this fashion, and live literally on the country for days and weeks, in delightful and refreshing companionship with Nature. It was this sort of life that we were all entering upon, in all its strange novelty and stimulating influences.

We found the Clear Creek valleys generally brisk and beautiful. Between mining and milling and the late floods, the north one is terribly torn to pieces, and looks rough and ragged. Black Hawk and Central City may be good places to get gold in, but there can be no genuine homes there. The valley is too narrow, a mere ravine, and all beauty is sacrificed to use; though after all beauty is truly use,—but to the mere use of washing out gold. Below and above, the valley widens and is finer; but over the divide on the South Branch, there is a very charming country to look upon and live in. Below Idaho, gulch mining, which is pretty lively and successful still, despoils the prospect so far as man can; but the dozen or fifteen miles from Idaho up by Fall River, Mill City and Empire to Georgetown, is quite the nicest bit of the inhabited portion of the mountains. The valley is not wide, indeed you can heave a stone across it in the narrower, and fire a rifle from hill to hill at its wider parts; but it breaks out frequently into little nooks of plateaus or bars; it opens up into seductive side valleys or canyons, and it winds and turns about, and sends up its high mountain walls in

Idaho Springs in the 1860s. Gold was discovered at the head of Chicago Creek in January 1859, and the townsite was laid out immediately. (WESTERN HISTORY DEPARTMENT, DENVER PUBLIC LIBRARY, NO. 43008)

Empire City, originally called Valley City. Gold was discovered here in 1864. (WESTERN HISTORY DEPARTMENT, DENVER PUBLIC LIBRARY, NO. 7273)

Founded as a gold mining camp in 1859, Georgetown became the most important silver mining town in Colorado (WESTERN HISTORY DEPARTMENT, DENVER PUBLIC LIBRARY, NO. 7097)

form and manner, to present a constantly varying but ever beautiful scene. At the upper end, winter confronts you in snow-covered peaks; below, nature looks warm and summer-like; and though the valley is from seven thousand five hundred to eight thousand five hundred feet high, the days are like June and October, and the winter is not long or severe. Till you reach Georgetown, where the hills shut in the valley sharply, and the rich silver section has its center, there is not much mining, and the villages are but neighborhoods of six to a dozen houses each. Idaho and Fall River have good hotels, and are favorite summer resorts. The former has a wonderful hot soda spring that furnishes most refreshing and health-giving baths. Over it rise a family group of three peaks, distinguishable in all mountain views, and known as the Chief, Squaw and Papoose,[18] and up from the valley here you rise to Chicago Lake[19] and Chicago Mountain, familiar as the foreground scene in Bierstadt's "Storm in the Rocky Mountains."[20]

All these mountains go sharply up from two to four thousand feet above the valley, often past the timber line, and end in snow or bare, grim rocks. They offer unending fascination to the lover of mountain-climbing and mountain views; while to lie on the grassy banks just above the river,—that, in practical parenthesis, it should be noted, runs swift and strong down the rapid descent of the valley, and is full of "water power,"—in the warm sun, and look through the snowy fleece of grass-hoppers, that with outstretched wings fill the air, up and among them,—masses of forest and rock and patches of snow,—to the line of brightened blue sky they border,—this is just comfort and rest, and is worth the coming to experience.

It was from here that, sending wagons and women,

tents and trunks, back to Denver, and coming down as the miners say to the "bed-rock" of flannel overshirts and a pocket comb for personal baggage, we started with a select masculine party for a week's trip over into the Middle Park.

We had a number of welcome Colorado volunteers for this expedition. There was a full dozen of us that gathered after breakfast on mule and horseback in the last camp of Governor Hunt and the young ladies, far up the Clear Creek valley, above Empire. The latter went back, we forward, led by Governor Hunt and Indian Agent Oakes.[21] Charley Utter, a famous mountaineer, trapper. Indian scout, rover, such a character as only the American border can breed, small and tough, wiry and witty, intelligent and handsome,—alike at home in your parlor or an Indian hut,—and to whom all these mountains and parks are as familiar as your own paternal acres are to yourself;[22] he and his assistant, Franklin Ashley,[23] provided our animals and outfit generally, and also came along with us, to guide and help us in our new and strange life. Two extra mules and a horse carried our blankets and provisions and cooking utensils, and the personal baggage of those not weaned yet from carpet bags.

Some experience as a traveler myself, and more valuable advice from those of larger, had taught me to rise superior to such aristocratic impediments. Indeed, it proved I was outfitted in quite a model way, and had more of what was necessary and less of what was not, than others of the inexperienced in camp and mountain travel. First, woolen stockings and winter under clothing; and of these, an extra set, with two extra handkerchiefs and two towels, soap, comb and tooth-brush and slippers, only moderately filled a pair of light saddle-bags on my own animal. Over the undershirt was worn a dark and thick cassimere shirt, with turn-over collar of same and pocket in breast, which, coming nowhere in contact with the body, may be worn for weeks without disrespect to your washer-woman. A pair of very thick, high top, riding boots, of extra size, my last winter's thick pantaloons and heavy sack coat, and an old soft hat flexible as a rag, and answering as well for a night-cap, completed my clothing. No vest or waist-coat, no suspenders; a strap around the waist held things together, and carried a revolver and a tin cup. Over the saddle-bags behind were strapped a thin woolen overcoat,—it better have been thick,—and a loose rubber cloth coat; both which were frequently in use, and were always valuable at night; and as often in mid-day they had the company around the saddle of the sack coat, and I rode under the warm sun in pantaloons and shirts. It was a neat, complete and compact personal outfit; everything that was needed for a trip of two or three weeks, and the only modification I would make, in going again, would be to substitute a pair of old shoes for the slippers, and to have the rubber overcoat so modified that it would closely cover the legs in the saddle down to the boot-tops. All this was carried on and around my own saddle; my bedding alone went on the pack animals, and this consisted of two pairs of heavy blankets, a buffalo robe, a rubber blanket and a pillow,—all strapped into a tight roll or bundle,—no more than one restless sleeper needs in the cold night of these outdoor mountains, but equally abundant for two square and fair sleepers who will turn over at one and the same time and don't kick the clothes off.

My mule,—did you ever ride a mule? There is no other experience that exactly fits one for this. As far as a mule's brains go, he is pretty sensible,—and so obstinate! But it

Charley Utter, "famous mountaineer, trapper, Indian scout, rover, such a character as only the American border can breed." (WESTERN HISTORY DEPARTMENT, DENVER PUBLIC LIBRARY, NO. 17276)

takes a long while to beat a new idea into his head, and when it dawns on him, the effect is so overpowering that he just stops in amazed bewilderment, and won't move on again until he is relieved of the foreign consciousness, and gets back to his own original possessions. The whole process is startingly human; it inspires you with faith in the idea of the transmigration of souls. I know *so* many people who must have been mules once, or will be,—else there is no virtue in the fitness of things! But my mule belonged to the best of the race; he was prudent,—he never went in any doubtful places until somebody else had gone before and proved the way; he was very patient,—he would always stop for me to get off, or to get on; he was very tough,—my spurs never seemed to annoy him one atom, and my riding him didn't wear any skin off of *his* backsides, not a bit. But after we grew acquainted, and he came to appreciate the more delicate shades of my character, we got on charmingly together for the first half of the day; in the afternoon, when he grew lazy and tired, and I nervous, we often had serious discussions,—sometimes with sticks,—but he generally got the best of the argument.

If a well-broken Indian pony or a "broncho" (a California half-breed horse) can be got, either is probably better than a mule; more springy in tread and quicker in movement, and equally careful in mountain-climbing and fording streams and ditches; but otherwise, the mule is the better animal for your work on these expeditions. A "States" horse can't stand the hard riding and tough climbing, and besides must have grain to keep him up, while the mule and the Indian and "broncho" ponies will live on the rich grasses of the country. The latter are apt to be wilful and wicked, and should only be taken, in preference to the mules, upon good references as to character and a trial to boot.

But "get up, Jenny." We are falling fast in the rear. The narrow valley rapidly narrows, and becomes a defile, a gorge, wooded and flowered, rock-strewed and briskly watered,—a wild Alpine scene. The mountains rise sharp and sheer, one thousand and two thousand feet above the road, and wide walls of red granite hang over it. The stream turns and twists and foams and we follow a half-made road along, over, in its rugged path. There was an attempt made a few years ago to build a stage road through the mountains and over into Utah by this route; many thousand dollars were spent upon it; but it was found too big a job,[24] and it is passable now for only a few miles farther on. It takes the traveler into and among rich mountain beauties; even to come up here and go back, without an objective point beyond, is abundant recompense.

After four or five miles of this road, we turn sharply from it up an abrupt mountain trail; in single file, along a mere path on a steep hill-side, a mis-step of the mule would send animal and rider rolling over and over among the sparse trees down the declivity,—but mules don't mis-step, and even the top-heavy pack jacks,—a mountain on a molehill, indeed,—carried their burden and themselves unharmed to the top. The thin and thinning air offered severer trial, however, and the beasts struggled like huge bellows for wind, and trembled beneath us in the effort to take in enough to keep going; to get off and walk was to undergo the same trial ourselves, and walking or riding, we had every few rods to stop and adjust the lungs of man and beast to the rare and growing rarer air. There was temptation to stop, too, in the widening view of the upper mountains; their snowy fields and gray or red or brown walls and peaks lifted into sight, on all sides, close and familiar, distant and stranger, but making us feel, for the first time, their real companionship,—that nearness to great and sublime nature that awes and uplifts like the presence of God himself.

Passing the sharp mountain side, we come, at a hight of ten thousand feet, to pleasant little park openings, ascending by easy grade, half-wooded, and whose bright grass and abundant flowers and deep evergreens tell of fertile soil and protecting hights around. Such spots are frequent in all these high mountain ranges, and are exceeding fair to look upon. They are in their glory at this season; it is but a little while back to last year's snows, and a few weeks forward to another wintry embrace; and they make the most of their stinted time. So in July and August they compress the growth and the blossom of the whole year; and we see at once flowers that are passed and flowers that are yet to come in the Plains below; dandelions and buttercups, violets and roses, larkspurs and harebells, painter's brush and blue gentian,—these and their various companions of spring, summer and autumn, here they all are, starring the grass, drooping over the brook, improving every bit of sunshine among the trees, jealous of every lost hour in their brief lives.

I wish I could repeat the roll of this army of beauties for the benefit of my flower-learned readers; I know most of them very well by sight, as the lad said of his unlearned alphabet, but cannot call them by name. Blue and yellow are the dominant colors; of the former several varieties of little bell and trumpet-shaped blossoms, pendant along stalwart stalks; again, a similar shaped flower, but more delicate,—a little tube in pink and white, seems original here; and of the golden hues, there are babies and grandbabies of the sun-flower family in every shade and shape. One of these, about the size of a small tea-saucer, holds a center stem or spike of richest maroon red, with deepest yellow leaves flaring away from it,—each color the very concentration and ripeness of itself, as if dyed at the very fountain head. The harebell is at home everywhere; drooping modestly and alone on the barren and exposed mountain side at eleven thousand or twelve thousand feet, as well as in the protected parks among all its rivals; but the fringed gentian is more fastidious, and grows only where nature is richer, but then in such masses, with such deep blueness and such undeviating uprightness of stems, as to prove its birthright here. The painter's brush, as familiarly called here, is a new flower to me; something like the soldier's pompon in form, it stands stiff and distinct on a single stalk, about six inches tall, with three inches' length and one inch in thickness or diameter of flower, in every shade of red from deepest crimson to pale pink, and again in straw colors from almost white to deep lemon. We picked on a single morning's ride seven of different shades of red. A bunch of the brightest of this flower, with sprinkling of those of milder hues and a few grasses, such as could be gathered in five minutes in many a patch of Alpine meadow we passed through, was enough to set a flower-lover crazy with delight. It was a beacon, a flame of color, and would make a room aglow like brilliant picture or wood fire on the hearth. But perhaps the most bewitching of the flowers we discovered was a columbine, generous but delicate, of pale but firm purple and pure white,—it was very exquisite in form and shading. Higher up, where only mosses could grow for rock and snow, these were in great variety and richness, with white, with blue and with pink blossoms.

All this wonderful wealth and variety of flower is marked with strength but not coarseness; the colors are more deep and delicate than are found in garden flowers; and though frost and snow may stiffen their blossoms every morning,—for at ten thousand feet high and above, the temperature must go down to freezing every night,—the dryness of the air preserves them through their season, and they keep on growing and flowering until their September and October winter fairly freezes them out.

There is no such variety and beauty in the forests of the Rocky Mountains as those of the East and the extreme West both offer. The oak, the maple, the elm, the birch, all hard woods are unknown. Pines, firs and spruces of various species, and the cotton-wood, a soft maple or poplar, with delicate white wood and a pale green and smooth leaf, are all that this region can offer for trees. Nor are these generally of large size. The forests seem young and the individual trees small, even by the side of those of New England; there is no hint among them of the giants of the Pacific coast. The probability is that they are young, that the Indians kept them well burned off, and that, with settlement and civilization, in spite of the wanton waste now in progress, and against which there should be some speedy protection, the forest wealth will increase. Perhaps not in these first years, but by and by, when coal takes the chief place for fuel, and self-interest and legislation work out their care of the trees, and prevent devastating fires. But many a fine grove of thick and tall pines, that would warm the heart of any ship-builder, have we passed through; and their deep colors and firm forms, contrasting with the light and free-moving cotton-wood, give a pleasing and animated life to the forest landscape.

But the silver spruce is the one gem of the trees; a sort of first cousin of the evergreen we call the balsam fir in our New England yards, but more richly endowed with beauty of shape and color. It is scattered plentifully through these mountain valleys, and looks as if a delicate silver powder had been strewn over its deep green needles, or rather as if a light white frost had fallen all upon and enshrouded it; and you cannot help wondering why the breeze does not shake the powder off, or the sun dissipate the frost, so ever present is the one illusion or the other. But it holds its birthright persistently,—a soft white-blue-green combination of positive power that comes into the rather hardish gray neutral coloring of the general landscape with most agreeable, even inspiriting effects. This and another spruce often throw themselves into a very charming form of growth; gathering around an old pine, they will shoot up numerous spires, thin and tall, thicker and shorter, and so shade down to a close, spreading mass in a wide semicircle around,—a bit of natural cathedral-like posturing in tree and shrub life, so often repeated as to suggest art, so effective as to call out the delight and envy of every landscape artist who sees it. Everywhere among these high mountains, in barren rather than in fertile spots, we unexpectedly find the "Mahonia Holly," a favorite but winter drying shrub of our eastern lawns; they call it here the Oregon grape, for it bears a little berry, and it is evidently killed to the root every winter, for it gets only a few inches of growth, and I do not find it massed at all. But in its freely scattered little specimens, its deep, smooth and hard green leaves kept company with us until we had passed the timber line, and come out among the snow fields.

V.

THE MIDDLE PARK

The Berthoud Pass—"Such a Getting Down" Hill—Our First Night in Camp—The Middle Park and Across it—An Indian Rescue and a Civilized Reception—The Mountain Raspberries—The Hot Douche Springs—Trout Fishing—Life with the Ute Indians.

HOT SPRINGS, MIDDLE PARK, AUGUST 1868

AFTER three or four hours' hard riding, from the upper Clear Creek, we suddenly came out of the trees into an open space of hardy green, bordered by snow, a gap or sag in the mountains,—and behold we are at the top of Berthoud Pass. The waters of the Atlantic and Pacific start from our very feet; the winds from the two oceans suck through here into each other's embrace; above us the mountain peaks go up sharp with snow and rock, and shut in our view; but below and beyond through wide and thick forests lies Middle Park, a varied picture of plain and hill, with snowy peaks beyond and around. To this point, at least, I would advise all pleasure travelers to Colorado to come; it is a feasible excursion for any one who can sit in the saddle; it can be easily made with return in a day from Empire, Georgetown or even Idaho; and it offers as much of varied and sublime beauty in mountain scenery, as any so comparatively easy a trip yet within our experience possibly can.

But to follow us down into the Park is another and

tougher affair; the Colorado ladies do it occasionally, but it needs real strength and endurance and an unfaltering enthusiasm. The descent is sharp and rocky, and thick with timber, and worse, wet and miry. Bayard Taylor, who came over in June, found the path heavy with snow, and impassable to any but heroic travelers;[1] now the snows are gone, and it is dryer than at any other season, but it is a rough and hard descent, almost perpendicular in steepness at times, and full of treacherous holes of water and mire. But we all got through without disaster, and found relief about two o'clock in an open, grassy meadow, with a trout brook on its border. The order to camp was grateful; animals were turned loose, and we lolled in the sunshine, made and drank coffee, and ate our lunch of bread and butter, ham and canned peaches.

But we were not in the Park yet, and after an hour's rest, we remounted and moved on,—on, on, the road seemed interminable, through thick woods, over frequent morass and occasional mountain stream; deceptive in glimpse of park that was not the Park; all, save our irrepressible mountain leaders, weary with the long, rough ride, and eager for the end. It was near dark, after traveling from twenty to twenty-five miles in all, when we stopped for the night, in the woods, just without the open section of the Park. A bit of meadow with tall grass was at hand for the animals, and, relieved of saddles and packs, away they went, without let or hindrance, to enjoy it. The only precaution taken is to leave the lariat, a rope of twenty to thirty feet long, dragging at their necks, by which to catch them the more easily in the morning. Only a portion of the herd are thus provided, however. They rarely stray away far from camp; and if they should, these people make little of an hour or two's hunt to find them, which they are quite sure of doing wherever the best grass grows. The animals are picketed only when there is danger from the Indians, or a prompt start is necessary.

A big fire is soon blazing; a part prepare the supper,—tea and coffee, bacon, trout, potatoes, good bread and butter, and, to-night, a grouse soup, the best use Governor Hunt can make of an old bird he shot on the road, to-day, and very good use it proved, too, by help of tin pail potatoes and butter;—others feed the fire, bring the water, and prepare the camp for sleeping. An old canvass cloth serves for table; we squat on our blankets around it, and with tin cups, tin plates, knife and fork and spoon, take what is put before us, and are more than content. Eating rises to a spiritual enjoyment after such a day; and the Trois Freres[2] or Delmonico does not offer a "squarer meal" than Governor Hunt. The "world's people" make their beds against a huge tree, and cut and plant boughs around the heads to keep out the cold wind; but the old campers drop their blankets anywhere around the fire; and after going back over the day and forward to the morrow in pleasant chat, sitting around the glowing mass of flame and coal, we crawl in under our blankets, in a grand circle about the now smouldering logs, say our prayers to the twinkling stars up through the trees, and,—think of those new spring beds invented in Springfield![3]

We broke up housekeeping and started into the Park by nine o'clock the next morning. It isn't an easy matter to make an earlier start, when we have to carry our homes with us; cook and eat breakfast; wash the dishes; catch the animals; pack up beds and provisions; clean up camp, and reconstruct not only for a day's journey, but for a family moving. A short ride brought us into miles of clear prairie, with grass one to two feet high, and hearty streams struggling to be first into the Pacific Ocean. This was the Middle Park, and we had a long twenty-five miles ride northerly through it that day. It was not monotonous by any means. Frequent ranges of hills break the prairie; the latter changes from rich bottom lands with heavy grass, to light, cold gravelly uplands, thin with bunch grass and sage bush; sluggish streams and quick streams alternate; belts of hardy pines and tender looking aspens (cotton-wood) lie along the crests or sides of hills; farther away are higher hills fully wooded, and still beyond, "the range" that bounds the Park and circles it with eternal snows. The sun shines warm; there are wide reddish walls of granite or sandstone along many of the hills; some of the intervales are rich with green grass; and the sky is deep blue; and yet the prevailing tone and impression of the Park is a coldish gray. You find it on the earth; you see it in the subdued, tempered, or faded greens of leaf and shrub and grass; it hangs over the distant mountains; it prevails in the rocks; you feel it in the air,—a certain sort of stintedness or withholding impresses you, amid the magnificence of distance, of hight and breadth and length, with which you are surrounded, and which is the first and greatest and most constant thought of the presence.

We scattered along wildly enough; some stopping to catch trout; others humoring lazy mules and horses; others to enjoy at leisure the novel surroundings,—meeting, with fellow-feeling, for lunch and the noon rest, but dividing again for the afternoon ride. All had gone before,—leaders, guides, packs, and were out of sight,—when my friend and especial companion on this trip, Mr. Hawkins of Mill City, of Springfield raising and relation,[4] and myself rose over the hill that looked down into the valley that was our destination. It was a broad, fine vision. Right and left, several miles apart, ran miniature mountain ranges,—before, six miles away, rose an abrupt gray mountain wall; just beneath it, through green meadow, ran the Grand River; up to us a smooth, clean, gradual ascent; along the river bank, a hundred white tents, like dots in the distance, showed the encampment of six to eight hundred Ute Indians,[5] awaiting our party with "heap hungry" stomachs; in the upper farther corner, under the hill-side, a faint mist and stream in the air located the famous Hot Springs of the Middle Park,[6]—the whole as complete a picture of broad, open plain, set in mountain frame, as one would dream of. It spurred our lagging spirits, and we galloped down the long plane, whose six miles seemed to the eye not a third so long in this dry, pure air.

Reaching the river, through the Indian encampment, whose mongrel curs alone gave fighting greeting, it looked deep and was boisterous; our animals hesitated; and we thought sympathetically of Bayard Taylor's sad fortune in making this hard journey into the Middle Park to see and try the Hot Springs, and then being obliged by the flood to content himself with a distant view from this bank of the river.[7] But our comrades had gone over; and the only question was where. Looking for their track, directly there came galloping to our relief a gaily costumed Indian princess,—we were sure she was,—bare-backed for her haste to succor, and full of sweet sympathy for our anxiety, and tender smiles for our—attractiveness in misfortune. Plunging boldly into what seemed to us the deepest and swiftest part of the stream,—as doubtless it was,—she beckoned us to follow, with every enticing expression of eye and lips and hand; and follow we, of course, did,—had it been more dangerous we should,—and by folding ourselves up on the highest parts of our animals, we got through without serious wetting. But it proved that we crossed in the wrong place, and that our beautiful Indian princess, with beads and feathers and bright eyes and seductive ways, was only a plain young "buck,"—not even a maiden, not so much as a squaw, not, to come down to the worst at once, so near to glory and gallantry as a relationship to the Chief. Nothing less than the welcome we had from one of the best women of Colorado,—whom we parted from last in Fifth Avenue, and now found spending the summer with her family in a log cabin of one room, with eight hundred Indians for her only neighbors,[8]—and the arrival of her husband from his afternoon's fishing with two bushels of fine trout packed over his horse's back,—here only was adequate soothing and consolation for our chagrin. And we didn't go into camp that night till after supper,—after supper of fresh biscuits, fried trout, and mountain raspberries!

Let me celebrate these high mountain raspberries before the taste goes from my mouth. They grow freely on the hill-sides, from seven thousand to ten thousand feet up, on bushes from six to eighteen inches high, are small and red, and the only wild fruit of the region worth eating. They are delicate and high-flavored to extreme; their mountain home refines and elevates them into the very concentration and essence of all fruitiness; they not only tickle but intoxicate the palate,—so wild and aromatic, indeed, are they that they need some sugar to tone the flavor down to the despiritualized sense of a cultivated taste. Yet they are not so sour as to require sweetening,—only too high-toned for the stranger stomach; after sharing their native air a few days, we found them best picked and eaten from the vines. It is one of the motives of family excursion parties into the mountains at this season to lay in a supply of raspberry jam for the year; while the men catch trout, the women pick raspberries, cook and sugar them in the camp-kettle, and go home laden with this rare fruity sweetmeat. Here in the Middle Park we were kept in full supply of the fresh fruit by the Ute squaws, who, going off into the hills in the morning, often two together astride the same pony, and a little papoose strapped on its board over the back of one, would come back at night with cups and pails of the berries to exchange with the whites for their own two great weaknesses, sugar and biscuit. But the bears get the most of the raspberries so far. They are at home with them during all the season, and can pick and eat at leisure.

The Hot Springs of the Middle Park are both a curiosity and a virtue. They are a considerable resort already by Coloradians at this season, and when convenient roads are made over into the Park, there will be a great flow of visitors to them. We found twenty or thirty other visitors here, scattered about in the neighborhood, while parties were coming and going every day. The springs for bathing, and the rivers for fishing, are the two great attractions. On the hill-side, fifty feet above the Grand River, and a dozen rods away, these hot sulphurous waters bubble up at three or four different places within a few feet, and coming together into one stream flow over an abrupt bank, say a dozen feet high, into a little circular pool or basin below. Thence the waters scatter off into the river. But the pool and the fall unite to make a charming natural bathing-house. You are provided with a hot sitz bath and douche together. The stream that pours over the precipice into the pool is about as large as would flow out of a full water pail turned over, making a stream three to five inches in diameter. The water is so hot that you cannot at first bear your hand in it, being 110° Fahrenheit in temperature, and the blow of the falling water and its almost scalding heat send the bather shrieking out on his first trial of them; but with light experiments, first an arm, then a leg, and next a shoulder, he gradually gets accustomed to both heat and fall, and can stand directly under the stream without flinching, and then he has such a bath as he can find nowhere else in the world. The invigorating effects are wonderful; there is no lassitude, no chill from it, as is usually experienced after an ordinary hot bath elsewhere; though the water be 110° warm, and the air 30° to 40° cold, the shock of the fall is such a tonic, and the atmosphere itself is so dry and inspiring, that no reaction, no unfavorable effects are felt, even by feeble persons, in coming from one into the other. The first thing in the morning, the last at night did we renew our trial of this hot douche bath during our brief stay in the neighborhood, and the old grew young and the young joyous and rampant from the experience. Wonderful cures are related as having been effected by these springs; the Indians resort to them a good deal, put their sick horses into them, and are loth to yield control of them to the whites; and in view of their probable future value, there has been a struggle among the latter for their ownership. They are now in the hands of Mr. Byers of the Rocky Mountain News at Denver, under a title that will probably defy all disputants. The waters look and taste precisely like those of the Sharon Sulphur Springs in New York.[9] The difference is that these are hot, those cold. They have deposited sulphur, iron and soda in quantity all about their path, and these are their probable chief ingredients.

William N. Byers (1831–1903), editor of the *Rocky Mountain News,* who played a leading role in Colorado's development. (FROM FRANK HALL, *HISTORY OF THE STATE OF COLORADO* [CHICAGO, 1889], 1:174)

Over a little hill from the springs, by the side of the Grand River,—the hill, the stream, and a half mile between us and the Indian encampment,—we settled down in camp for two days and a half, studying Indian life, catching and eating trout, taking hot douche baths in the springs, and making excursions over the neighboring hills into side valleys. The river before us offered good fishing, but better was to be found in Williams Fork,[10] a smaller stream a few miles below, where a half day's sport brought back from forty to sixty pounds of as fine speckled trout as ever came from brooks or lakes of New England. They ranged from a quarter of a pound up to two pounds weight each, and we had them at every meal.

The Indians were very neighborly; hill, stream and distance were no impediment to their attentions; their ponies would gallop with them over all in five minutes; and from two to a dozen, men and boys, never the squaws, were hanging about our camp fires from early morning till late evening. Curiosity, begging and good-fellowship were their only apparent motives; they did no mischief; they stole nothing, though food and clothing, pistols and knives, things they coveted and needed above all else, were loosely scattered about within reach; they only became a nuisance by being everlastingly in the way and spoiling the enjoyment of one's food by their wistful observation. Mrs. Browning says, you remember, that observation, which is not sympathy, is simply torture.[11] And not a bit of sympathy did they show in our eating except as they shared. We were as liberal as our limited stores would allow; but the capacity of a single Indian's stomach is boundless; what could we do for the hundreds?

These Utes are a good deal higher grade of Indian than I had supposed.[12] They are above the average of our Indian tribes in comeliness and intelligence; and none perhaps are better behaved or more amenable to direction from the whites. There are seven different bands or tribes of them, who occupy the mountains and parks of Colorado and adjoining sections of New Mexico and Utah. The bands number from five hundred to one thousand each. This one consisted of about seventy-five "lodges" or families, each represented by a tent of cloth stretched over a bunch of poles gathered at the top, and spreading around in a small circle. The poles leave a hole in the top for the smoke of a fire in the center beneath, and around which the family squat on their blankets and pile their stores of food and skins and clothing. Probably there were six hundred in the camp near us, men, women and children. They look frailer and feebler than you would expect; I did not see a single Indian who was six feet high or would weigh over one hundred and seventy-five pounds; they are all, indeed, under size, and no match in nervous or physical force for the average white man. Some of both sexes are of very comely appearance, with fine hands and delicate feet, and shapely limbs, with a bright mulatto complexion, and clear, piercing eyes; but their square heads, coarse hair, hideous daubs of yellow and red paint on the cheek and forehead, and motley raiment,—here a white man's cast-off hat, coat or pantaloons, if squaw a shabby old gown of calico or shirt of white cloth, alternate with Indian leggins and moccasins, bare legs and feet, a dirty white or flaming red blanket, beaded jacket of leather, feathers, and brass or tin trinkets hanging on the head, from the ears, down the back or breast,—all these disorderly and unaccustomed combinations give them at first a repulsive and finally a very absurd appearance. The squaws seem to be kept in the background, and, except when brides or the wives of a chief, dress much more plainly and shabbily than the bucks. They are all more modest and deferential in appearance and manners than would be expected; and I saw no evidence of or taste for strong drink among this tribe,—none of them ever asked for it, while their desire for food, especially for sugar and biscuit, was always manifest. The sugar they gobble up without qualification, and such unnatural food as this and fine flour breed diseases and weaknesses that are already destroying the race. Coughs are frequent, and dyspepsia; sickness and deaths are quite common among the children; and this incongruous mixture of white man's food and raiment and life with their own, which their contact with civilization has led them into, is sapping their vitality at its fountains. To make matters the worse, they have got hold of our quack medicines, and are great customers for Brandreth and other pills,[13] with the vain hope of curing their maladies. In short, they are simple, savage children, and in that definition we find suggested the only proper way for the government to treat them.

Their wealth consists in their horses, which they breed or steal from their enemies of other tribes, and of which this tribe in the Middle Park must have a couple of hundred. They live on the game they can find in the parks and among the mountains, moving from one spot to another, as seasons and years change, the proceeds of the skins of the deer and other animals they kill, roots, nuts and berries, and the gifts of the government and the settlers. It is altogether even a precarious and hard reliance; the game is fast disappearing,—save of trout we have not seen enough in all our travels among the mountains to feed our small party upon, if it had all been caught; and the government agents are not always to be depended upon in making up deficiencies. Our neighbors had lately come over from the North Park, where they had hunted antelope to some purpose and with rare fortune, killing four thousand in all in two or three weeks, half of them in a single grand hunt. They cut the meat into thin slices and dry it, so that it looks like strips of old leather; and as we went about their camp we saw the little, weakly children pulling away at bits of it, apparently with not very satisfactory results. Our tribe was in trouble about a chief; the old one was dead, and there were two or three contestants for the succession; but the wrangle was not half so fierce as would arise over a contested election for mayor of a white man's city.

Affairs always seemed very quiet in the Indian camp in the day-time; the braves played cards, or did a little hunting; the squaws gathered wood, tanned skins, braided lariats, or made fantastic leather garments; the boys chased the ponies; but at night they as invariably appeared to be having a grand pow-wow,—rude music and loud shouting rolled up to our camp a volume of coarse sound that at first seemed frightful, as if the preparatory war-whoop for a grand scalping of their white neighbors, but which we learned to regard as the most innocent of barbaric amusements. Though these Utes are quite peaceful and even long-suffering towards the whites, they bear eternal enmity to the Indian tribes of the Plains, and are always ready to have a fight with them. Each party is strongest on its own territory,—the Arapahoes,[14] Comanches[15] and Cheyennes[16] on the prairies, and the Utes among the hills; and each, while eager to receive the party of the other part at home, rarely go a-visiting. The Plains Indians are better mounted and better armed; chiefly because, keeping up nearly constant warfare with the whites, they have exacted prompter presents and larger pay from the government. The Utes complain, and with reason, that their friendliness causes them to be neglected and cheated; while their and our enemies thrive on government bounty.

There is now a plan for all the Ute tribes to go together into the south-western corner of Colorado,[17] away from the mines and the whites, and there, upon abundant pastures and fruitful mountains, engage in a pastoral and half agricultural life; to set up stock-raising on a large scale, and such tillage as they can bring themselves to, under the protection and aid of the government. The scheme is a good one; the Indians agree to it; and the bargain has been made by the government agents here,—all that is needed is for the authorities at Washington to furnish the means for carrying it into execution. So far as our observation extends, the greatest trouble with our Indian matters lies at Washington; the chief of the cheating and stupidity gathers there; while the Indian agents here upon the ground are, if not immaculate, certainly more intelligent, sensible, and practical, and truer to the good of the settler and the Indian than their superiors at the seat of government.

VI.

FROM THE MIDDLE PARK BY BOULDER PASS

The Longing Lingering in Middle Park—Professor Powell and his Explorations—The Canyon of the Colorado—Over the Boulder Pass in a Snow Storm—A Cold Night and a Warm Noon Camp—Night in a Barn—By Boulder and Central to Mill City and Georgetown.

MILL CITY, COLORADO, AUGUST, 1868

WE were loth to leave the Middle Park. I counted the hot douche sulphur baths, and tried to multiply them by six, then by two; but it was of no use,—the Vice-President travels by time-table; and the ladies were in Denver, and the grand expedition to South Park was ahead. I looked longingly through the hills up the valley of the Grand; beyond I knew there lay a wilder country than we had seen, and under the shadow of Long's Peak, Grand Lake itself, a large and fine sheet of water, alive with trout, and rich in commanding beauty.[1] We galloped over the bare hills the other way, and looked off down the valley. Bits of rare stone, agates and jaspers and crystals and petrifactions, lay everywhere about; and over the river, a dozen miles off, was the famous "moss agate patch," where these peculiar crystallizations covered the ground; Williams Fork came rollicking down the opposite hill-sides through a line of trees, with innumerable breakfasts of uncaught trout, and a wide green meadow at the mouth for camping ground; while far on in the landscape, the

Grand found magnificent pathway for twenty-five miles through a broad field of heavy grass,—the gem, the kernel of the Middle Park; then turning abruptly west, it shot through the mountains by a canyon, lapped up the Blue on the other side,[2] and, thus strengthened, poured out southward for the Colorado and the Pacific Ocean. It was this way we should have gone out,—down the Grand and up the Blue, all within the capacious boundaries of the Middle Park,—but time and the provision bag forbade. Yet there was nothing inviting in the return by the Berthoud Pass; there could be nothing worse than its mire and its rough ascent; another way would at least be new,—and we voted to go out by its rival for a railroad track, the Boulder Pass.[3] The Governor (Hunt) and the Indian agent, finding their talk with the Indians not eloquent enough to convince by lack of food and blankets, had gone back by the old route, taking a dozen or twenty of the leading braves with them, to seek arguments where the freight was not so expensive. The Indian sees the point of an idea always through a full stomach and a warm back, and it required a whole beef and several barrels of flour and sugar and a dozen blankets to prove to them that a petty technical amendment by the Senate to their last treaty was just right.[4]

We had made familiar and friendly acquaintance with Professor Powell's scientific exploring party, from Illinois, while in the Middle Park.[5] They were in camp there for some time, and made it the end of their summer and the beginning of their winter campaign. The party comprises a dozen or more enthusiastic young men, interested in one department or other of natural science, or eager for border experiences, mostly from Illinois, and giving their time and labor to the expedition for the sake of the education and the health. Professor Powell, the originator and head, does more; the government furnishes food, allowing it to be drawn from the supplies of the nearest post, and the Illinois University and Natural History Society contribute small sums of money;[6] but he draws upon his private purse for all deficiencies, and these must be many thousands of dollars before he gets through. The summer has been spent among the higher Mountains and in the Parks,[7] taking careful notes with barometer and thermometer, collecting flowers and birds and larger animals, and studying the rare geological phenomena of the country. Their collection of birds is very full and valuable, and numbers over two hundred different specimens.

Professor Powell, two or three of his assistants, and Mr. Byers, of the Denver News, who knows all these mountains better than any other man, probably, have just accomplished the ascent of Long's Peak.[8] This is the prominent north-eastern mountain of the Coloradian series, is seen from the Railroad, and is fourteen thousand feet high, and has heretofore defied all the efforts of explorers and mountaineers to reach its top. They had a terribly hard climb of it, but felt amply paid in the glory of the fact, and more in the glory of the landscape spread before them at the summit.[9] The plains and mountains to the north beyond the Railroad, the unending eastern plains, with Denver and the intervening settlements below and to the south, the whole of Middle Park, and the surrounding and far-beyond mountains,—all Colorado, as it were, and part of Wyoming, lay beneath their eyes. Streams flowed out from the mountain in all directions, and no fewer than thirty-nine lakes on that and the neighboring mountain sides, nearly all of and above the altitude of ten thousand feet, were visible from their commanding height.

From here the explorers will follow down the Grand River, out of the Park into western Colorado, and then strike across to the other and larger branch of the great Colorado River, the Green, and upon that or some of its branches, near the line of Utah, spend the winter in camp, studying up their past achievements, and preparing for the next summer's campaign.[10] The great and final object of the expedition is to explore the upper Colorado River and solve the mysteries of its three hundred mile canyon.[11] They will probably undertake this next season by boats and rafts from their winter camp on the Green; but they may postpone the adventure till another year, and meantime discover and reveal the mountains and plains of western Colorado and eastern Utah, which are so little known. But the mocking ignorance and fascinating reports of the course and country of the Colorado ought to hasten them to this interesting field. The maps from Washington, that put down only what is absolutely, scientifically known, leave a great blank space here of three hundred to five hundred miles long and one hundred to two hundred miles broad. Is any other nation so ignorant of itself? All that we do know goes to show that, beginning with the union of the Grand and the Green Rivers, the Colorado is confined for three hundred miles within perpendicular walls of rock averaging three thousand feet high, up which no one can climb, down which no one can safely go, and between which in the river, rapids and falls and furious eddies render passage frightful, certainly dangerous, possibly impossible.

The general conviction of the border population is that whoever dares venture into this canyon will never come out alive. But we have an authentic account this season of a man who made the trip last year and lives to tell the tale. He and a companion prospecting for gold in southwestern Colorado, and driven by Indians, took to the Grand River just before its union with the Green, made a raft and committed themselves to the waters. Foaming rapids and a whirlpool swept the companion and all the provisions off, and they were lost, while White, the surviving hero's name, without food, passed seven days more, a second seven days, upon these strange waters, between frowning walls, over dangerous rapids, through delaying eddies, before he reached Callville in Arizona, the first settlement and the head of navigation on the river.[12] His entire journey upon the river must have exceeded five hundred miles, and he represents that for most of the distance it was through these traditional high walls, impassable as a fortress, a dungeon over a cataract.

Nearly all of the rivers of Colorado and Utah run for brief distances, from one to twenty-five miles, through these gorges of rock; or they "canyon," as, by making a verb out of the Spanish noun, the people of the country describe the streams as performing the feat of such rock passages, where their banks are inapproachable, and trails or roads are sent over or around; but this rock-guarded career of the great river of the interior basin of the Continent is the grand canyon of the world, and one of its most wonderful marvels. Its passage in well protected boats by careful navigators can scarcely be deemed impracticable, however dangerous, and the country will await the Powell movement through it with eager interest.

The whole field of observation and inquiry which Professor Powell has undertaken is more interesting and important than any which lies before our men of science.

The wonder is they have neglected it so long. Here are seen the central forces that formed the Continent; here more striking studies in physical geography, geology, and natural history, than are proffered anywhere else. New knowledge and wide honors await those who catalogue and define them. I can but think the inquiry, vast and important as it is, is fortunate in its inquirer. Professor Powell is well educated, an enthusiast, resolute, a gallant leader, as his other title of Major and an absent arm, won and lost in the war, testify,—seemingly well-endowed physically and mentally for the arduous work of both body and brains that he has undertaken. He is every way the soul, as he is the purse of the expedition; he leads the way in all danger and difficulty, and his wife, a true helpmeet, and the only woman with the party, is the first to follow.

But while talking with the Professor, our reduced party has chosen a new leader,—General R. F. Lord of Georgetown,[13]—and is packed, bridled and saddled for the start. We cross the river, look gratefully and regretfully for the last time on the Hot Springs, pass through the Indian encampment, and go lingering back over the long hill that we had galloped down so gladly three days before. Two-thirds the day's ride was the same we had passed over in coming in;[14] then we turned to the left, the Boulder Mountain lying on the opposite side of the lower end of the Park from Berthoud; and soon we passed into a succession of woods and open meadows, alternating with picturesque effects, as we gradually ascended the mountain, and offering fine views of sections of the Park from occasional bluffs. The grass was thicker and greener than in the more exposed parts of the Park; the pines and firs and cotton-wood were in full variety and beauty; and the flowers grew gayer,—altogether it was a pleasanter country to ride leisurely through than we had yet met with.

At the end of some twenty-five miles, we camped for the night, in the edge of the woods, fronting an open area of water-courses, grass and willows, with plenty of evidence that the beavers had a settlement there. An old bower of evergreens was cleared up and strengthened to lay our blankets under; and big fires kept off the cold of a ten thousand feet elevation, until three to four o'clock in the morning, when, by their subsidence and the increasing chill, everybody was in a shiver, and glad enough that an early call to morning duty soon summoned us up and astir. The water was freezing and the grass and shrubs were stiff with frost, so stiff and yet so dry from lack of moisture in the air, that neither then, nor after the sun had softened them, was there wet to be won by walking among them. It was a perfectly dry freeze, and this is why these summer frosts do no more harm to vegetation, and delicate flowers thaw out and go on in their sweet short life in these high mountains.

The clouds gathered, and the rain-drops fell, as we finished breakfast and packed and saddled for the cold hard ride over the mountains.[15] In an hour we were out of the timber, and a dreary waste of rock, relieved only by a thin grass at first, then by mosses, and always by flowers, lay before and all around us. The storm grew thick and fast, hail and snow; the trail wasted itself in the open area; the ground was being rapidly covered with the white snow; straggling was forbidden, and "close up" and "push on" were the orders from the front. The promised view of park and plains, of range on range, was lost; only thick, dark clouds, hanging over impenetrable abysses, were around and below us; the storm bit like wasps; beards gathered snow and ice; the mules and horses winced under the blasts,—it was a forlorn looking company for a pleasure party.

But there was exhilaration in the unseasonable struggle; there was something jolly in the idea of thus confounding the almanacs, and finding February in August. At the summit of the Pass,—thirteen thousand feet high,—the storm abated its intensity to let us dismount and pick out of the snow the little yellow flowers that crept up among the rocks everywhere. Then it rolled over again, and now with thunder and lightning, pealing and flashing close around us. Here our laggard pack mules with their drivers came hurrying up and forward; Charley Utter saying as he spurred them by that perhaps we might like it, but for him "hell was pleasanter and safer than a thunder-storm on the range."

But as we descended the elements calmed; the clouds opened visions of the new valleys, and flashes of sunlight unveiled the great mysteries of the upper mountains. Summer was again around us; and though it was hardly noon, the spot we had reached was so rarely charming, and the sun so refreshing, that we halted, loosed our animals, made our coffee, lunched, and basked on the rocks in the sunshine for a long, delightful hour. We were on a narrow crest of the mountain, shooting out into the valley, and not over twenty feet wide. On either side, there was a sharp almost perpendicular descent for at least one thousand feet in one case, and seven hundred and fifty in the other. At the foot on our right were two lovely lakes,[16] one almost an absolute circle, rock and grass bound, fed by great snow-banks between us and them, and feeding in turn the South Boulder Creek. On our left, a grassy slope, so steep that it was impossible to walk down except in long zigzags, and far away at the bottom among the trees ran the North Boulder from out the mountains. Everywhere about us, where the snow and the rocks left space, were the greenest of grass, the bluest of harebells, the reddest of painter's brush, the yellowest of sunflowers and buttercups. All, with brightest of sun and bluest of sky, made up such a contrast to our morning ride that we were all in raptures with the various beauties of the scene, and feel still that no spot in all our travel is more sacred to beauty than this of our noon camp on Boulder.

But, as if to frame and fasten the picture still more strongly, we were hardly in the saddle again, before the storm set in anew, and we rode all the afternoon under snow or rain. There is what is called a road over into Middle Park by this Pass, and strong wagons with oxen or mules make the passage; but the difficulties they encounter are frightful,—mud and rocks, rivers and ravines,—it is hard to imagine how any wheels can surmount them and remain whole,—and few do. Our trail followed the road only in part; it made short cuts over hills, through woods, and across valleys, and was full of variety, annoyance, sometimes of difficulty; but we found all less vexations than the descent of Berthoud Pass, and, following the South Boulder Creek, came at last, wet and weary, into the nearly deserted mining village of South Boulder.[17] Here we found welcome around the fire of the post-office; a deserted cabin was thrown open to us for our baggage and our meals; and a big barn's loft with fresh hay furnished a magnificent bedroom. We dried, we ate, having fresh meat, cream and vegetables added to our bill of fare, and we slept, all in luxury. Half the village was pre-occupied by a large party of men and women, some twenty to thirty, from the villages farther down the valley, on their way into the Park by the road we had come out. They had ox teams for their baggage, saddle animals to carry themselves, and a cow to furnish fresh milk; and thus generously equipped were jollily entering upon camp life among the mountains for ten days or a fortnight.

An early start the next morning, and a rapid gallop of ten miles over good roads, across the hills, by scattered saw-mills, farm-houses, and mining-camps, brought us into the valley of North Clear Creek, and to the higgledy-piggledy but brisk town of Central City in season for the morning stage to Denver. Our old friends here gave us hearty welcome, but stared at our costumes in grim dismay, and some took us for "honest miners" come to town from the mountains for fresh supplies. Here, too, the party separated; the Vice-President going on to Denver with some of the others; but the Governor (Bross) and myself and our Georgetown friends, first eating a French dinner by way of contrast to camp diet and manners, rode on over another range of hills into the South Clear Creek valley. And here, again, a bath at the Idaho warm springs, and a couple of days' rest and recreation at Mill City and Georgetown have prepared us for another and still more select expedition into the highest mountain tops of the country.

VII.

OVER GRAY'S PEAK TO SOUTH PARK

A Private Outfit for a Grand Mountain Excursion—Gray's Peaks and What They Showed Us—The Finest Mountain View in the World—Saturday Night Camp in the Snake River Valley—Sunday Travel with Commodore Decatur—A Butter Ranch—How Life Goes in Camp, and What it Costs—The Blue River Valley—Breckenridge, and over the Range into South Park through Thunder and Lightning, Hail and Rain.

SOUTH PARK, COLORADO, AUGUST, 1868

WHILE the Vice-President, Governor Hunt, and a considerable party of Denver friends were to accompany our ladies into the South Park by the usual wagon road from that point,[1] Governor Bross, General Lord and myself made a short cut but rougher journey over two high ranges of mountains, much of the way impassable to vehicles, and met them here. Our chief object was to ascend Gray's Peaks, the highest summits yet accurately measured in the Colorado mountains, and from their central position commanding the widest and most majestic views to be obtained in the country. Such a load as we put on our single pack mule: a great overtopping cube of blankets and sacks of meat and bread, and four little feet sticking out beneath, were all that could be seen as it went shaking along on a mysterious trot. Sending the outfit and our outfitter, Ashley Franklin, by an easier path over to where we intended to camp for the night, we three started early

Saturday morning[2] from Georgetown,—distance fifteen miles to Gray's Peaks, and, by virtue of mines among the mountains, a good wagon road two-thirds the way. It was an object to get to the summit as early as possible, before afternoon haze or cloud should dim the view, and we galloped rapidly through aspen groves, then among larger pines, by the side of rapidly descending streams, around and around, up and up, and finally out above the trees, where grass and flowers had all life to themselves, and again above these and only thin mosses lived among the stones, and yet still higher, where the mountains became great walls of rock, or immense mounds of broken stone, as if they had been run through a crusher for the benefit of Mr. Macadam.[3] Such was the character of Gray's Peaks. Great patches of snow divided place with the rocks, and fed the clear, cold rivulets that started out from every sheltered nook or side of the mountains; but they only added to the cold dreariness of the scene. The only life was grasshoppers,[4]—here they were still by thousands, by millions, sporting in the air and frisking over the snow, but the latter's chill seemed soon to overcome their life, for they lay dead in countless numbers upon its white surface. In some places the dead grasshoppers could have been shoveled up by the bushels, and down at the edges of the snow cold grasshopper soup was to be had *ad libitum*.[5] There was a feast here for the bears, but we could see none enjoying it.

Gray's Peaks,—great mounds or monuments of loose, broken stone,—shoot up sharply from a single base, in the midst of very high mountains all about. Their sharpness increases the appearance of the fact of their superior height. Below, the two seem but a rifle shot apart; above, they are manifestly several miles away from each other;

but their common paternity, their similarity in form, effect and views, entitle them to bear the common name. It was probably given originally to the lower peak alone by Dr. C. C. Parry of St. Louis,[6] who has been, so far, the most thorough scientific explorer of the higher mountain regions of Colorado, and in honor of the distinguished Cambridge botanist, Professor Gray; but though there are persistent rivals for the name of the other and higher peak,—Dr. Parry himself, we believe, has suggested that of Professor Torrey for it,—the local judgment insists that they shall go together with the name of Gray. There are now trails for horses to the top of each,—that to the higher was nearly finished while we were there; and though the path to the lower is the more easy and familiar, our ambition was not content with anything less than the highest, and spite of fatigue and cold we stuck out for it. Going through a snow-drift at least fifteen feet high, and coming out above all snow deposits, we fastened our animals with stones at the end of the path, and slowly toiled the remaining quarter of a mile over the loose rocks,—the thin air obliging us to stop every three minutes to gain our breath,—and at high noon sat upon the highest peak of the highest known mountain of the great Rocky Mountain range. Dr. Parry made the lower peak fourteen thousand two hundred and fifty-one feet high; the highest must be at least fourteen thousand five hundred.

The scene before us was ample recompense for double the toil. It was the great sight in all our Colorado travel. In impressiveness,—in overcomingness, it takes rank with the three or four great natural wonders of the world,—with Niagara Falls from the Tower, with the Yosemite Valley from Inspiration Point. No Swiss mountain view carries such majestic sweep of distance, such sublime combination of hight and breadth and depth; such uplifting into the presence of God; such dwarfing of the mortal sense, such welcome to the immortal thought. It was not beauty, it was sublimity; it was not power, nor order, nor color, it was majesty; it was not a part, it was the whole; it was not man but God, that was about, before, in us. Mountains and mountains everywhere,—even the great Parks, even the unending Plains seemed but patches among the white ranges of hills stretching above and beyond one another. We looked into Middle Park below us on the north; over a single line of mountains into South Park, below us on the south,—but beyond both were the unending peaks, the everlasting hills. To the west, the broadest noblest ranges of mountains,—there seemed no breaks among them except such as served to mark the end of one and the beginning of another, and no possible limit to their extension. The snow whitened all, covered many, and brought out their lines in conspicuous majesty. Over one of the largest and finest, the snow-fields lay in the form of an immense cross,[7] and by this it is known in all the mountain views of the territory. It is as if God has set His sign, His seal, His promise there,—a beacon upon the very center and hight of the Continent to all its people and all its generations. Beyond this uplifted what seemed to be the only mountain in all the range of view higher than the peak upon which we stood. It is named Sopris Peak upon some of the maps,[8] but has never been explored,[9] and is more completely covered with snow than any other.

Turning to the east we find relief in the softer and yet majestic and unending vision of the Plains,—on, on they stretch in everlasting green and gray until lost in the dim haze that is just beginning to rise along the horizon. Directly below us, great rough seams in the mountain sides, as if fire and water had been at work for ages to waste and overturn; dreary areas of red and brown and gray rocks; masses of timber; bits of green in the far-down valley; flashes of darkness where little lakes nestled amid the rocks, fed by snow, and feeding the streams,—Nature everywhere in her original forms, and her abounding waste of wealth, as if here was the great supply store and workshop of Creation, the fountain of Earth. Looking from side to side, above, below, and around,—impressed, oppressed everywhere with the presence of the Beginning; it was almost unconsciously and instinctively that we turned again and at last, as Mrs. Browning makes Romney Leigh, "toward the east:"—

> "——where faint and fair,
> Along the tingling desert of the sky,
> Beyond the choice of the conscious hills,
> Were laid in jasper-stone as clear as glass
> The first foundations of that new, near Day,
> Which should be building out of heaven, to God."[10]

It was difficult to leave this citadel of earth, this outpost of heaven; but our time and our strength were both exhausted. The long gallop, the hard climb, more, the excitement of the vision of earth and sky at this elevation of over fourteen thousand feet above the ocean level had used up our nerve-power; the cool breezes, too, chilled us; and after lunching, we regained our horses, and pushed down the other side of the mountain from that we came up.

There was only a dim trail to follow, running hither and thither around and among the hills, and then across and along the valleys of the streams that came in from every mountain crevice and snow-bank. We crossed Colfax Park, a little gem of grass and flowers, with Colfax Lake at its head,[11] a great rock bowl of clear water, high in the hill-side, and pouring its surplus over a sharp natural wall of stone,—so named by an enthusiastic and appreciative miner in the lower valley, who would hardly be reconciled with us that we had not brought the Vice-President to witness how happily and fitly he had been honored here. We passed also through many a beaver village; but the inhabitants gave us no visible welcome; they modestly let their works speak for them. The woods grew thick and mellow; the aspen tender, the spruces silver-hung and silver-tongued; and we came at last,—a long ten miles from the summit of Gray's Peak,—to our proposed camping spot, the junction of two forks of the Snake River and of the two trails from Georgetown.[12]

Here, the grass was abundant, the stream ran pure and strong, unpolluted by miner's mud, fuel was plenty, even the mosquitoes sang a welcome, but no Ashley Franklin, no pack-mule was to be seen, no blankets, no food, no nothing, that belonged to us, but weariness and hunger. We sounded the war-whoop of the country,—a shrill, far-reaching cry; and back the voices came, not only from our lagging outfit, but from miners here and there among the hills, just finishing their day's work, and wondering who had come into their wilderness now. The mules took up the refrain, and bellowed from "depths that overflow" their welcome to each other. Soon we were at home, the coffee brewing, the ham stewing, and a hole through the peach can; Commodore Decatur, the prince of prospectors, the character of all Colorado characters, dropped in to bid us welcome to his principality, on his way from mine to cabin;[13] under the frosts of night and the smoke of the camp fire, the merry mosquitoes flew away; our tent was raised, our blankets spread; and the peace of Saturday night and a day richly spent reigned over us four and no more.

But camp life is not all comfort. This very blessed Saturday night on the Snake River, the wind took turns in coming out of the three or four valleys that converged upon our camping-ground, and blew the virulent smoke in upon us. Shift the fire, change the blanket, still the smoke followed us, as if charmed, and was discomfort and sleeplessness to all, poison to at least one. There was a yearning for something delicate for the Sunday morning breakfast,—a bit of cream toast, or a soft egg, and some milk ameliorated coffee; but the knurly little "Jack," that carried our "bed and board," had no provision for sensitive stomachs, and we had to take our victual and drink "straight,"—plain ham and bread and butter and black coffee,—or go without. But that best and cheapest of doctors and nurses, the sun came to our relief; and later in the day a pitcher of butter-milk completed and capped his healing triumphs. Mr. Richardson records my sarcastic contempt for buttermilk three years ago, but I take it all back now,—no cup of it shall ever pass from my lips again other than empty.[14] It comes to a faint and forlorn stomach like woman's sympathy to a bruised heart.

Governor Bross galloped back into the hills to make a call at a solitary cabin half a dozen miles away; Commodore Decatur dropped in with the Lord's blessing on his lips, and picked me up for a ride down the river,—whither we were bound;—General Lord followed along with his fishing-pole, lingering over the streams; and the mule and his master strolled more leisurely after, to protect the rear and gather in the Governor. There was a rough wagon road most of the way, chiefly through woods, occasionally across an open park, frequently over or in the stream, but the hills kept close guard, and the eye was not allowed to wander far away for beauty. But the "Commodore," who, to thirty years of school and civilization, has added twenty of border life in Mexico, in Nebraska and in Colorado, living at times among the Indians, and for many a season in his solitary cabin in these elevated valleys, kept me entertained with his original experiences, his keen observations on men and manners, and his quaint yet rich philosophies. He is an old Greek philosopher,—with an American variation; as wise as Socrates, as enthusiastic as a child, as mysterious in life and purpose as William H. Seward[15] or an Egyptian sphynx, as religious as a Methodist class-leader,—he ranks high among the individual institutions and idiosyncracies of Colorado, such as Governor Hunt, Editor Goldrick[16] and Charley Utter, whom not to know is to miss the next piquant things to its Mountains and Parks.

We sauntered thus through ten miles in four hours, gathering up at last the stragglers in the rear, and came out then into a grand opening in the valley. The timber disappeared; the hills sharpened into a dead wall on one side, and swept away in soft rolling outlines on the other; a wide stretch of intervale lay between, while pretty groves of trees tempered the distant knolls and broke the abruptness of forests beyond. We were again, indeed, in Middle Park, though a high range of mountains and a long, hard ride separated us from that part of it which we visited the week before.

Away under a bluff, a speck in the distance, was a log-cabin,—"the Georgia Ranch,"[17] towards which we now rode with freshened speed. Here in a cabin of two rooms, with a log milk-house outside, the only dwellers in this rich pasture park, were a man, his wife and daughter; their home and farm were in Southern Colorado, but they had come up here in the spring with forty or fifty cows, and were making one hundred and forty-five pounds of butter a week, and selling it to the miners in the cabins and camps among the hills ten to fifteen miles around, for seventy-five cents a pound; when the snows begin to fall in October, they will drive the herd back to their southern pastures,—the increase of the cows will pay all expenses, and the one hundred dollars a week or more cash for butter and milk, is clear profit. The dairy cabin was a "sight to behold," such piles of fresh golden butter, such shelves of full pans of milk,—there wasn't room for another pound or pan; and yet the demand far exceeds the supply,—it was a favor to be allowed to purchase the treasures of "Georgia Ranch." It was our "Commodore's" Sunday diversion to ride down these dozen miles, fill his weekly butter-pail and his milk-can, and gallop back in season for a Sunday night supper with his cabin comrade of "mush and milk."

These mining hermits in the mountains manage to live well,—they become adepts in cooking; with flour and meal and fresh meat, potatoes and onions, dried and canned fruits, the bill of fare is appetizing; and the cost of the "best tables" is from seventy-five cents to one dollar a day. Nor are they always thus exiles from society; their season in the hills, hunting new lodes or developing old ones, is confined to the summer; when cold and snow come, they flee to the villages or to Denver,—to live as leisurely and luxuriously as what they have made the past season or hope to make the next will permit.

We "packed" a bottle of cream, filled our water canteen with milk, took Decatur's Methodistic benediction,—

"May the Lord take a liking to you,"—with a hearty "amen," and rode down the valley, by numerous soda and other mineral springs, three or four miles farther, to our camp for the night. This was at a still more picturesque spot,—a trinity of rivers, a triangle of mountains. The Blue and the Snake Rivers and Ten Mile Creek all meet and mingle here within a few rods;[18] each a strong, hearty stream, from its own independent circle of mountains; and while the waters unresisting swam together, the hills stood apart and away, frowning in dark forests and black rock, and cold with great snow-fields, overlooking the scene, which green meadows, and blue sky, and warm sun mellowed and brightened. A neck of land, holding abundant grass and fuel, between the three rivers at the point of junction, offered a magnificent camping-ground. It is a spot to settle down upon and keep house at for a week. Ten Mile Creek overflows with trout; General Lord took ten pounds out of a single hole in a less number of minutes,—a single fish weighing about three pounds; and deer and game birds must be readily findable in the neighborhood. The Blue isn't blue,—its waters have been troubled by the miners, and it gives its name and mud color to the combined stream, which flows off through an open, inviting valley to join the Grand, and thence to make up the grand Colorado of the West.

We had a lesson in precaution, after unloading, and proceeding to make camp here, by finding that nobody had any matches; we could not shoot flame out of our metallic-cartridge pistols; nor had we the Indian accomplishment of rubbing fire out of two sticks; so the best mule was put over the road to the "Ranch" and back at a very un-mule-like-gait, to bring us the means of kindling our camp fire. But we had a sumptuous supper, of cream toast and trout, with milk for our coffee, and a sweet night in camp, though lulled to sleep by the roll of thunder and the patter of a brisk shower, with high wind and sharp lightning; and we turned reluctantly up the valley of the Blue, the next morning, with the resolution to come to stay at this point another season.

We had come this way through a little obstinacy of our own, instead of taking the common and short cut over the hills, from the valley of the upper Snake to Breckenridge,[19]—sure that the conjunction of the Blue, the Snake and Ten Mile must offer something worth seeing in the way of valley and mountain scenery; and so we were quite proud of our generous repayment, and desire all future travelers to make a note of our route, and follow it. The valley of the Blue, both above and below where we struck it, is altogether one of the most interesting scenic sections of the territory;[20] it should be taken in going into or out from the Hot Springs; there is no route so rich in interest and beauty as that through it from the Middle to the South Park, or vice versa, or from Georgetown over Gray's Peaks into either Park,—and we were sorry not to have time for wider exploration of its lines.

Our day's ride now followed up the river to its very head in the mountains. The first eight miles was through a fine open grazing country, and we found a magnificent herd of fat cattle, strongly marked with Durham blood, enjoying its rich grasses. They had been sent up here to fatten for the summer from some of the ranches of the lower valleys, and, perhaps, to furnish fresh beef to the mining camps, which are quite numerous among the side valleys of the neighborhood. Nearly all our day's ride we were in sight of the ditches that had been built to carry water to the rich beds of sand that were in course of being washed over for gold deposits at various localities in the valleys. One of these ditches is twelve miles long; tapping the Blue away up in the mountains, it takes a vigorous stream along and around the mountain sides, up and down, from gulch to gulch, parting with portions at different points on the route to little companies of miners at so much per foot; and, deployed into sand-banks, swept through long boxes, tarried in screens and by petty dams, it does its work of separating the tiny particles of gold from the earth, and finds its way back to the parent stream, miles from where it left it, but bringing the pollutions of the world and of labor with it. Many thousands of dollars are invested in these ditches; sometimes they are made and owned by individuals, who also work the mines or deposits of gold to which they lead, but oftener now they belong to companies that have no other interest than to sell water from them to those who mine alone. Generally they have passed out of the hands of their builders, who rarely realized anything but expectations, vast and vain, from them.

At Breckenridge we got above the washings,[21] and the river was clear again. This is the center of these upper mining interests, but a village of only twenty or thirty cabins, located ten thousand feet high, and scarcely habitable in winter, though many of the miners do hibernate here through the season of snow and cold that begins in early October and ends in June. There is a good hotel here, of logs to be sure, with a broad buxom matron, and black-eyed beauties of daughters,[22] to whom, after dinner, we consigned Governor Bross, with warning against his fascinations, while General Lord and myself, with our guide, went on over the range into the South Park. The

Breckenridge, founded in August 1859 with the discovery of gold on the Blue River. (PHOTOGRAPH BY G. CHAMBERLAIN, DENVER; COLORADO HISTORICAL SOCIETY, NO. 7836)

miners were to be gathered in the next night for speeches from the Vice-President and the Governor, and the latter awaited the occasion and the former's arrival.

There was a good wagon road all our way, leading from Breckenridge to the summit of Breckenridge Pass,[23] through open woods, flower-endowed meadows, a broken, various and interesting mountain country, often giving majestic views of the higher and snow-crowned peaks, with glimpses of valleys and parks below and beyond. The Pass is just above the timber line, about twelve thousand feet high, and as we mounted it, a cold storm gathered upon the snow-fields above us, wheeled from peak to peak in densely black clouds, and soon broke in gusts of wind, in vivid lightning, in startlingly close and loud claps of thunder, in driving snow, in pelting hail, in drizzling rain. We were below the storm's fountain, but near enough to see all its grand movements, to feel its awful presence, to be shaken with fear, to gather inspiration. The rapidity of its passage from side to side, from peak to peak, was wonderful; the crashing loudness of its thunderous discharges awful; one moment we felt like "fleeing before the Lord," the next charmed and awed into rest in His presence.

But it was dreary enough, when the thundering and the flashing ceased, and the clouds stopped their majestic movement, and hung in deep mists over all the mountains and the valleys, and the rain poured ceaselessly down. The poetry was gone, and gathering overcoats and rubber closely about us, we bent our heads to the undeviating shower, and pushed gloomily and ghastily on. It seemed a long ride down mountain side and through valley to Hamilton,[24]—woods that made us feel even more pitiful; open valleys that made the rain more pitiless; streams twisted out of place and shape by ruthless miners; desolated cabins, doorless, windowless,—even the storm was more inviting; Tarryall, where thousands dug and washed sands for gold three and four years ago, and now only two or three cabins, mud-patched and turf-warmed, sent forth the smoke of home; a solitary dirt-washer trudging along from his day's mountain work, with dinner-pail and pickax,—out at last, where, through the opening mists, we could see the long, level reaches of South Park, and into Hamilton,—fifty or more vacant or decaying cabins and two log hotels,—where one thousand men mined in '60 to '64, and gayety and vice reigned, and now a dozen or twenty men and three or four women were the entire population; a grimy, dirty looking village of the past, for all the world in the storm like an old Swiss mountain village, with manure heaps in front of the houses, and a few sorry looking horses and mules scattered about the pastures.

It was a comfortless promise after so comfortless a ride. We passed on by the village to a plateau above the river, and tried to make camp; but everything was wet,—the water especially so and very muddy; we couldn't start a fire; our guide was obstinate for going to the hotel, and after long struggling against it, we capitulated and went. We gained shelter and warmth, and a good supper, and chapters of country experiences around the fire with the tobacco, and a small bed for two; but there are more real comfort and better air and greater cleanliness and real independence in camp than in these pent-up mountain inns. It was hard to accept such compromise with civilization after the luxuries we had enjoyed in our ground and tent homes.

VIII.

THE SOUTH PARK AND MOUNT LINCOLN

Sunshine and Reunion in the South Park—The Beauties of the Park—Camping Experiences—The Ascent of Mount Lincoln, the Mother of the Mother Mountains—A Snow Storm on the Summit—Montgomery and Fairplay—The Everlasting Plattes—Over the Range again into the Arkansas Valley.

UPPER ARKANSAS VALLEY, AUGUST, 1868

WITH the morning[1] at Hamilton came sunshine and beautiful views of the South Park country, that lay spread out before us in unending stretches of green prairie; here lifted up by a perfect embankment to a new level and going on again in another plain; there rolling off into hills with patches of evergreen; now bringing down from the mountains, still through pastures green, tributaries to the main river; offering on every hand glimpses of beckoning repetitions of itself through and over hills; while all around in the distant horizon huge mountains stood sentinel, guarding this great upper garden-spot of the territory, as if jealous lest its frontiers be invaded, its lands despoiled. No so fine a combination of the grand beauty of the plains, of the lovely beauty of the hills, of the majestic beauty of the mountains ever spread itself before my eyes. Water-courses were abundant, groves and forests were placed with sufficient frequency to diversify the scene and relieve and kindle the eye, while mountains, near and remote, gave their impressive sanction and completeness to the picture. The coloring was brighter yet softer than in Middle Park; and we felt that Colorado and indeed reserved her choicest landscape treasures for us to the last.

Before noon, six miles away,[2] we caught sight of our companions from Denver, coming over the hill,[3]—some on horseback, some in light carriages, and the rest in wagons with the baggage. They looked like one of the patriarchal families of Old Testament times, sons and daughters, servants and asses, moving from one country to another, in obedience to high commandment; and as if representatives of another tribe, we rode out to greet and welcome them to our goodly land. We propitiated their stomachs with our treasured big trout; and after lunch upon the open prairie, the grand caravan moved on, in somewhat disorderly array.[4]

We made a dozen miles, along the northern line of the Park, over a rich, rolling country, starred by occasional lakes, darkened by frequent forests, shadowed by the everlasting snow fields of the mountains. The inevitable afternoon storm came upon us midway, and we rode into Fairplay,[5] the most considerable town of the South Park country, variously wet and considerably disgusted. The ladies stopped by the hospitable fires of the village, while the men went on, and made camp on a hill overlooking the valley, shaded by a few old and stunted pines, and circled by a miner's ditch full of furiously running water. Here half a dozen fires were kindled, as many tents stretched, and, the storm passing away, everybody came into camp, and sleep followed supper to the satisfaction of all.

We moved but a dozen miles the next day, up into the mountains more closely, and near Montgomery,[6] from whence some of us were to ascend Mount Lincoln the day after.[7] These winding valleys, leading out from the Park proper to the mountains, are very beautiful, and the road between Fairplay and Montgomery, which lies close under the highest mountains, offers a succession of brilliantly picturesque mountain and valley views. The valleys are broad, and fertile with green grass, and bright with flowers, and broken with forest patches, while the mountains rise all about in every attitude, and reach up on every hand to snow-fields, flashing in the morning and reddening in the evening sun.

Our camp was a gay one that night,—it lay scattered along a green hill-side, a few rods from a river, and directly under a forest;[8] fuel was abundant, and the fires burned bright and high in all directions; we were not worn with the day's travel; anticipation of the mountain excursion the next morning, was keen and exhilarating; and song and speech and dance around the central camp fire exhausted the hours till bed-time.

It was a happy thought to call the parent mountain of this region, of the whole Rocky Mountain range proper, for the President who guided the Nation so proudly through civil war and slavery to peace and freedom. Peer among presidents and mother among mountains is LINCOLN. The higher Gray's Peak is as high, possibly a hundred or two feet higher; but Mount Lincoln is broader, more majestic, more mountainous. Out from its wide-spreading folds stretch three or four lines of snow-covered mountains; within its recesses spring the waters of three great rivers, the Platte, the Arkansas and the Colorado, that fertilize the plains of half the Continent, and bury themselves, at last, two in the Atlantic and the third in the Pacific Ocean. This is the initial point in our geography, and a fountain-head of national wealth and strength.

Fairplay, founded in 1859, had become "the most considerable town of the South Park country" by the time of Bowles's visit in 1868. (WESTERN HISTORY DEPARTMENT, DENVER PUBLIC LIBRARY, NO. 8486)

This geographical parentage, the representative association of its name and office, and the enthusiasm kindled by our accounts of the view from Gray's Peak, spread a zest among our party for climbing Mount Lincoln; and though the morning was strewn with showers, and huge black clouds hung over the mountain tops in alternation with great rifts of sunshine, these revealing fresh-fallen fields of snow, we determined to take our chances, and galloped off, a dozen strong, women and men, up the valley to Montgomery.[9]

The rain poured relentlessly through these five miles; but then the sunshine came out, and joined by half a dozen more at that point, we turned directly up the mountain side. For two or three miles there is a rough wagon road; beyond that not even a trail that is fixed. Catching sight of the distant goal, we scattered irregularly over the intervening slopes and ravines; first through richest grasses and most abundant and high-colored flowers; then across huge snow-fields, so soft under the summer sun, that our animals could not bear us without floundering in dangerous depths, and we had to dismount and walk and lead; next over wide but steep fields of thin mosses, delicate in leaf and blossom to the last degree, pink and white and blue,—the very final condensed expression of nature; all beauty, all tenderness, all sweetness in essence; and at last, beyond all growth, beyond all snow, out upon miles of broken stones, immeasurably deep, as steep as they could lie.

To ascend over these was tough work; the wind blew biting cold; clouds charged with hail and snow every few minutes swept over, through us; the air was so rare that the animals labored for breath at every step; the sides so steep and the stones so loose as to render the footing fickle,

Montgomery, established with the discovery of gold in 1859, could boast some 250 houses by 1862. (WESTERN HISTORY DEPARTMENT, DENVER PUBLIC LIBRARY, NO. 5904)

even dangerous; we could only make upward progress in slow degree by long, zigzag courses back and forth; and every few minutes the panting, trembling horses and mules would come to a stubborn stop in very fear of their footing. Then we had to dismount and reassure them by leading the way, or find firmer paths. But at last we got as far as horses could go; and a climb of five hundred feet remained for ourselves of even steeper and still loose-lying rocks to the summit. Then we found our hearts and lungs, if never before; work as fast as they could, shaking our very frames in the haste to keep up with their duty, we still had to stop and rest every thirty or forty feet, and let them get even with the air.

Finally on the very crest of the mammoth mountain, the one spot higher than all others, than all around so far as could be seen.[10] Our hopes our fears belied, our fears our hopes in turn; the sweep of the horizon was broken by thick clouds; and we could not compare the view with its rival, from Gray's Peak; but the contending elements lent a new majesty, almost a terror to the scene. Sunshine and storm were continually at war; clouds and clearness constantly changing places; now it was all light to the east, and Gray's Peak and all the intervening mountains to the Plains, the Plains themselves. Denver itself glowed in golden sunshine, while in the west everything was shrouded in blackness and despair; then the clouds came upon and over us, pelting us with snow, and passing by opened great lines of brightness to the west, and we could see on to indefinable distances of snow-covered mountains,—Sopris Peak, the mountain with the snow cross, a continent of rocks and snow, dreary yet beautiful in color, majestic yet fascinating in form. So we caught long narrow glimpses of the South Park, and the Arkansas valley, south of us; and Pike's Peak in one direction and Long's Peak in another were not denied us,—sentinels of nature in the far off corners of the territory, rising above clouds, over intervening storms; while deep chasms, yawning recesses opened in ghastliness through the clouds below us on every side.

The whole vision, fickle, forbidding in many features, always surprising, never satisfying, piquing us by what was withheld, astonishing us by what was given, though disappointing our hopes, yet was vastly finer than our fears. It was the wildest of mountain views and mountain experiences,[11] such as may be welcomed as a variety, though not chosen as the reward for a single excursion. Similar experiences in the high Alps are tamer every way; there is less variety in the landscape; less color in the mountains and the atmosphere; above all, less sweep of distance, less piling of mountain on mountain, through the long openings in the clouds.

We waited as long as the freezing air and the driving snow would let us for wider views of earth and sky; but clouds and storm growing denser, and having finished our lunch of sandwiches and sardines, pickles and peaches, and, coffee being out of the question, a necessary flask of whisky, we retraced the tedious, hard-going way to the valley. Far up, where only rocks reigned, beautiful white and blue birds, like large doves, but called mountain partridges, trotted or flew tamely about us; and a revolver sadly repaid the faith of some of them. Back among the flowers, we gathered large bouquets of bright painter's brush, harebells, fringed gentians, lupins and quaint grasses, and rode into Montgomery aglow with color and excitement, and wet alike from perspiration, snow and rain.

The whole excursion up from and back to Montgomery occupied five hours. The distance cannot be more than six miles to the top; and the hight of the mountain, though never exactly measured, must exceed fourteen thousand feet above the sea level. The wildest estimates are made by the local population of these higher peaks of Colorado; but unless it be Sopris Peak in the far West, it is not probable that any one of them rises as high as Mount Whitney in the Sierra Nevada of California,[12] which is known to be above fifteen thousand feet. Gray, Lincoln, Pike's and Long's Peaks are the four great mountains of explored Colorado; they are all above fourteen thousand feet high, but probably no one goes higher than fourteen thousand five hundred.

Montgomery, which lies close at the foot of Mount Lincoln, on the inside, and is about ten thousand feet high, is another of the deserted mining towns of Colorado. There are a hundred or two houses standing, but only one now occupied.[13] Several years ago, the mines in the hill-sides were rich and remunerative, and a population of two or three thousand were gathered there. There was an opera house, and saloons and stores by the dozens; but the more readily worked ore gave out, there were no means to reduce profitability what followed in the mines, and fresher discoveries elsewhere invited the people "to move on." "Buckskin Joe" is another similar town, five miles off, under another spur of Mount Lincoln.[14] There are good and rich mines at both places, and new ones are even still being discovered; but like most of the ores of Colorado, they await cheaper labor and simpler and more searching processes of treatment for their profitable use.

The solitary family in Montgomery, cultivated, tasteful people, such as we find everywhere among these mountain recesses, gave us a rich hospitality,[15]—which means a "square meal" and a hearty welcome,—and, sunshine being now permanently the victor, we had a pleasant afternoon ride down the valley, by our now deserted camp of the night before, along the clear-running juices of old Lincoln, winding about among her child-hills, their snow-tops reddening under the descending sun, and giving depth and richness to the verdure of valley and forest. Reaching Fairplay at dusk, we found the rest of the party,—those who did not go up Mount Lincoln,—had gone ten miles farther on, with tents, bag and baggage, and left us to the miserable resource of a night's life in town. But the long-stretching log hotel and the country habit of close-packing,—no house is ever full here, so long as any bed has less than four in it, or there is a vacant corner to lay a blanket,—made accommodations for us all, even though the village was unusually crowded that night by reason of Mr. Colfax and Governor Bross stopping over to make speeches.[16] But we missed the better victual, the wider space, the purer air of camp, and duly anathematized Governor Hunt and his various "little Indians," for running away from us.

The Platte River divides, subdivides, and redivides almost indefinitely; and when we get up here among its head waters, the brain fairly grows confused with the number of its forks or branches. The same name extends to the remotest subdivision; and we have the north branch of the south fork of the South Platte; and the middle fork of the north branch of the south fork of the South Platte, and so on *ad infinitum*. I wish the Coloradians would abolish the sinuosities and multiplications, and put the Plattes into numerals, as Platte 1, 2, 3, 4, 5, and so on. I verily believe they would run up to the hundreds; but

Joseph Myer's home in Montgomery, where Schuyler Colfax and William Bross spent the night of August 26, 1868. (WESTERN HISTORY DEPARTMENT, DENVER PUBLIC LIBRARY, NO. 8469)

that would be better than the "Peter Piper picked a peck of pickled peppers" nomenclature. Perhaps, though, they mean to make their geography take the place of classics as a discipline for the youthful mind; if so, they have hit upon a very ingenious substitute, not to say improvement. As between learning the Plattes and conjugating a Greek verb, where's the choice for hardness? All the time we were in the South Park, we were among Plattes, and getting to the heads of Plattes, and each was big enough and independent enough to go alone, and to deserve a name to itself. Fairplay lies on the Platte, and so did every one of our camping grounds for a week.

I believe I have exhausted my adjectives and every known variety of picture frame in trying to set the South Park landscapes in the mind's eye of the reader. But their soft coloring, their rich variety of outline, their long sweep of distance, their greyish-green grasses, their deep-green evergreens, their silvery-green aspens, their summer pictures in their winter frames,—here August, there rising around always January,—only seeing can be feeling and believing. Especially beautiful and exhilarating to sense and spirit are the approaches to the mountains out from the central basin or prairie. First, over slight and soft-rolling hills, through wide valleys, around spurs of the mountains into new valleys, each succeeding one narrower, finally into canyons or chasms, and then up the abrupt hill-side; flowers that had deserted the plains now beginning, then trees ceasing, and snow-banks appearing; and finally catching the cold western wind as it sweeps over the crest of pass or hill. Occasionally, in the open prairie country, a ranch where some successor of David tends his flocks; in the narrow valleys, or on the hill-sides, the deserted cabins of gold-hunters, who had passed on; every six or eight miles a new Platte to cross; and at each ascended mountain-top the beginning of a new Platte, running through tender grass out of a little round lake, or oozing from under a huge snow-bank.

These were our observations the next day, as we galloped savagely on after the head-quarters of the camp. We surprised it at lunch by our rapidity, and then all pushed on "over the range" that divides South Park from the Arkansas valley.[17] The South Park country is free from rocks or stones; the waste of the mountains is broken and pulverized before it reaches the valleys; and even when we mount above grass and trees and earth, the "rock-ribbed hills" are simply great deposits of small stones, or, more correctly, broken rocks. This is one great element in the softness of its scenery. But as we go over the mountains into the Arkansas valley, there is a change; the roads become rough with stones; boulders lie along the path or in the hill-sides, and the water-courses have thrust themselves through high walls of solid rock. There is more ruggedness and coarseness in nature; and while the want of it was not felt, now we welcome the new materials in the landscape. Our heavy baggage teams were slow in working up the huge hills and down, and we went into camp at the first passable widening of the side valley.

IX.

AN INDIAN SCARE—THE TWIN LAKES

Alarming Indian Reports—The Savages on our Track—Scenes and Thoughts in Camp—A Nervous Night and its Sufferings—The Indian Question Generally—The Old False, the New True Policy—The Relief of the Next Morning—The Arkansas Valley and its Greetings—The Twin Lakes and their Beauties—Sunday and Short-Cake—Taylor and Trout.

TWIN LAKES, UPPER ARKANSAS VALLEY,
SEPTEMBER, 1868

THE circle of our Colorado and border travel experience has been made complete by an Indian scare. We have shared the horrible excitement of the settlers, when the hostile Indians put on their war-paint, raise their war-whoop, and dash wildly upon the life and property of the whites. Just as we were going into camp,—weary with mountain travel, and our heaviest teams far behind,—this side the range, there dashed in, on a gaunt white horse, a grim messenger from Denver, with official advices to Governor Hunt that the Indians of the Plains,—the Cheyennes, Araphoes and Sioux,—were on the "war-path;"[1] that from seeming friends they had suddenly turned again to open foes; and were raiding furiously all among the settlements, east, north and south of Denver, stealing horses and shooting the people.[2] We were besought to keep among the mountains,—the homes of the friendly Utes,—as the only place of safety, for our company of territorial and federal officials would be a tempting prize for the red men; but the messenger, who proved to be a villainous sensationist,[3]—though of course we did not know this then,—added to his written reports the alarming story that he had met the hostile Indians in the mountains, only that very day, that they had pursued and shot at him,—the rascal even showing as proof the bullet-holes in his saddle,—that he barely escaped by rapid riding, and that they were probably but a few miles back, and on our path.

Here was serious business, indeed, for such a party; burdened with overloaded wagons, tired horses and defenseless women and children; and all on pleasure and not on war intent. Messengers were sent back to hasten to camp all stragglers, and to warn the Indian agent, with his load of goods and rifles in the Park, to be on his guard, and to come forward. The secret could be kept from no one; the confusion and the excitement quickly grew intense; and that peculiar recklessness or indifference as to ordinary matters that follows the presence of a deep emotion, was singularly manifest. Tents were shabbily put up; camp was disorderly made; supper was eaten in that mechanical, forced way, without regard to quantity, quality or clean plates, that happens when death is in the house; and elaborate toilets were dispensed with. But we huddled close in together; the animals were picketed near at hand; our fire-arms were put in good order; and up and down the road, trusty sentinels were posted. On each side were high abrupt hills; it was a "lovely spot" for an ambuscade; but the nearest anybody came to being killed was when one of our sentinels, during the midnight blackness of storm, suddenly entered upon the ground of the other. Indian-shod in sandals, and moving with that noiseless, stealthy tread that hunters unconsciously adopt, the one was almost upon the other before the latter discovered a foreign presence. There was a sudden click of the rifle's cock, a peremptory demand for "personal explanation" without delay, and then,—a friendly instead of a deadly greeting.

But it was a night to remember,[4] with a shiver,—lying down in that far-off wilderness with the reasonable belief that before morning there was an even chance of an attack of hostile Indians upon our camp, more than half of whose numbers were women and children,—after an evening spent in discussing the tender ways Indians had with their captives, illustrated from the personal knowledge of many present; aroused after the first hour's feverish rest by a new messenger from another quarter, galloping into camp, and shouting, as if we were likely to forget, that "the Indians were loose, and hell was to pay;" followed by the coming of furious storm of rain and hail and thunder and lightning, sucking under our tents, beating through them, to wet pillows and blankets,—at any other time a dire grievance, now hardly an added trial; every ear stretched for unaccustomed sound, every heart beating anxiously, but every lip silent; all eagerly awaiting the slow-coming morning to bring renewal of life and the opportunity to go farther on and to safer retreats. To confess the unprosaic individual fact,—while I report the general truth,—this deponent had the soundest, sweetest night's sleep he had had in the mountains. Some natures will be perverse, and if one must be nervous, it is a great help to be conscious of it.

The experience brought serious thought to us all of the whole Indian question, that puzzle to Congress and eastern public opinion generally. And the failure, which this unexpected outbreak brings to the last and most promising experiment with the so-called but miscalled "peace policy," will probably lead to a more intelligent study and understanding of the whole subject by the country, and in the end to a resolute reformation of our past treatment of it. The truth here, as in many another dispute, lies between the two extremes of opinion and policy. The wild clamor of the border population for the indiscriminate extermination of the savages, as of wolves or other wild beasts and vermin, is as unintelligent and barbarous, as the long dominant thought of the East against the use of force, and its incident policy of treating the Indians as of equal responsibility and intelligence with the whites, are unphilosophical and impracticable. The conflict between these two theories, with the varying supremacy of each, has brought us nothing but disaster and disgrace; we have alternately treated these vagrant children of the wilderness as if we were worse barbarians than themselves or downright fools. It is time we respected ourselves and commanded their respect. Now we do neither.

In the first place, the care of the Indians should be put into a single department at Washington. Its division between the war and interior secretaries is the cause of half our woes. The war office, as representing force, which is the first element in any successful dealing with ignorance and dependence, should monopolize their care. Then we should stop making treaties with tribes, cease putting them on a par with ourselves. We know they are not our equals; we know that our right to the soil, as a race capable of its superior improvement, is above theirs; and let us act openly and directly our faith. The earth is the Lord's; it is given by Him to the Saints for its improvement and development; and we are the Saints. This old Puritan premise and conclusion are the faith and practice of our people; let us hesitate no longer to avow it and act it to the Indian. Let us say to him, you are our ward, our child, the victim of our destiny, ours to displace, ours also to protect. We want your hunting-grounds to dig gold from, to raise grain on, and you must "move on." Here is a home for you, more limited than you have had; hither you must go, here you must stay; in place of your game, we will give you horses, cattle and sheep and grain; do what you can to multiply them and support yourselves; for the rest, it is our business to keep you from starving. You must not leave this home we have assigned you; the white man must not come hither; we will keep you in and him out; when the march of our empire demands this reservation of yours, we will assign you another; but so long as we choose, this is your home, your prison, your play-ground.

Say and act all this as if we meant it, and mean it. If the tribes would go and submit peaceably, well and good; if they would not, use the force necessary to make them. Treat them just as a father would treat an ignorant, undeveloped child. If necessary to punish, punish; subject any way; and then use the kindness and consideration that are consistent with the circumstances. Use the best of these white men of the border, these Indian agents, many of whom are most capable and intelligent and useful men, to carry out and maintain this policy, so far as is possible; use the army so far as is necessary to enforce it, but withhold the soldiers whenever it is not,—for their presence on an Indian reservation is demoralizing to both parties,—but let all authority proceed from a single head, and that head represent a single force.

Above all, stop the treaty-making humbug. It is the direct parent of all our Indian woes and theirs too. Neither party keeps the bargain.[5] The Indian is cheated; the Senate changes the provisions; a quiddling secretary of the interior or Indian commissioner refuses to carry it out; and from secretary down through contractors and agents, something is taken off the promise to the ear by each, till it is thoroughly broken to the hope of the poor savage. What the Indian wants is to be fed and clothed; the treaty and those who fulfil it on our part may or may not do this for him, oftenest not; he cannot tell what or how much he wants beforehand for these ends, and if he did, and bargained for it, the chances are ten to one that he fails to get it; or getting it, squanders it at once, and now, hungry and naked, he goes forth to seek relief by the simplest law of nature; and hence his excuse and the excuse of his white sympathizers for war.

But establish Force for Bargain; Responsibility for Equality; Parentage for Antagonism; see that he is put apart and kept apart from the tide of settlement and civilization; that he has food and clothing, not in gross, but in detail; supplying him the means to help himself in the simplest forms possible,—stock raising is practicable to all the tribes, and tilling the soil possible to most,—and furnishing the rest from day to day; add such education as he will take, such elevation as he will be awakened to, and then let him die,—as die he is doing and die he must,—under his changed life.

This is the best and all we can do. His game flies before the white man; we cannot restore it to him if we would; we would not if we could; it is his destiny to die; we cannot continue to him his original, pure barbaric life; he cannot mount to that of civilization; the mongrel marriage of the two that he embraces and must submit to, is killing him,—and all we can do is to smooth and make decent the pathway to his grave. All this is possible; and it need not cost so much as the mixed state of war and bargaining that we have heretofore pursued. In the beginning there must be the display and the use of power to unlearn in the Indians the false ideas our alternately cowardly bargaining and cowardly bullying policy towards them has engendered; but once inaugurated, it will be simple and successful,—it will give us both peace and protection, and the Indians an easier path to the grave than lies before them now. More briefly and soldierly, General Sherman, now alive at last to the true nature of the question, expresses the new and necessary policy: "Peace and protection to the Indians upon the reservations; war and extermination if found off from them."[6]

But to get back to our camp and ourselves. The scare wore off under the tonic of a cool, clear morning, with splendid visions of fresh fields of snow glancing in the sunlight, the arrival of our load of rifles and Indian goods safe,[7] a good breakfast of trout and Governor Hunt's best griddle-cakes, and the following summons to horse for the Twin Lakes.[8] Never party moved out of camp more gladly; and a few miles farther on, the Arkansas valley welcomed us into a new country, full of the light and the freshness and the joy of a newly awakened nature. There was a California roll to the hills that led down to the river; the sage bush that covered them was greener and more stalwart that that of the Middle Park; and the river bottom held a deeper toned grass, and was alive with grazing cattle; while the Sahwatch range of mountains, that divides the Arkansas valley from the Pacific waters,[9] was continuously higher than any we had yet looked up to, and its bold majestic peaks bore and brought far down their middles that thin new snow, which is such a touching type of purity, and is never seen without a real enthusiasm. Governor Bross and Vice-President Colfax, who had been off spending the night among the miners of an upper gulch,[10] greeted us, too, with felicitations on our safety, and with a company of volunteer cavalry, that did not desert us until all apprehensions of danger had passed away.

Crossing the river, descending the valley, and then turning up among the western hills, over one, two lines of them, racing and roystering along with our new companions, and in our new joys, we suddenly came out over the Twin Lakes, and stopped. The scene was, indeed, enchanting. At our feet, a half a mile away, was the lower of two as fine sheets of water as mountain ever shadowed, or wind rippled, or sun illuminated. They took their places at once in the goodly company of the Cumberland Lakes of England, of Lucerne in Switzerland, of Como and Laggiore in north Italy, of Tahoe and Donner in California, and no second rank among them all. One is about three miles by a mile and a half; the other say two miles by one; and only a fifty-rod belt of grass and grove separates them. Above them on two sides sharply rise,—dark with trees and rocks until the snow caps with white,—the mountains of the range; sparsely-wooded hills of grass and sage brush mount gracefully in successive benches on a third,—it was over these that we came into their presence; while to the south a narrow, broken valley, pushed rapidly by the mountains towards the Arkansas, carries their outlet stream to its home in the main river. Clear, hard, sandy beaches alternate with walls of rock and low marshy meadows in making the immediate surroundings of both lakes. The waters are purity itself, and trout abound in them.

Here we camped for that and the next day, which was Sunday;[11] restored our Indian-broken nerves; caught trout and picked raspberries; bathed in the lakes; rode up and around them; looked into their waters, and on over them to the mountains,—first green, then blue, then black, finally white, and then higher to clouds, as changing in color under storm, under sun, under moon, under lightning. Every variety of scene, every change and combination of cloud and color were offered us in these two days; and we worshipped, as it were, at the very fountains of beauty, where its every element in nature lay around, before, and above us.

Also, not to live forever in poetry, we patched our clothes, greased our boots, washed our handkerchiefs and towels,—one would dry while another was being washed, in the dry, breezy air,—and ate boiled onions and raspberry short-cake to repletion. Bayard Taylor's letters are at least a guide to the opportunities for good dinners in Colorado;[12] and ostensibly with the purpose to explore the lakes, and see the falls in the river above, possibly with a thought to fall upon such hospitality as he experienced in the little neighboring village of Dalton,[13]—another collection of vacant cabins, with a new court-house, and only two occupied tenements,—a few of us stole quietly off for a Sunday excursion.

We circled the lakes, as beautiful in detail as in grand effect; picked out many a charming camping-ground for future visits; found along the shores one or two resident families, and a tent with a stove-pipe through it, where a Chicago invalid was spending the summer, gaining vigorous strength and permanent health, and drying quantities of trout,—think of trout so plenty as to suggest drying them!—followed up the bed of the stream two miles or more above the lakes to a very pretty waterfall, and a deep pool, worn out of solid rock, thick with visible trout, whom we could poke with long sticks, but could not seduce with fattest of grasshoppers; lunched off the mountain raspberry vines; tracked a grizzly bear; and looked up the far-stretching gorge through rocks and bushes and vines that were very seducing,—but came back to Dalton in time to get our invitation to dinner. There was white table-cloth, and chairs, and fresh beef-steak, and mealy potatoes, and soft onions, and cream for coffee, and raspberry short-cake "to kill," and a lady and gentleman for hostess and host; everything and more and better even than Taylor had two years before. Going back by the lakes to camp just at sunset, they were in their best estate of color, of light and shade; and water and mountain and sky met and mingled, and led on the eye from one glory to another, till the joy of the spirit overcame and subdued and elevated the satisfaction of the senses.

X.

FROM THE TWIN LAKES TO DENVER

Down the Arkansas Valley—A Picturesque Scene—A Sensation—Over into South Park—Who were with us, and How we Made Camp and Spent the Night—Governor Bross Grinding Coffee—Governor Hunt's "Slapjacks"—An Evening in Camp with the Indians—Out of the Park, and into the Plains—Through "the Garden of the Gods"—Grand Entree into Denver.

DENVER, COLORADO, SEPTEMBER, 1868

WE entered the Arkansas valley so far up that its head was visible. It leads to the lowest pass in all the mountains over to the Pacific slope, not rising above the timber line. Like all the passes of the range, it is ambitious of a railroad, and certainly seems more reasonably so than many others. But for many years to come our continental railroads will find lower and smoother paths both north and south of Colorado.

The plan of our journey was to go from the Twin Lakes down the Arkansas, around the outside of South Park, so nearly as the rock-bound banks of the river would allow, through Canon City[1] and Colorado City,[2] and up by the Plains, under the eastern line of the mountains, to Denver. Thus we should have circuited all the great central portions of the state, and except San Luis Park, which we should have left in the south, have seen all the principal centers of her population, all the distinguishing features of her geography and her natural beauty. But this would have taken us directly into the path of the now rampantly hostile Indians; so we drew in our lines, and made a narrower circle across the South Park, and up to Denver. We lost little or nothing that was distinctive, though some repetitions and modifications of beautiful scenery already or to be made familiar to us. But I urge all who come after us to follow our intended route, and even to extend their trip over into San Luis Park. Here, though the testimony is contradictory, will be found a country rich in beauty and resources, and with some features not characteristic of the other great Parks.

First we rode some twelve miles down the valley. With a mounted escort of about twenty gallant young gold miners, and the addition of two or three camping parties that sought our company home as a sedative to the nervousness of the Indian stories, we made up a grand "outfit." All together, there were from seventy-five to one hundred persons, and as many animals, as it moved back over the mountains into South Park again. The first eight miles were through a broken, hilly country, the mountains coming down to the river on each side in great gashes or rolls, occasionally a broad inclined plain, frequently a dry ravine. The soil was light and cold, and sage bush and coarse grass and thin forests were its products, other than gold. Of the latter it holds in deposit a plentiful sprinkling almost everywhere; and we passed the prosperous mining villages of Granite[3] and Cash Creek,[4] their peoples tearing up the ground all about in eager search for the precious metal.

Little canyons and big canyons drove our road away from the river and over hills and bluffs for much of these eight miles; but at the end we came down into a wider and richer opening, and there spread before us a fine agricultural section, the garden of the upper Arkansas. For thirty-five miles now, the river, hugging the hills on the east, lays open a broad, clean, rising plain of from one to ten miles in width, before the rocks and forests of the western mountains begin. Beyond these thirty-five miles, the river canyons again for a long course, and farming is at an end, and travel down the valley is turned off into South Park till the stream emerges again from its rock embrasures. Tributaries of the main stream slash and fertilize this great meadow; and it bears large crops of grain, grass and roots. Some twenty farmers have brought under profitable cultivation about seven hundred acres of this valley; the mines in the valleys above and over in South Park furnish the markets; a Frenchman, one of the first of these ranchmen, and whose bread and milk we devoured as we went by, returned an income of from twelve to fifteen thousand dollars two years ago, as the results of a single season's farming, crops being good and prices high; and, spite of grasshoppers and drouth, the business is uniformly more successful than mining.

Crossing the river through the hospitable Frenchman's grounds, we turned up the hills, and began to leave this inviting country almost as soon as we had entered it. It beckoned us back by scenes of exquisite beauty, clothed in warm sunshine, and at every convenient spot in the ascending hills, we lingered for longing looks, up and down, and across its lines. All around on the lower hills, down to the river, guarding its passage, were magnificent ruins of mountains; huge boulders; fantastic shaped columns; lines of palisades; the kernels which water could not wash nor abrasion wear away; groves of rocks; fortresses upon the river shore,—the Rhine is not more thickly peopled with ruined castles; with pines and aspens and coarse bushes growing upon and among them all, including a new species, called *pinyon,* a stunted, sprawling, thick-growing pine, looking, as set in a grove a little way off, like an old apple orchard. Starting from the opposite bank, the open, rising meadow, a great inclined plain of gray and green, stretching miles away up the sides of the grand Sahwatch Mountains, whose tops formed a line of snow fields that overlooked and cooled the whole warm scene of sunshine and life below. Up and down hills we toiled all the afternoon, refreshed only and yet tantalized by occasional glimpses of the beautiful valley behind, which seemed to spread out all its beauty of form, of scene, of color, to harrow us for so early deserting it.

The only other sensation of the afternoon's ride was the sudden dashing into our line from behind of a dozen or twenty Ute chiefs and warriors.[5] As we had not learned to know one kind of Indians from another, their galloping in among us stirred the blood a trifle; but we soon found they were friends, and pairing off among our mounted men, they were grunting and gesticulating their story into all our ears. They proved to be the leaders of a band of Utes living down in the San Luis Park country, who had learned, in the mysterious and speedy manner of savages and wildernesses, of the uprising of the hostile Indians of the Plains, and of the presence of Governor Hunt and our party in this region, and so, traveling day and night, they had hurried up to meet us, and see if they were wanted, either to protect us, or take the field against their and our enemies. Not without a selfish thought, too, perhaps, for blankets and beef. They camped with us that night, were well-fed and well-promised, and went back home the next day. The Governor had neither authority nor means to put them into the field against the Plain Indians; nor was it clear that there was any occasion for it.

We pushed up near to the tops of the mountains, riding far into the evening, before camping, and finally pitched our tents in a great meadow, heavy with grass, and interspersed with little wooded knolls,[6] within and around one of which we built our fires and laid our blankets for the night. We needed them all, for it was dreary cold before morning, and water froze in our cups on the way from the brook half a mile off. But the forenoon's sun and saddle brought summer warmth back; and we were not long in getting over the range and down into South Park. We entered it about at the middle, and it seemed tamer and less green than in the upper sections. Alkali and salt deposits whitened the surface in great patches, and so rich are the springs with salt at one spot, that a large establishment for evaporating the water and making salt is in operation, and holds a profitable monopoly of the salt market of the state. We made a fine noon camp by one of the everlasting Plattes,[7] and trout-catching was brisk for an hour.

Here, too, we had another Indian raid,—the outposts of our old Middle Park Utes, who had heard the story of the Plain Indians coming up into the South Park, and moved over in a body to dispossess them, came wildly and joyfully riding in upon us, a dozen or two, with some white friends from Fairplay. So our escort doubled, and we traveled across the Park with as large and as motley a retinue as ever Oriental prince moved among over the deserts of Asia. Only, with true American individuality, we scattered wildly about, and lingered or hurried at pleasure over the wide open plains, dotted with occasional hill and lake, the latter repeated by mirage in the distance, or by the deceptive resemblance of an alkali field, and circled by the far-distant, far-reaching mountains. Everything else failing or fatiguing, from sheer abundance,—mountain, field, grass, forest, color, the atmosphere remained, a feeling of beauty that ministered to several senses without ever palling the appetite of either.[8]

We made grand camp that night about a mile beyond Fairplay, on a gently sloping plateau,[9] backed by a thick aspen grove, watered at its base by a fresh stream, fronted by the broad Park meadows, looking towards sundown, and taking the best light of the full moon through its nightly circle of the horizon. The dozen or twenty Utes enlisted to go through with us to Denver, and made a camp for themselves a few rods away among the trees. The mounted men were usually the first in camp; they stripped their animals of saddles and bridles and blankets, and sent them galloping off for grass and water. As fast as the wagons came up, they took their places in the grand circle of the camp-ground, and were unloaded of tents, baggage and provisions, and their horses loosened to join the others. Smooth spots were chosen for the tents in a semi-circle, and the tents put up by the most adroit in that business. There was one for Governor Hunt and his family; another for Mr. Witter and his,[10] consisting of himself, his wife (Mr. Colfax's sister), a babe eight weeks old,[11]—think of that, you tender mothers in four-walled and close-roofed houses in civilization!—and Mr. Colfax's mother and father;[13] a third for the young ladies; Governor Bross and the Vice-President used one of the large covered wagons for lodgings; my friend Lord and myself had a little tent by ourselves; and the rest, despising such paltry interventions of effeminacy, lay around in the softest, shadiest places, under the wagons, under trees, always near the fires. The little sheet-iron cooking-stoves, one for each of the two messes into which our original party was divided, were simultaneously planted and fired up. The open fires were located, and the Vice-President, Governor Bross, Mr. Thomas of the Rocky Mountain News,[13] and any other idle and otherwise incompetent persons were detailed to fetch wood for them. Soon a huge fire blazed in front of each tent. Then the wood-haulers became water-carriers. Next the fastidious made their toilets; and Governor Hunt called for assistant cooks.

This night we were to have an extra meal. To start with, and especially to provide quantity for the capacious Indian stomachs, a herd of cattle were driven up from the meadow, and Mr. Curtis,[14] the Indian interpreter, passing them in review, rifle in hand, and, choosing a fat young cow, sent a ball unerringly into her forehead, and she fell dead instantly. It was the first time I had ever seen this speedy, humane manner of butchering; and Mr. Bergh,[15] the anti-cruelty man, ought to demand its universal use. The animal was soon cut up, and a few choice pieces brought to our camp, but the Indians carried off the bulk to theirs, and, with forked sticks and open fire, and a little salt, were soon filling up their waste places. The village furnished us cream and fresh supplies of sugar. Soon we had beefsteak frying, mush and milk in proper progress, oyster soup and tomatoes stewing, hominy warming, a huge section of ribs of beef roasting on a forked stick before the fire, coffee and tea brewing, biscuits baking at one mess, and slapjacks browning at another. Governor Bross earned his supper by grinding coffee for half an hour, and afterwards, his hand having grown supple, you could have seen him, seated on an empty whisky-keg, turning the griddle-cakes to perfection; and your correspondent won his glory and victual by making the "long-sweetening," *i.e.* white sugar melted into a permanent syrup. Then there were canned peaches and raspberries for desert. All this, seated on our haunches on the ground or on bended knees around the board and box that served for tables, each with a tin plate and cup, and knife and fork and spoon to match, and all with appetites worthy the food. We generally "boarded around," that is ate at the mess which happened to have the most inviting meal, and as there is no knowledge so satisfactory as the experimental on such a subject, it commonly resulted in our eating at both. It is surprising how excellent food can be had in such a camping expedition with a little painstaking and tact in providing and cooking. Governor Hunt was master of all the arts of camp-life, and under his care we "fared sumptuously every day." The slap-jacks and their "long-sweetening" were an incomparable dish, and took the place of bread at Governor Hunt's table.[16]

Supper over, and the dishes washed, in which last operation "equal rights" were sometimes allowed the women, all gathered around the central campfires, with shawls, buffalo robes and blankets for protection from the ground; our friends traveling in company, who had made separate camps adjoining, came over to spend the evening; to-night our escort party from the Arkansas valley had supped with us, and were about to say farewell; and their Indian successors, having become happy and hilarious, were invited and welcomed into the circle; and thus re-enforced and diversified, we made a gala night of it. It was a very curious scene indeed. The blaze of the camp-fire contrasted sharply with the light of the moon, and brought out in fine relief all the hundred varying faces and strange costumes gathered around. Speeches were made and songs sung; Mr. Colfax addressed the Utes, and his words were interpreted to them by Mr. Curtis, and the reply of their chief to us; and then we called for songs from them.[17] Stimulated by a pile of white sugar that Governor Hunt threw down at their feet, they got up and responded with spirit. Standing in a row, shoulders touching, and swaying to and fro in a long line by one motion, they chanted in a low, guttural way, all on one key, and only musical as it was correct monotone. Then there were more songs and sentiments from the whites; the Indians were dismissed; our kind friends from the Arkansas said good-by; and soon the fires of camp were dull, and all its life still in sleep,—a sleep of trust and safety, there under the open sky, with a village of all sorts of people a mile away, and a band of savages within six rods. It was all so incongruous and anomalous to our home thought and life; and yet we felt as safe, and were as safe, as in double-bolted houses on police-patrolled streets. Only the contrasts forced themselves into the wakeful moments of night and morning, as we turned over and refastened the blankets, and piled more baggage over chilly feet, and peered out into the dead stillness of the camp, broken may-be by the dull snoring of a heavy sleeper, and the far-off browsing of a greedy mule; sounds brought near and made loud by the hush of human life, and the reign of nature's peace.

Out of the Park and into the hills that separate it from the Plains the next day. The way was familiar, the road for the most part good. We scattered along, two or three together, through five or six miles; closing up for lunch, and again for night camp. Our Indian escort familiar with every rod of the country, roamed at will, taking short cuts over the hills, and appearing first in the rear, then far in advance. We had a beautiful camp, after twenty-five miles ride, in a narrow but long little valley, that bowed the sun out at one end, as it welcomed the moon up at the other. The next day, too, all among the hills, riding another twenty-five miles; the roads improving; ranches thickening,—no lack now of buttermilk or cream; travelers grew numerous; daily newspapers coming in; and the end dawning. It was a pleasant mountain country, open, free, lightly wooded, abundantly watered, and the valleys rich for grass and grain. The streams, too, hold trout, and the hills are thick with raspberries,—it is up here that the Denverites come for their briefer mountain excursions, and this is the common road for commerce and for pleasure into the South Park.

Our night camp now was the last of the excursion.[18] It was near the junction of the roads leading to Denver by the Plains and to Idaho through the mountains. There was a rivalry among the cooking-stoves for the best farewell supper; but the slapjacks gave Governor Hunt the victory,—there was no equalling, no resisting them. Around the camp-fire, we "talked it over;" hilarious with a vein of sadness; humorous with a touch of pathos; Mr. Colfax made his excellent speech, beginning, "this is the saddest moment of my life;" we sang auld-lang-syne, and prepared for an early start in the morning.

The breakfast dishes were packed dirty,—"after us the Deluge,"—and camp was broken by eight o'clock with the cry, "Ho, for Denver." The going out of the mountains was very fine. The several miles through Turkey Creek Canyon, the road winding along with the stream at the bottom of a high gorge of rocks, were fresh and exhilarating; we had gone around canyons before, painfully and laboriously; now to follow one by a narrow but firm road offered new and picturesque views. This was not unlike the Via Mala of Switzerland;[19] and coming out, the road circled a high precipitous hill midway in its side, an expensive and excellent bit of road-making, such as is rarely seen anywhere in America.

Here we overlooked the grand ocean of the Plains, and came upon the struggles of nature to leave off mountain and begin plain. Along here, as at other points below, there seems to have been an especial and antagonistic fold thrown up almost abruptly from the level plain. Pike's Peak, which is distinct from the main range, is the chief endeavor or culmination of this throe of the formation. And around it, as here, are grouped monuments or remains of mountains, alike grotesque, commanding, impressive; taking all shapes, and giving the thought that somebody greater and higher than man had made here familiar home. The collection of these ruins near Pike's Peak and Colorado City, which we missed seeing because of the Indian war, is called "The Garden of the Gods," and the name not unfitly clothes the impression they make.[20] They are not boulders or piles of rock, but what is left of mountains washed and worn away by waters and winds. The body is a fine reddish granite; and they stand sentinelled about upon the bare closing bluffs of the hills, with forms of such majesty and such personality, as arouses one's wonder and deepens curiosity into awe.

Down into the last ravine, and out upon the long rolls of the Plains. The Platte and its branches wind with their gardens of grain and their groves of trees about in the far distance, making a pleasantly variegated map of green of the vast picture. Bear Creek especially offers a charming principality of its own.[21] And far in the thin haze the steeples and blocks of Denver stand upon the sky. Herds of grazing cattle are scattered along on both sides of the road; and with a common hunger for home and civilization, beasts and drivers spur each other into rapid gait. Our day's ride of twenty-five miles is finished by two o'clock, and we stop before entering the town to "serry the ranks," and try the unaccustomed draughts of a suburban brewery.

A circus would have been a poor show compared to the procession that then passed into Denver.[22] First were the faithful Utes, gay with bright blankets and yellow and red paint; a bride among them, beaded and bespangled from head to foot; then our own cavaliers and cavalieresses, their plumage not over gay after a fortnight's mountain use, their animals worn and sorry from hard riding and no oats; next carriages, ambulances and baggage-wagons, out of which peered flapping sun bonnets and browned faces, with every other wheel bound in huge sticks from the forest to keep them from dropping to pieces; and finally Governor Evans's carriage,[23] altogether minus two wheels, and just lifted from the ground by two poles that dragged their slow length along behind. Despite the solemnity of the town over the Indian raids; despite the dignity of demeanor due to high officials, Ute chiefs, Colorado chiefs, Illinois chiefs, Washington fathers,—the street broke into a horse, neigh a mule laugh that rolled along from block to block, and turned the back doors out in affright lest Cherry Creek had come to town again.[24] And then we were dismissed to assure our friends of our identity, and reconstruct ourselves.

XI.

MINES, MINING, AND MINERS

Review of the Mining Interests of Colorado—Present Condition of Affairs in the Quartz Centers—Central City, Georgetown, Mill City, Empire City, etc.—Renewal of Gulch-Mining, its Profits, and its Promises—Present Yield of Gold and Silver, and its Certain Increase—Population of Colorado, and the Idiosyncracies of its Miners.

DENVER, COLORADO, SEPTEMBER, 1868

IT remains for me to speak of the industrial interests, growth, prosperity, and promise, of Colorado. These have only been incidentally alluded to so far; but they deserve special exhibition. The change in its material affairs and prospects, since we were here three years ago, is most marked and healthy. Then, the original era of speculation, of waste, of careless and unintelligent work, and as little of it as possible, of living by wit instead of labor, of reliance upon eastern capital instead of home industry, was, if not at its hight, still reigning, but with signs of decay and threatening despair. The next two years, 1866 and 1867, affairs became desperate; the population shrunk; mines were abandoned; mills stopped; eastern capital, tired of waiting for promised returns, dried up its fountains; and the secrets of the rich ores seemed unfathomable. Residents who could not get away, were put to their trumps for a living; and economy and work were enforced upon all. Thus weeded out, thus stimulated, the population fell back on the certainties; such mining as was obviously remunerative was continued; the doubtful and losing abandoned; the old and simple dirt washing for gold was resumed, and followed with more care; and farming rose in respectability and promise. The discovery and opening of specially rich silver mines near Georgetown kept hope and courage alive, and freshened speculation in a new quarter; but the main fact of the new era was that the people went to work, became self-reliant, and, believing that they "had a good thing" out here, undertook to prove it to the world by intelligent and economic industry.

These were the kernel years of Colorado; they proved her; they have made her. Her gold product went down, probably, to a million dollars say, in each of 1866 and 1867; but it began at once, under the new order of things, to rise; and agriculture also at once shot up and ahead, and directly assumed, as it has in California, the place of the first interest, the great wealth. No more flour, no more corn, no more potatoes at six cents to twelve cents a pound freight, from the Missouri River; in one year Colorado became self-supporting in food; in the second an exporter, the feeder of Montana, the contractor for the government posts and the Pacific Railroad; and now, in the third year, with food cheaper than in "the States," she forces the Mississippi and Missouri valleys to keep their produce at home or send it East. She feeds the whole line of the Pacific Railroad this side the continental divide, and has even been sending some of her vegetables to Omaha. Her gold and silver product is up to at least two millions this year, got out at a profit of from twenty-five to fifty per cent, is now at the rate of nearly if not quite three millions, and will certainly surpass that sum in 1869. Her agricultural products must be twice as much at least, certainly four millions for 1868, and perhaps six millions; though it is difficult to make as certain estimates in this particular, and the Indians have worked great mischief with the ingathering of the crops this fall.

Central City, in the midst of the mountains on the north branch of Clear Creek, continues to be the center of the gold quartz-mining; and business there was never more healthily prosperous than now. All its stamp mills are in operation, and more are being erected; for after wearily waiting through two or three years for more effective processes for reducing the ores, their owners have set these in operation again, simplified, perfected and economized their working, and, from about one hundred and forty mills and seven hundred and fifty stamps, are now producing near fifty thousand dollars of gold a week, at a cost for both mining and milling of from two-thirds to three-quarters that sum. Another season will see say fifty mills and one thousand stamps at work in this valley. The most valuable ores of the neighboring mines are not put through this process, but are sold at about one hundred dollars a ton to Professor Hill's smelting or Swansea works,[1] now established here, and working the richer and sulphuretted ores with an economy and completeness that the plain stamp mills cannot do. The ores worked in the latter form the principal product of the mines, and produce under the stamps about twenty-five dollars a ton, while the cost for mining and milling is about fifteen dollars. If steam is used the cost goes up to twenty dollars. The Swansea and the plain stamp mill are the only "processes" now in use in this valley. Professor Hill has proved the success and profit of the former, at least for all high-class ores. He is giving from eighty to one hundred and twenty-five dollars a ton for such ore, and probably makes from thirty to forty dollars a ton on it; and his purchases amount to some twenty thousand dollars a month. He is already doubling his furnaces. But the problem is to apply his process profitably to lower class ores; to such as hold from twenty-five to fifty dollars a ton, and of which there are almost literally mountains in Colorado. The free or simple gold ores of this grade can be worked well enough by stamps and amalgamation, as in Central City and California, and the cost thereof can be ultimately reduced to probably one-half of present prices; but these constitute only a fraction of the rich ores of Colorado. Most of them hold both silver and gold, combined with sulphurets of iron, and a process which gets one leaves the other, except, of course, smelting, which at present is too expensive for any but highly-freighted ores. This is why thousands of mines are unworked to-day; why scores of mills with unperfected processes, or plain stamps, stand idle, rotting and rusting in all parts of the territory; and why deserted cabins and vacant villages lie scattered in all the valleys about,—telling their tragic tales of loss and disappointment, monuments of the enthusiasm and the credulity of miner and capitalist, who labored and invested wildly and before their time.

Some silver mine discoveries have recently been made in the Central City region; indeed, there is silver in all the gold ores, and gold in all the silver ores of the territory, and lead and copper in most besides; but the head-quarters of the silver business is at Georgetown, ten or a dozen miles over the mountains from Central City, at the head of the south branch of Clear Creek. Around and above this now thriving and most beautifully located of the principal mining villages of Colorado; at nine thousand, ten thousand, or even to twelve and thirteen thousand feet above the sea level, almost unapproachable save in summer, and then only by pack mules or on foot, are many marvelously rich silver veins in the rocks. Hundreds of mines have been opened; but only a dozen or twenty are now being actually worked with profitable results. The rest await purchasers from their "prospectors," or capital to develop them. The ore from the leading mines ranges from one hundred to one thousand dollars a ton. Only two mills for reducing the ore are in operation; one treats the second class ore, such as will average say two hundred dollars a ton, reducing it by crushing or stamping, then washing with salt to oxidize it, and then amalgamating with quicksilver, at a cost of from fifty to one hundred dollars a ton; and the other smelting the higher priced ores, at a cost probably of one hundred to two hundred dollars a ton. The latter establishment buys outright most of the ore it reduces, and has paid all the way from five hundred to six hundred and seventy-five dollars a ton for it. Both processes get out from seventy-five to ninety per cent of the assay value of the ore; but they are imperfect and expensive, and much of the best ore is sent East for treatment. The Equator mine, owned by a party of railroad men from Chicago, is one of the two or three prizes here,[2] and sends its first-class ore, worth from nine hundred to one thousand dollars a ton, all the way to Newark, N.J., to be reduced. Thirty tons were packed for shipment the day I was there. The superior yield under the closer and more economical treatment at Newark more than pays for the freight, which is but forty-eight dollars a ton. The Equator mine claims to have yielded one hundred thousand dollars' worth of ore this season, and brags of a million next. Only a portion of its ore taken out is yet worked. There are several, perhaps half a dozen other mines nearly as good as this.

Georgetown now has a population of about three thousand, and the best hotel in the territory. It is one of the places that every tourist should visit, partly for its silver mines, partly because the road to it up the South Clear Creek is through one of the most interesting sections of the mountains, and partly that it is the starting-point for the ascension of Gray's Peaks. The traveler can go up to the top of that mountain and back to Georgetown between breakfast and supper; and if he will not take his tour by the Snake and Blue Rivers to the Middle or South Park, he should certainly make this day's excursion from Georgetown. Central City and its neighborhood are much less interesting to the mere pleasure traveler. That town, with its four thousand or five thousand inhabitants, is crowded into a narrow gulch, rather than valley, torn with floods, and dirty with the debris of mills and mines that spread themselves over everything.

Scattered about, in Boulder District, on the Snake, over on the Upper Arkansas, up among the gulches of the South Park hills, are a few more quartz mills, some in operation, more not; but the principal business of quartz mining is done in the sections I have named, in Gilpin and Clear Creek counties. Mill City, Empire, and Idaho are villages in this section, with their mines and mills, doing a little something, struggling to prove their capacity, but hardly in a single case making money, partly because of the poverty of the ore, but chiefly because it is refractory, and will not yield up its possessions to any known and reasonably cheap process. Time, patience, and cheaper labor will bring good results out of many of these investments; but others will have to go to swell the great number of failures that stand confessed all over this as all over every other mining country.

There are great tunneling schemes proposed or started in the Georgetown silver district, by which the various ore veins of a single mountain are to be cut deep down in their depths, and their wealth brought out of a single mouth in the valley, at a much cheaper rate than by digging down from the top on the vein's course and hauling up. The "Burleigh drill" from Massachusetts, that has been in use in the Hoosac tunnel, has been introduced here for this purpose;[3] and successful mining on a grand scale will soon take this form, not only here, but in Nevada, and indeed in most of our mining States.

The other form of mining, known as gulch-mining or dirt-washing, is increasing again, and has employed full three hundred men this season. Fifty to seventy-five of these are at work in the Clear Creek and Boulder valleys; but the great body of them are scattered through Park, Lake, and Summit counties, on the Snake and other tributaries of the Blue River; on the upper Plattes in South Park; and on the upper Arkansas and its side valleys. They have averaged twelve dollars a day to a man; but the season for this kind of mining is less than half the year, in some places because of ice and snow; in most for lack of water. The year's product from gulch-mining will certainly foot up half a million dollars, probably a hundred thousand more. New gulches and fresh "bars," or deposits of sand, brought down from the hills by the streams, have been opened this year in preparation for another year's work; and it is not unreasonable to look for a million dollars from gulch-mining next year.

These figures seem small compared with the amounts reported to be got out in the years following the first gold discoveries of 1859.—in '60 to '64,—when one year's production ran up as high as six or eight millions, and for several years averaged probably four; when hundreds if not thousands of eager miners were gathered in a single gulch, and ran over its sands with a reckless waste, taking off the cream of the deposits, and then moving on to new places, and, finally exhausting both their own first enthusiasm, and all the best or most obvious chances, turning away in disgust at a "played out" territory. But the business is now resumed in a more systematic, intelligent and economical way; labor is cheaper; miners are satisfied with more moderate returns; and there is really almost no limit to these valleys and banks, under the hills and along the rivers, whose sands and gravel hold specks of gold in sufficient quantity to pay for washing over." An intelligent investigator of the subject tells me that the whole of South Park would pay three to four dollars a day for the labor of washing it over. But I pray it may not be done while I live to come to these Mountains and the Parks; for gold-washing leaves a terrible waste in its track.

In the valley of the Blue and its tributaries, more extensive works for gulch-mining exist than in any other district; there, not less than eighty-four miles of ditches to bring water to wash out the gold with have been constructed, and the amount of water they carry in the aggregate is eight thousand seven hundred and fifty inches. One of these ditches is eleven miles long; two others seven miles each; another five, and so on; and they cost from one thousand to twelve hundred dollars a mile. Says Mr. Thomas of the Rocky Mountain News, from whose careful and elaborate investigations this summer and fall, I draw many of the facts of this letter:—"The facilities and opportunities for gulch-mining in this country (Summit) are equal if not superior to any in Colorado.[4] Many of the gulches, now worked, will last for years to come, while much ground remains yet untouched. The Blue River will pay for ten miles or more, at the rate of five to ten dollars per day to the man. Many places will pay from three to five dollars per day to the man, and will be worked when labor becomes lower and living cheaper."[5]

In the Granite district of the Upper Arkansas, quartz gold is found in simple combinations, or "free," as in California, which can be mined and reduced for eight to ten dollars a ton, while it yields from fifteen to one hundred dollars; but these are ores from near the surface, and it is yet a problem whether they will not change on getting down in the veins, as in other Colorado mines, and become "refractory," and impossible of working at a profit by any yet known process.

The Cinnamon mines,[7] just over the southern border in New Mexico, have attracted much attention for the last two years. Several quartz mills are in operation there, but the main yield, so far, is from the gulches, and the total product this year is about a quarter of a million dollars. San Luis Park, too, is believed to be rich in mineral deposits; some promising discoveries have already been made there; and indeed in almost every quarter of the state are the beginnings of developments that inspire great faiths, each in its own particular circle of prospectors and prophets.

There is apparently no limit, in fact, to the growth of the mineral interests of Colorado. The product this year is from two millions to two and a half; next year it will be at least a million more, perhaps a million and a half, or four millions; and the increase will go on indefinitely. For the business is now taken hold of in the right way;

pursued for the most part on strictly business principles; and every year must show improvements in the ways and means of mining and treating the ores. The mountains are just full of ores holding fifteen to fifty dollars' worth of the metals per ton; and the only question, as to the amount to be got out, is one of labor and cost as compared with the profits of other pursuits.

The settled population of Colorado is now at least fifty thousand, perhaps sixty thousand. About one-quarter is Mexican, all in the southern section, and ignorant and debased to a shameful degree. The rest are as good a population as any new state can boast of. They are drawn from all eastern sources; but the New England leaven, though possibly not the New England personality, is dominant in their ambition, their education, their morality, their progressive spirituality. The pioneer miners, the "prospectors," are a class of characters by themselves. Properly they never mine; to dig out and reduce ore is not their vocation; but they discover and open mines, and sell them, if they can; at any rate move on to discover others. Men of intelligence, often cultivated, generally handsome, mostly moral, high-toned and gallant by nature, sustained by a faith that seems imperishable, putting their last dollar, their only horse, possibly their best blanket, into a hole that invites their hopes, working for wages only to get more means to live while they prospect anew and further, they suffer much, and yet enjoy a great deal. Faith is comfort, and that is theirs; they will "strike it rich" some day; and then, and not till then, will they go back to the old Ohio, Pennsylvania or New England homes, and cheer the fading eyes of fathers and mothers, and claim the patient-waiting, sad-hearted girls, to whom they pledged their youthful loves. The vicious and the loafers, the gamblers and the murderers, have mostly "moved on;" what is left is chiefly golden material; and the men and the mines and farms of Colorado, all alike and together, are in a healthy and promising condition, and insure for her a large growth and a generous future. The two things she lacketh chiefly now are appreciation at the East and women; what she has of both are excellent, but in short supply; but the Railroad will speedily fill the vacuums.

XII.

THE AGRICULTURE OF COLORADO: CONCLUSION

The Farming Interests of Colorado; their Great Attainment and Greater Promise—Details of the Harvest and of Prices—Stock-Raising—The Birth and Growth of Manufactures—The Colorado Bread—Coal and Iron—Professor Agassiz among the Mountains, looking after his Glaciers—End of the Vacation—Summing Up of its Experiences—Colorado the Switzerland of America—How to Travel There.

DENVER, COLORADO, SEPTEMBER, 1868

INEXHAUSTIBLE as is Colorado's mineral wealth; progressive as henceforth its development; predominant and extensive as are its mountains; high even as are its valleys and plains,—in spite of all seeming impossibilities and rivalries, Agriculture is already and is destined always to be its dominant interest. Hence my faith in its prosperity and its influence among the central states of the Continent. For agriculture is the basis of wealth, of power, of morality; it is the conservative element of all national and political and social growth; it steadies, preserves, purifies, elevates. Full one-third of the territorial extent of Colorado,—though this third average as high as Mount Washington,[1]—is fit, more, rich for agricultural purposes. The grains, the vegetables and the fruits of the temperate zone grow and ripen in profusion; and through the most of it, cattle and sheep can live and fatten the year around without housing or feeding. The immediate valleys or bottom lands of the Arkansas and Platte and Rio Grande and their numerous tributaries, after they debouch from the mountains, are of rich vegetable loams, and need no irrigation. The uplands or plains are of a course, sandy loam, rich in the phosphates washed from the minerals of the mountains, and are not much in use yet except for pastures. When cultivated, more or less irrigation is introduced, and probably will always be indispensable for sure crops of roots and vegetables; but for the small, hard grains, I have no idea it will be generally found necessary. It is a comparatively dry climate, indeed; but showers are frequent, and extend over a considerable part of the spring and summer.

At a rough estimate, the agricultural wealth of Colorado last year was a million bushels of corn, half a million of wheat, half a million of barley, oats and vegetables, 50,000 head of cattle, and 75,000 to 100,000 sheep. The increase this year is at least 50 per cent; in the northern counties at least 100. Indeed, the agriculture of the northern counties, between the Pacific Railroad at Cheyenne and Denver, which has grown to be full half that of the whole state, is the development almost entirely of the last three years. South, in the Arkansas and Rio Grande valleys, the farming and the population are older, going back to before the gold discoveries. This is the Spanish-Mexican section, and was formerly a part of New Mexico. Its agriculture is on a large but rough scale, and only the immense crops and the simple habits of the people, chiefly ignorant, degraded Mexicans, permit it to be profitable. The soil yields wonderfully, north and south. There is authentic evidence of 316 bushels of corn to the acre in the neighborhood of Denver this season; 60 to 75 bushels of wheat to the acre are very frequently reported; also 250 bushels of potatoes; and 60 to 70 of both oats and barley. These are exceptional yields, of course, and yet not of single acres, but of whole fields, and on several farms in different counties. Probably 30 bushels is the average product of wheat; of corn no more, for the hot nights that corn loves are never felt here; of oats say 50, and of barley 40, for the whole state. Exhaustion of the virgin freshness of the soil will tend to decrease these averages in the future; but against that we may safely put improved cultivation and greater care in harvesting.

The melons and vegetables are superb; quality, quantity and size are alike unsurpassed by any garden cultivators in the East. The irrigated gardens of the upper parts of Denver fairly riot in growth of fat vegetables; while the bottom lands of the neighboring valleys are at least equally productive without irrigation. Think of cabbages weighing from 50 to 60 pounds each! And potatoes from 5 to 6 pounds, onions 1 to 2 pounds, and beets 6 to 10! Yet here they grow, and as excellent as big.

Let me borrow, in further illustration of the farming development of this country, some statistics of this year's cultivation in a few of the leading river valleys north and south. They are from Mr. Thomas's personal collections for the Denver News: The Cache-a-la-Poudre is the most northern side valley of Colorado, and markets at Cheyenne; it has at least 200,000 acres of tillable lands, and probably not 5,000 are in use yet; but among its chief products this year are 25,000 bushels of oats, 5,000 wheat, 5,000 potatoes, 2,500 corn, 2,500 tons of hay, and 15,000 to 20,000 pounds of butter. The oat crop averaged 48 1–2 bushels per acre; and the cows have generally paid for themselves in butter this season. The

Big Thompson, another of the northern valleys, has about 2,000 acres under cultivation, and yields this year 33,000 bushels potatoes, with an average of 165 bushels per acre cultivated; 27,000 bushels oats, 8,000 bushels wheat, 3,300 bushels corn, 1,400 tons hay, and 7,500 pounds of cheese from a single dairy. One farmer has 700 to 800 head of cattle, and 100 to 200 horses and colts. In the Platte valley, for sixty miles north of Denver, or to the mouth of Cache-a-la-Poudre, there were raised this year 15,000 bushels wheat, 27,000 bushels oats, 5,000 bushels barley, 3,000 bushels corn, 7,000 bushels potatoes, and 1,500 tons of hay, and about 23,000 pounds of butter made. In the valley of the Platte, south of Denver, twenty miles long, there are 3,000 acres under cultivation, nearly half in wheat, and a quarter in oats, with crops of barley at 66 bushels to the acre, of wheat 70, and of oats 65, and the average being 30 to 35 of wheat, 35 to 40 of oats and barley. Bear Creek, just south of Denver, has 1,225 acres cultivated, divided about as those of the Platte are. In the main valley of the Arkansas are nearly 6,000 acres of cultivated land, half corn, and a third wheat;[2] in Fontaine qui Bouille,[3] a branch of the Arkansas also 6,000, with almost exactly the same division among crops. The St. Charles, another tributary, cultivates 1,500 acres, half corn, a third wheat, the rest oats. In the Huerfana valley, still another tributary of the Arkansas, are 5,000 acres under tillage, with the usual southern division, corn largely dominating, and here are some of the largest farms in the state, ranging up to 1,500 acres in cultivation, and so requiring but few farmers to make up the total. In this valley, the corn crop averages from 30 to 50 bushels the acre, wheat 20 to 40, and oats 40 to 45. These are but specimens of twice as many valleys above and below

Denver, in which farming has been begun, but only begun, yet with such profitable results as insure rapid development.

I now quote the prices of agricultural produce this week at Denver; they will be likely to recede as the crops come into market: Barley 3c. a pound, corn 3 1-2 to 4 1-2 c., cheese 20 to 22c., corn meal 5c., eggs 50 to 60c. a dozen, flour $7 to 9 a sack of 100 pounds, oats 3c. a pound, potatoes 2 to 3c. a pound, fresh tomatoes 3c. a pound, wheat 3 3–4c. a pound, cabbages 1c. a pound, butter 45c. a pound retail, chickens $5.50 a dozen, good beef 12 to 15c. a pound. At Cheyenne, on the Pacific Railroad, prices are somewhat higher,—like these, for instance, for vegetables: Cabbages 6 to 8c. a pound, onions 6 to 8c. a pound, turnips 2 to 4c. a pound, beets 5 to 7c. a pound, tomatoes 20 to 25c. a pound, squashes 4 to 7c. a pound, cucumbers 40 to 50c. a dozen. Beef is, on the whole, the cheapest grown and the cheapest selling food here. It costs about half the New York and Boston retail prices.

Stock-raising on the Plains is simple and profitable business. The animals can roam at will, and a single man can tend hundreds. The only enemies are the Indians and the diseases that the Texas cattle bring up from the South.[4] But the former are the great evil; the confusion, danger and loss they have created this season sum up a serious blow not only to stock-raising, but to all farming. Even if the evil is suppressed hereafter, this season's raids are a year's loss to the agricultural interests of Colorado. Many farmers have given up in despair from danger and disaster, and retired from the field; others hesitate and refuse to come, who otherwise would be here at once and in force of capital and energy, to enter upon the business.

These great interests of mining and farming shade naturally into others, and already there are the beginnings of various manufacturing developments, as there are the materials and incentives for such undertakings without stint. Some fifteen or twenty flouring-mills are in operation throughout the state. The Colorado wheat makes a rich hearty flour, bearing a creamy golden tinge; and I have eaten no where else in America better bread than is made from it. There is a baker in Georgetown, whose products are as rich and light as the best of German wheat bread. The wheat will rank with the very best that America produces, and is more like the California grain than that of "the States." Coal mines are abundant, and several are being profitably worked along the lower range of the mountains; as, indeed, they have been found and opened at intervals along the line of the Pacific Railroad over the mountains, and are already supplying its engines with a most excellent fuel,—a hard, dry, brown coal, very pure and free-burning; in Boulder valley and Golden City, iron is being manufactured from native ore; at Golden City,[5] there is a successful manufactory of pottery ware and fire brick; also a paper-mill and a tannery, and three flouring-mills; the state already supplies its own salt; soda deposits are abundant everywhere, and will be a great source of wealth; woolen mills are projected and greatly needed, as wool-growing is the simplest of agricultural pursuits here; a valuable tin mine has been lately discovered and its value proved, up in the mountains; and next year the Railroad will be one of Colorado's possessions, and bring harmony and unity and healthy development to all her growth, social, material, and political. Also, by that time she will be a state, and so responsible for her own government, be it good or bad.

As we go out, Professor Agassiz[6] leads a new party

of eastern notables[7] from over the Plains and into the Mountains. He is already seething with enthusiasm; all Brazil was nothing, he says, to what he has seen of natural beauty and scientific revelation in crossing the Plains; but the half is not told him. When he comes face to face with the mountains,—the mountains in perfection and the mountains in ruin,—and their phenomena of parks and wealth of verdure, then indeed he may feel he is among the "Gardens of the Gods." The professor finds abundant materials to sustain his wide-spread glacial theories; all these vast elevated plains, from Missouri River to Mountains, from Montana to Mexico,—the very heart of the Continent,—are but in his eye the deposit of great fields of ice, stretching down from these hills and washing down their hights. What must they have been once to have lost so much and remain so Titanesque!—to be still the Mother Mountains of the Continent?

Here rests the record of our Summer Vacation in the Rocky Mountains. The stage ride back to Cheyenne,—now hardened to long journeys and open air life,—was a long eighteen hours' pleasure under warm sun and cool stars; and we tumbled into the tender berths of Pullman's palace car, waiting on the railroad track, at three o'clock in the morning, with a keen gratitude to Colorado and all its kind friends for what rare joy of new experience and rich hospitality they had given us, and as keen a welcome to steam locomotion, beds, and the near home. Two days of the Pacific and the North-western Railroads brought us to Chicago, and there we separated, as we gathered, about the hospitable tables of Governor Bross.

Life was fresher to all of us, new to some, for the health and the sentiment of the thin pure air of the Mountains and the Parks. Their skies and their waters repeat the fabled fountain of perpetual youth. It is to them that America will go, as Europe to Switzerland, for rest and recreation, for new and exhilarating scenes, for pure and bracing air, for pleasure and for health. They offer no wonderful valley like the Yo Semite; no continental river breaking through continental mountains like the Columbia; no cataract like Niagara; no forests like those of the Sierra Nevada range, no nor the equals, in diversified form and color and species, of those of New England or of Pennsylvania; and yet I am greatly mistaken if the verdict of more familiar acquaintance by the American people with America is not, that here,—among these central ranges of continental mountains and these great companion parks, within this wedded circle of majestic hill and majestic plain, under these skies of purity, and in this atmosphere of elixir, lies the pleasure-ground and health-home of the nation.

Smoother ways will soon be provided, but no philosophic or accustomed traveler need wait for them. The true aroma of the country is to be found in the saddle and in the camp. It is not necessary to travel with such numbers and with such protection of authority as was our fortune. A smaller party, more independent of time and circumstances, is on many accounts even more desirable. If of men purely, four to eight is a fit number for an expedition; if the two sexes are combined, about double these limits will be found desirable. We met in the Middle Park a young man from Yale college, who was making a thorough journey of two months through the Mountains and Parks without any companions but such as he picked up from day to day or week to week. He had bought a pony and blankets and coffee-pot in Denver, and for the rest bargained for his daily rations en route, stopping for the night at ranches and hotels where he found them, and in cabins or tents, if the doors were open and there was room, and under a hospitable tree when all else was denied him.

August is the best month to come, for that is nearest summer in the high mountains; the streams are lower, purer and more readily forded; the weather most uniformly clear. But any time from June 15 to September 15 will answer for visiting either or both the great Parks; and I beg every "Across the Continent" traveler to give at least a week and if possible a month to the interior regions of Colorado. But do not come unless you will visit one of the Parks at least, go over one or two of the high passes, and ascend either Gray's Peak or Mount Lincoln. Else you will discredit my enthusiasm, and deny yourself when you talk of having seen Colorado.

NOTES

Editor's Introduction

1. Samuel Bowles, *Our New West: Records of Travel between the Mississippi River and the Pacific Ocean* (Hartford, Conn.: Hartford Publishing, 1869), p. 68.

2. Ibid., p. 39.

3. Albert D. Richardson, *Across the Mississippi: From the Great River to the Great Ocean* (Hartford, Conn.: American Publishing, 1867), p. 442.

4. Willard H. Smith, *Schuyler Colfax: The Changing Fortunes of a Political Idol* (Indianapolis: Indiana Historical Bureau, 1952), p. 293.

5. Quoted in Smith, *Schuyler Colfax*, p. 293.

6. According to Bross, "As Chairman of the Post-Office Committee of the House of Representatives, he [Colfax] had brought in the 'Overland Daily Mail' and 'Pacific Telegraph' bills. He had also used all his influence to pass the Pacific Railroad bill, and he wanted to see what further legislation was necessary to develop the Pacific States of the Republic" (*Address of the Hon. William Bross, Lieutenant-Governor of Illinois, on the Resources of the Far West, and the Pacific Railway* [New York: J. W. Amerman, 1866], p. 4). Bross's address, reprinted in this thirty-page pamphlet, had been originally given before the New York Chamber of Commerce on January 25, 1866. Arrangements for the 1865 trip were made by Ben Holladay, owner of the Overland Mail and Express Company, who sent his agent George K. Otis to accompany the party. According to Willard H. Smith, "Part of the stimulus came from Ben Holladay and other proprietors of the overland mail route who wished to recognize Colfax's part in the improvement of the western mail service" (Smith, *Schuyler Colfax*, p. 210).

7. After coming together in Atchison, the party departed by stagecoach on May 22 for the five-day trip to Denver. There Colfax visited his sister and brother-in-law, Clara and Daniel Witter, repeated at

Governor Evans's request his much-celebrated eulogy of Abraham Lincoln, and spent a week visiting the mining camps along Clear Creek, speaking on demand along the route. The next stopping place was Salt Lake City, seven days out from Denver, though they were forced "to lie over two nights, and once twenty-four hours, on account of Indians" (Ovando J. Hollister, *Life of Schuyler Colfax* [New York: Funk & Wagnalls, 1886], p. 258). By June 26 they were in Virginia City, Nevada, and by July 1 arrived in San Francisco. The final sixty-mile leg of their journey was over the new Pacific railroad. The trip north to Vancouver consumed the month of July. By August 2 the party was back in California, where they spent a month touring, before departing for home by steamship on September 2, 1865. See also Richardson, *Across the Mississippi,* pp. 327–436, and Smith, *Schuyler Colfax,* pp. 210–17.

8. Samuel Bowles, *Across the Continent: A Summer's Journey to the Rocky Mountains, the Mormons, and the Pacific States, with Speaker Colfax* (Springfield, Mass.: Samuel Bowles & Company, 1865), pp. iii–iv.

9. Ibid., pp. v–vi.

10. Ibid., pp. 272–73.

11. By 1860 the combined circulation of both the daily and weekly editions reached 18,000 copies, 2,000 of which went outside New England. Personal sacrifice and hard work (Bowles on one occasion reportedly worked forty-two hours without rest) also contributed to Bowles's success, as did his good fortune in being in Springfield at the right time. Thanks to the presence in the city of the United States Arsenal, the Civil War proved to be a boon. Manufacturing of the famous Springfield rifle increased from 800 per month in 1861 to 26,000 a month in 1864, while the arsenal's work force grew from something like 200 to 3,000. By 1865, Springfield's total population had increased by more than half, to 22,000. Meanwhile, the circulation of the *Daily Republican* doubled (Richard Hooker, *The Story of an Independent Newspaper: One Hundred Years of the Springfield Republican* [New York: Macmillan, 1924], p. 88).

12. Bowles to H. L. Dawes, February 26, 1861 (George S. Merriam, *The Life and Times of Samuel Bowles,* 2 vols. [New York: Century, 1885], 1:318). George Merriam (1843–1914), a native of Springfield and an author in his own right, was a friend and part-time employee of Samuel Bowles. His two-volume "life and times" biography of Bowles is clearly hagiographic, but it nonetheless remains an indispensable source for biographical information and Bowles's

surviving correspondence. A helpful, if not definitive, analysis of Bowles's journalistic and political career is Stephen G. Weisner's more recent study, *Embattled Editor: The Life of Samuel Bowles* (Lanham, Md.: University Press of America, 1986). Hooker's study, noted above, traces the history of the *Springfield Republican* from 1824 to 1915 under three generations of men named Samuel Bowles. Hooker was the son of Bowles's eldest daughter, Sallie. For a brief study of Bowles's political views, see Richard A. Gerber, "Liberal Republicanism, Reconstruction, and Social Order: Samuel Bowles as a Test Case," *New England Quarterly* 45 (September 1972): 393–407.

13. Richardson, *Across the Mississippi,* p. 442.

14. Hooker, *Story of an Independent Newspaper,* p. 132.

15. Bowles suffered three breakdowns (the first at the age of nineteen, the year after he took over the *Republican*). As Weisner notes, "Dyspepsia, bowel difficulties, sciatica, severe headaches (probably migraine), frequent lung problems, and other ailments dogged him throughout his life" (*Embattled Editor,* p. 142).

16. Hooker, *Story of an Independent Newspaper,* p. 133.

17. Richardson, *Across the Mississippi,* pp. 404, 380.

18. Bowles, *Across the Continent,* p. 45.

19. Bowles to John Pierce, September 8, 1867 (Merriam, *Samuel Bowles* 2:55).

20. Bowles, *Across the Continent,* pp. 45–46.

21. In writing to New York lawyer David Dudley Field in 1871, Bowles made his responsibilities as a journalist clear: "The gathering and publication of facts is but one part of its vocation. To express opinions is a higher and larger share of its duties. The conduct of public men, before the public, is the legitimate subject of its discussion" (quoted in Merriam, *Samuel Bowles* 2:99).

22. Ibid., pp. 46, 47.

23. Lloyd Wendt, *Chicago Tribune: The Rise of a Great American Newspaper* (Chicago: Rand McNally, 1979), p. 87.

24. Bowles, *Across the Continent,* p. 46.

25. Hollister, *Life of Schuyler Colfax*, p. 326.

26. Colfax to W. E. Chandler, August 10, 1868 (Smith, *Schuyler Colfax,* pp. 294–95). Just how well Colfax and Bross adhered to this plan may be judged from an account of the speeches they delivered to the residents of Breckenridge on the evening of August 24, as subsequently reported in the *Rocky Mountain News*. Colfax went first and delivered a half-hour address that "was frequently interrupted by the most enthusiastic applause." "Avoiding entirely the political issues

of the campaign," the report continued, "he spoke in glowing language of the resources, progress, and prospects of our Territory, and of the warm interest which he had always taken in our growth and prosperity. He declared in the strongest terms his continued devotion to the principles and cause with which he has ever been identified, and concluded his short address by expressing his warmest wishes for the future of Colorado, and for the welfare of its people."

Bross followed, and "in a manner at once humorous, logical, and eloquent, he proceeded to discuss the great political questions involved in the present contest. After a few introductory remarks, which excited laughter and drew the attention of his audience, Gov. Bross reviewed the history of the Democratic party, and charged home upon it the numerous crimes of the past ten years, challenging at every point a denial, but none was given. He discussed most thoroughly the questions of reconstruction, negro suffrage, and finance, and pointed out the duty of live men in the coming election, closing with an eloquent appeal to the young men of Colorado to array themselves on the side of the Republican party, and its national principles" (*Rocky Mountain News,* August 31, 1868, p. 4).

27. Carl Abbott, Stephen J. Leonard, and David McComb, *Colorado: A History of the Centennial State* (Boulder: Colorado Associated University Press, 1982), p. 67.

28. The *Rocky Mountain News* reported that Bowles "is in rather feeble health, though his looks don't say so" (August 8, 1868, p. 4). Part of Bowles's reason for coming to Colorado was clearly his health. Earlier that year he had written that "it seemed as if the bottom was falling out" (Merriam, *Samuel Bowles* 2:80).

29. *Rocky Mountain News,* August 10, 1868, p. 4. On Saturday, August 15, the *News* reported that the ladies from the Speaker's party had returned the previous evening. "They camped out every night but one while gone, one time in a smart rain. Yesterday morning they took saddle horses from Black Hawk, and rode to the top of Bald Mountain, head of Nevada gulch, which affords as fine a view as any place we know of" (p. 4).

30. Frank Hall, *History of the State of Colorado,* 4 vols. (Chicago: Blakely Printing, 1889), 1:442.

31. For an account of mining in Colorado during this period, see James E. Fell, Jr., *Ores to Metals: The Rocky Mountain Smelting Industry* (Lincoln: University of Nebraska Press, 1979); Stanley Dempsey and James E. Fell, Jr., *Mining the Summit: Colorado's Ten Mile District, 1869–1960* (Norman: University of Oklahoma Press,

1986); Louise C. Harrison, *Empire and the Berthoud Pass* (Denver: Big Mountain Press, 1964); Virginia McConnell, *Bayou Salado: The Story of South Park* (Denver, Sage Books, 1966); and William S. Greever, *The Bonanza West: The Story of the Western Mining Rushes, 1848–1900* (Norman: University of Oklahoma Press, 1963), pp. 157–82.

32. See pp. 65 and 165 above.

33. Abbott, Leonard, and McComb, *Colorado,* p. 71.

34. Much of this highly colored journalism reflected existing bias and hostility toward the Indian, combined with propaganda aimed at influencing the government to send more soldiers into the West, enriching local merchants in the process. See Elmo Scott Watson, "The Indian Wars and the Press, 1866–1867," *Journalism Quarterly* 17 (December 1940): 301–12.

35. The best existing study of Alexander Hunt and his role as governor in attempting to deal with Colorado's Indian problems is Jess Augustin Castro, "Alexander Cameron Hunt: Colorado Territorial Governor, 1867–1869" (master's thesis, University of Denver, 1957).

36. See Robert G. Athearn, "Colorado and the Indian War of 1868," *Colorado Magazine* 33 (January 1956): 42–51; Wallace B. Turner, "Frank Hall: Colorado Journalist, Public Servant, and Historian," *Colorado Magazine* 53 (Fall 1976): 328–51; Hall, *History of the State of Colorado* 1:453–62. For Colorado's Indian wars in their larger context, see Robert M. Utley, *The Indian Frontier of the American West, 1846–1890* (Albuquerque: University of New Mexico Press, 1984).

37. Wallace Stegner, *Beyond the Hundredth Meridian: John Wesley Powell and the Second Opening of the West* (Boston: Houghton Mifflin, 1954), p. 26.

38. Byers's movements of July and August toward his rendezvous with the Powell party at the camp at the top of Berthoud Pass, his trip into Middle Park, and the expedition to Longs Peak by way of Grand Lake and Wild Basin can be traced in his unpublished diary of 1868, located in the Western History Department of the Denver Public Library, as well as in the series of articles he wrote for the *Rocky Mountain News*.

39. Byers eventually gained title to 160 acres on both sides of the Grand River (now the Colorado), where he laid out and promoted the town of Hot Sulphur Springs. Though he spent considerable time and money pursuing this dream, the scheme was never a major success, in part because Middle Park remained inaccessible by railroad until

after Byers's death. Hot Sulphur Springs is now the county seat of Grand County.

40. See *Rocky Mountain News*, September 1, 1868, p. 1. Four years earlier, in August 1864, Byers had made an unsuccessful attempt to reach the summit. Bowles errs in discussing his meeting with Powell and Byers in Middle Park, where he characterizes them as having "just accomplished the ascent of Long's Peak" (p. 106 above). In reality, both parties left Middle Park on August 17.

41. P. 144 above.

42. P. 153 above.

43. Bowles to Mary Bowles, September 6, 1868 (Merriam, *Samuel Bowles* 2:57–58).

44. Merriam, p. 81. In 1869, Bowles combined this book with his earlier travel narrative of 1865, publishing the result as *Our New West: Records of Travel between the Mississippi River and the Pacific Ocean,* which he dedicated to Colfax. *Switzerland of America* reportedly sold eight thousand copies; *Our New West,* twenty-three thousand.

45. Pp. 138 and 140 above.

46. Albert D. Richardson, who had visited the Clear Creek diggings in 1859, noted on his return visit with Bowles and Colfax in 1865 that "thousands of acres, which at my first visit had been covered with stately pines, were now utterly bare. The wood had been consumed for fuel in Denver, and by the mountain quartz mills." In other areas he noted "vast fire-swept expanses" where "blackened armless trunks of trees stand weird and ghastly" (*Across the Mississippi,* p. 334). Like most of his generation, Bowles did not sense the ultimate incompatibility between exploiting and despoiling the environment in the name of economic progress, on the one hand, while simultaneously extolling its natural beauty as the equal of Switzerland's on the other.

47. Pp. 146–47 and 148 above.

48. Bowles has somewhat less to say than the surviving accounts of his contemporaries about the subsequent encounter with the Utes in South Park and the colorful events that transpired around the campfire that evening, including the attempt by Chief Washington to trade four horses and a squaw for the raven-haired Sue Matthews. These accounts include those written by Sue Matthews (later Mrs. Frank Hall), Clara Witter, and Isa Hunt (Governor Hunt's eldest daughter, later Isa Hunt Stearns): Mrs. Frank Hall, "Seventy Years Ago—Recollections of a Trip Through the Colorado Mountains with the Colfax Party in 1868," ed. LeRoy R. Hafen, *Colorado Magazine* 15 (September 1938): 161–68; Mrs. Daniel Witter, "Pioneer Life," *Colorado Magazine* 4 (Decem-

ber 1927): 165–74; and Isa Stearns Gregg, "Reminiscences of Isa Hunt Stearns," *Colorado Magazine* 26 (July 1949): 183–93.

49. P. 165 above.

50. Robert G. Athearn, *The Coloradans* (Albuquerque: University of New Mexico Press, 1976), p. 108.

51. Pp. 112, 117, and 140 above.

52. Schuyler Colfax married Ellen Wade on November 16, 1868, at the home of her mother in Andover, Ohio, with the bride described by the *Indianapolis Journal* as being "of medium size, good figure, dark hair, brown eyes, . . . a pleasing face, indicating goodness and intelligence" (quoted in Smith, *Schuyler Colfax,* p. 312). The wedding ring was reportedly made of gold dust that had been presented to Speaker Colfax in the mountains by a miner the previous summer (Hollister, *Life of Schuyler Colfax*, p. 327). Interestingly enough, the newlyweds spent their first Christmas with Samuel and Mary Bowles in Springfield.

Stories about Colfax's courtship of Nellie Wade were long remembered by various members of the party. Isa Hunt (1856–96), the oldest child of Governor Alexander Hunt, wrote shortly before her death that "the engagement of [Colfax and Wade] occurred one night [in South Park] when we had camped early and father had sent Mr. Colfax to the river after water. Miss Wade accompanying him, they were gone a long time. On his announcing their engagement to my mother later I was present and child-like I quickly added, 'I know when it was. It was when you went to get the water.' He laughingly added I was right" (Gregg, "Reminiscences," p. 189). She also remembered Bowles as "a jovial, delightful man and a child's friend in every sense of the word."

The other two marriages involved Sue Matthews and Frank Hall, and Carrie Matthews and Ovando Hollister. Sue Matthews (b. 1852) met Frank Hall (1836–1917), then territorial secretary and a man sixteen years her senior, at the Witter home during their visit. "When I came down the stairs, there was Mr. Hall," Sue Matthews later recalled. "It was the first time I ever met him. I thought he was terribly old. But I changed my mind later." They were married in Buchanan, Michigan, on October 4, 1871 (Hall, "Seventy Years Ago," p. 164).

Ovando Hollister (1834–92) was an associate editor of William Byers's *Rocky Mountain News* and in that capacity accompanied the Colfax party into South Park on its first day out. It is not clear how or when he first came to know Carrie Matthews, but "on that day he and Miss Matthews became engaged" (Hollister, *Life of Schuyler Colfax,*

p. 327n). They were married a few months later. Somewhat earlier, in 1863, Hall and Hollister had been partners in editing the *Black Hawk Mining Journal*. Hall sold out his interest in 1865. Hollister eventually left Colorado for Utah. Later, in 1886, he wrote the first biography of the man who had become his brother-in-law, Schuyler Colfax.

William Todd (1846–1919), Speaker Colfax's secretary and yet another member of the party of 1868, also returned to Colorado, where he was elected to the state legislature and became one of the founding members of Denver's Union Trust and Deposit Company.

53. Bowles to Sallie Bowles, July 27, 1869 (Merriam, *Samuel Bowles* 2:145). Samuel and Mary Bowles (1827–93) would return to Colorado yet once more in the autumn of 1871, when they visited their old friends General and Mrs. John Pierce. In the spring of 1873, Bowles and his wife also made a six-week tour of California.

54. See James F. Willard and Colin B. Goodykoontz, eds., *Experiments in Colorado Colonization, 1869–1872: Selected Documents Relating to the German Colonization Company and Chicago-Colorado, St. Louis-Western, and Southwestern Colonies* (Boulder: University of Colorado, 1926), pp. xxiv–xxx, 135–330. Bross was elected treasurer at the November 22, 1870, organizational meeting, which took place in Chicago. "On taking the chair, Mr. Bross . . . said that he was one among the first who believed in the mineral and agricultural wealth of that territory. The mineral resources were especially rich—the richest of any in the world. On the other hand, the barns of Colorado contained some of the finest wheat that ever was grown. The climate was particularly healthful. The speaker had slept out of doors in that territory night after night, and he fancied that he had not fallen into a decline" (*Chicago Times*, November 23, 1870, quoted in ibid., p. 233). The agent for the Chicago-Colorado Colony was none other than the other inveterate booster of Colorado, William Newton Byers.

55. Colfax to Samuel Bowles, March 10, 1874 (Smith, *Schuyler Colfax*, p. 433).

56. P. 35–36 above.

AUTHOR'S PREFACE

1. Bowles's book is composed of eleven letters originally written for the *Springfield Republican*. The letters were published between August and December 1868 as follows: August 19; September 17; October 5, 12, 21, 28; November 11, 18, 25; December 7, 16. Chapter

1 of Bowles's book was essentially new, but except for a few editorial additions, the content of book and letters is substantially the same. A comparison does suggest that Bowles took the responsibilities of authorship seriously, for he rearranged portions of his material to strengthen its flow as narrative, improved transitions, and made alterations in individual words and phases in the interest of style.

2. Bowles published his 1865 observations in book form as *Across the Continent*.

3. The allusion is to Bayard Taylor's *Colorado: A Summer Trip* (New York: G. P. Putnam and Son, 1867). Taylor (1825–78) was a well-known nineteenth-century poet, novelist, journalist, diplomat, and inveterate traveler who published books recounting his experiences in England, France, Germany, Austria, Switzerland, Egypt, Syria, Palestine, Norway, Lapland, Africa, India, China, and Asia Minor, as well as in California and Colorado.

4. The word "park," in the parlance of the mountains, means valley.

5. Bowles had taken a six-month European trip in 1862, two months of which he spent in Switzerland.

6. The Union Pacific Railroad, which would meet the Central Pacific at Promontory, Utah, on May 10, 1869, to complete the first transcontinental railroad, was built through southern Wyoming, some one hundred miles north of Denver, bypassing Colorado completely.

1. THE PACIFIC RAILROAD

1. Bowles's allusion is to the Continental Divide (or "Great Divide"), the ridge of Rocky Mountain summits stretching from Canada to New Mexico, separating streams flowing into the Atlantic from those flowing into the Pacific.

2. The Pacific Railroad Act of July 1, 1862, authorized the Union Pacific Railroad to build a line from Nebraska to Utah, where it was to connect with the Central Pacific Railroad, chartered in 1858. By the end of 1865, however, the Union Pacific's tracks extended only 40 miles beyond Omaha. Then, thanks to competition from the Central Pacific, the pace of construction began to accelerate rapidly. Some 260 miles were built in 1866, 240 in 1867, and nearly 500 in 1868.

3. As noted above, the Pacific railroad was completed on May 10, 1869.

4. "Our little party of four" consisted of Bowles, Vice President Schuyler Colfax (1823–85), William Bross (1813–90) of the *Chicago Tribune*, then serving as lieutenant governor of Illinois, and Albert D.

Richardson (1833–69), the star correspondent for Horace Greeley's *New-York Tribune*. Bowles describes all four in some detail in *Across the Continent,* pp. 44–49. They were accompanied by George K. Otis, a special agent for Ben Holladay's Overland Mail and Express Company, which hosted the trip.

5. They were actually a party of ten: Bowles and his eldest daughter Sallie; Bross; Colfax; Colfax's mother, stepfather, and half sister (Carrie Matthews); her cousin Sue Matthews; Ellen Wade; and Colfax's secretary, William Todd.

6. Colfax was then serving as chairman of the House Committee on Post Offices and Post Roads, so that his trip constituted an official trip of inspection.

7. As noted in the Introduction, William Bross, like Schuyler Colfax, enjoyed a considerable reputation as a public speaker.

8. Albert D. Richardson. As a correspondent for the *Boston Journal,* Richardson had visited Denver and the Gregory diggings at Central City in 1859 in the company of Horace Greeley and Henry Villard of the *Cincinnati Commercial Inquirer* and subsequently confirmed the discovery of gold in Colorado. He later became a Civil War hero when he escaped from a Confederate prison after some twenty months in captivity.

9. George W. Pullman (1831–97), was the industrialist inventor who in 1863 built "Pioneer," the first specially constructed railroad sleeping car. Four years later, in 1867, he organized the Pullman Palace Car Company.

10. Delmonico's, a fashionable New York restaurant located at the corner of Fifth Avenue and Fourteenth Street. As New Yorker Abraham C. Dayton wrote, "To lunch, dine, or sup at Delmonico's is the crowning ambition of those who aspire to notoriety, and no better place for study of character does the city afford than that expensive resort at almost any hour of the day" (*Last Days of Knickerbocker Life in New York* [New York: G. P. Putnam's Sons, 1897], p. 140).

11. As a base camp, Omaha, Nebraska, became the first western town to feel the benefits of the Union Pacific Railroad. As early as the fall of 1865, materials for the railroad began to pile up, and during the months that followed shop buildings were constructed capable of building railroad cars.

12. The lack of a railroad bridge over the Missouri at Council Bluffs was a source of consternation and remained so until the end of 1870, for it meant that western travelers had to disembark, be ferried across the river, and reboard another train. At one time during the spring of

1870, it was reported, some eight hundred passengers were forced to wait on the Iowa side for transportation across the river. The delay, caused by a political dispute between Omaha and Council Bluffs over which city should be the eastern terminus of the Union Pacific, was resolved by late 1870 with the erection of a temporary bridge. Two years later a permanent bridge was constructed at the cost of nearly three million dollars.

13. Ever since 1810, when Zebulon Pike published the journal of his expedition to the Rio Grande, American advocates of western expansion had been consistently warned about the existence of the "great American Desert," an uninhabitable desert area east of the Rocky Mountains that limited the advance of the agricultural frontier.

14. Bowles's train carried no dining car, making it necessary to stop at such places for meals, one of which, Sue Matthews recalled, was North Platte (Hall, "Seventy Years Ago," p. 162).

15. Fort Kearney, the military outpost on the south shore of the Platte River near the western end of Grand Island, was established by the U.S. Army in 1848 to protect emigrants bound for Oregon and to keep peace between the Sioux and Pawnee.

16. Julesburg, in the extreme northeast corner of Colorado, was named for Jules Beni, who established a trading post at the "upper crossing" of the Platte prior to 1860 at the junction of the Oregon and Overland trails. In 1859 it became an Overland Stage station. Six years later, in January and early February of 1865, Julesburg was attacked twice and burned by large parties of Arapahos, Cheyennes, and Sioux in reprisal for the infamous Sand Creek massacre of November 1864 (see note 16 in chapter 5 below).

17. On July 3, 1866, Congress had authorized the Union Pacific's Eastern Division (which later became the Kansas Pacific Railroad) to build along the Smoky Hill branch of the Republican River and connect with a branch line from the Union Pacific run south to Denver. The first passenger train arrived in Denver from Kansas City on August 15, 1870.

18. Hastened by the construction of the Union Pacific, Wyoming became a territory on July 25, 1868. By that date track had been laid as far as the present-day town of Rawlins in central Wyoming.

19. The Union Pacific crossed the Black Hills (Laramie Mountains) of Wyoming, a high, rugged spur of the Rockies, at Sherman's Pass, some thirty-five miles west of Cheyenne. It was named in 1866 by its discoverer, Major General Grenville M. Dodge (1831–1916), chief engineer for the Union Pacific, in honor of Civil War hero William

Tecumseh Sherman (1820–91), who from 1866 to 1869 commanded the Division of Missouri, which included the Great Plains. It was Sherman's assignment to protect the route of travel for emigrants moving west as well as the railroads then under construction. Dodge had served with Sherman on the famous march on Atlanta. Though the pass at times also carried the name of James A. Evans, the Union Pacific's division engineer, ultimately Sherman's name carried the day. Though at the time Sherman Pass was the highest point reached by any railroad in the country, within a decade it yielded that honor to railroads in Colorado. In 1903–4 the Union Pacific was rerouted several miles to the south at a slightly lower elevation of 8,013 feet.

20. Fort Laramie, located at the junction of the Laramie and North Platte rivers, protected travelers moving west to Oregon, California, or Utah. Founded as a fur trading post and supply depot in 1834, Fort Laramie served as an army post from 1849 to 1890. It has now been reconstructed as a living museum by the National Park Service.

21. Pelion and Ossa are mountains in ancient Thessaly, where, according to Greek mythology, giants made war upon the gods.

22. Bitter Creek rises in the Rocky Mountains in the southeastern part of what is now Wyoming's Sweetwater County and flows about eighty miles north and west past the town of Rock Springs into the Green River.

23. According to Chief Engineer Dodge, the Union Pacific Railroad generally employed between eight and ten thousand laborers (Grenville H. Dodge, *How We Built the Union Pacific, and Other Railway Papers and Addresses* [New York? 1910?], p. 16).

24. Benton, some 695 miles west of Omaha, where the last crossing of the North Platte was made, was one of a number of short-lived Wyoming border towns called into being by the railroad as a supply base. The irony, as T. A. Larson has noted, is that "three of the larger communities—Benton, Bryan, and Bear River City—survived only a short time, while smaller communities—Rawlins, Rock Springs, and Evanston—put down strong roots" (*History of Wyoming* [Lincoln: University of Nebraska Press, 1965], pp. 41–42). By mid-August 1868 the Union Pacific was open from Omaha to Benton, with daily passenger trains running between Benton and Cheyenne.

25. The Green River flows south from near Fremont Peak in the Wind River Range, through western Wyoming and eastern Utah to the Colorado River south of Moab, a distance of 730 miles.

26. Church Buttes are a series of eroded sandstone cliffs that rise in the form of a cathedral some seventy-five feet above the surrounding

hills. They are located in the southwestern corner of Wyoming, some forty-five miles southwest of Rock Springs. Bowles had passed the Church Buttes on his way to California in 1865 and pronounced them "the most marvelous counterfeit of a half-ruined, gigantic, old-world Gothic cathedral, that can be imagined" (Bowles, *Across the Continent,* p. 76).

27. Fort Bridger, located on the Black Fork of the Green River, southwest of Church Buttes, was a frontier trading post and later a U.S. Army fort. It was named after trapper-scout Jim Bridger (1804–81), who, together with his partner, Louis Vasquez, built the fort in 1843 as a place of rendezvous for their fellow mountain men. Under the army, which took over Bridger's post in 1858, Fort Bridger became a way station for emigrants bound for Oregon, California, and Utah. It was abandoned in 1890.

28. Two deep and spectacular canyons in north central Utah. Bowles described Echo Canyon in *Across the Continent* as "a very miniature Rhine valley in all but vines and storied ruin" (p. 81).

29. The Wasatch Mountains of Idaho and Utah extend for some 250 miles from the bend of the Bear River in Idaho on the north, southward past the Great Salt Lake in Utah.

30. Brigham Young (1801–77) organized the Mormon exodus of 148 "Saints" from Missouri to the valley of the Great Salt Lake in July 1847. Thousands of other Mormons soon followed. "He is," Bowles noted in 1865, "a very hale and hearty looking man, young for sixty-four, with a light gray eye, cold and uncertain, a mouth and chin betraying a great and determined will—handsome perhaps as to presence and features but repellent in atmosphere and without magnetism" (*Across the Continent,* p. 86).

31. Bowles had devoted considerable attention in *Across the Continent* to satisfying the nation's "curious excitement" over the Mormon experiment.

32. The valley of the Humboldt River (or the Great Basin, as it is called) lies between the Wasatch Mountains on the east and the Sierra Nevadas on the west and includes the western third of Utah and most of Nevada. It was crisscrossed by emigrant trails to Oregon and California.

33. The Sierra Nevada mountain range of eastern California extends more than four hundred miles from Lassen Peak at the south end of the Cascade Range in the north to Tehachapi Pass near Bakersfield in the south. The highest point in the range is Mount Whitney (14,495 feet).

34. Though the transcontinental railroad was to be built privately, Congress provided a partial subsidy that included a grant of twenty sections of land (a total of 12,800 acres) for every mile built and thirty-year 6-percent government bonds scaled, as Bowles suggests, according to the difficulty of the terrain. The government obligated itself for half the costs; the railroad was to raise the remainder through its own bond offering. Both types of bonds were to be released for sale only after government commissioners certified that twenty-mile sections of track had been completed, except in mountain regions, where bonds could be released before construction.

35. Just how "gigantic" the speculation and the railroad's profits at government expense had been became apparent in the fall of 1872, with the revelation that prominent members of Congress had accepted bribes in the form of stock from the Crédit Mobilier of America, a construction company organized in 1864 to build the Union Pacific. As noted in the Introduction, the scandal effectively ended the career of Schuyler Colfax, then serving as Grant's vice president.

2. To Denver and There

1. Construction for the 106-mile Denver Pacific Railroad linking Denver and Cheyenne was begun on May 18, 1868, one mile north of the city as then defined, with a formal ceremony and celebration that, it was said, attracted a thousand people. It was completed on June 22, 1870. See Thomas J. Noel, "All Hail the Denver Pacific: Denver's First Railroad," *Colorado Magazine* 50 (Spring 1973): 91–116.

2. The stage stop at Laporte was located on the Cache la Poudre, about five miles northwest of present-day Fort Collins.

3. Virginia Dale, just south of the Colorado-Wyoming line on the North Fork of the Cache la Poudre River, was established in 1862 as an Overland Stage station by Joseph A. ("Jack") Slade, who named it for his wife, Virginia. Bowles, Colfax, and party were detained there by Indian raids during their trip of 1865. Bowles wrote on that occasion that "only the station of the stage line occupies the Dale; a house, a barn, a blacksmith shop; the keeper and his wife, the latter as sweet, as genteel and as lady-like as if just transplanted from eastern society, yet preparing bountiful meals for twice daily stage-loads of hungry and dirty passengers; the stock-tender and his assistant,—these were all the inhabitants of the spot, and no neighbors within fifteen miles" (*Across the Continent,* p. 58).

4. Sue Matthews (Mrs. Hall) recalled the episode in much the same

way. "Along in the night, somebody suggested that we stop and have something to eat. They didn't serve all night at the stations, but someone remarked that Mr. Colfax, being such a diplomat, could get the woman to prepare a meal. He was a widower and very popular. He approached the woman and said, 'Couldn't you get us something to eat?' At first she was pretty cross, but she finally agreed to serve us. That was on the St. Vrain" (Hall, "Seventy Years Ago," 162–63).

5. According to the tradition Bowles alludes to, the Cache la Poudre River, which flows northeast out of Poudre Lake to the east of the Continental Divide at Milner Pass (10,758 feet), was so named in 1836 by a party of French trappers from St. Louis who over the course of one winter safely deposited some of their supplies, including a quantity of black gunpowder, close by its banks. The Poudre flows north and east and enters the South Platte east of Greeley.

6. The Saint Vrain Creek rises in two branches near Mount Audubon (13,233 feet) in the Front Range and flows east and northeast for sixty-eight miles past Lyons and Longmont respectively before entering the South Platte.

7. The Big Thompson River flows out of Forest Canyon in Rocky Mountain National Park, through Estes Park, and makes its way through rugged Big Thompson Canyon to Loveland and, eventually, the South Platte.

8. The Little Thompson River, whose sources lie in a cluster of hills some six miles east of Longs Peak, gradually makes its way eastward until it joins the Big Thompson.

9. The several branches of Boulder Creek have their source in a series of lakes along the Continental Divide west of Boulder and then flow east and northeast past Boulder to the Saint Vrain River near Longmont (or Burlington, as it was then known).

10. Clear Creek rises in several branches near Grays Peak (14,270 feet) in the Front Range and flows sixty-eight miles past Idaho Springs and Golden to the South Platte, north of Denver.

11. For the last ten-mile leg of the trip into Denver, the stage company furnished six perfectly matched dapple gray horses.

12. Denver, which was first settled in the fall of 1858, was named for General James William Denver (1817–92), then governor of the territory of Kansas. Fueled by the discoveries of gold in the Clear Creek valley in 1859, Denver quickly became a base camp for those entering the mountains.

13. Professor William H. Brewer, who visited Denver in the summer of 1869, concurred with Bowles's view.

> Denver is not at all the place my fancy painted it—I had not read Bowles' book except by extracts, but kept it for the trip, and when I would have read it during the last week, it has been in the lost trunk [Brewer left the Union Pacific at Cheyenne; his trunk went west to Utah]. I had supposed a lively mining town, in the mountains, with rough miners within and rougher mountains without. Not at all so. A quiet little village of perhaps four or five thousand inhabitants, lying out on the plain some dozen or sixteen miles from the base of the great chain—rather dull just now for a mining town, or even a western town. No miners about, or at least conspicuously, and no trees about it.
>
> . . . The old mining excitement has ceased, the old Overland stage has stopped and its business rushes past on a railroad a hundred miles north. Business is dull, the town quiet, almost as an eastern village. I see scarcely a new house going up, plenty of places 'To Let'; yet it will perhaps start again and have healthy growth, although I see no reason to predict an especially brilliant future.
>
> . . . The place is better built, perhaps, than any other place between Omaha and the Salt Lake. Many of the stores are two-story and brick, and we have been stopping at a brick three-story hotel. (*Rocky Mountain Letters, 1869,* ed. Edmund B. Rogers [Denver: Colorado Mountain Club, 1930], pp. 14–15)

Brewer (1828–1910), professor of agriculture at Yale, had served as principal assistant on the Whitney survey of California between 1860 and 1865, and then as chief of the field party that explored the central high Sierra in 1864, before coming to Colorado with Whitney for two months of exploration among the Rockies during July and August 1869. Brewer, who brought with him a copy of Bowles's book, covered much the same ground as the Massachusetts editor, and his letters to his wife, published by the Colorado Mountain Club in 1930, thus provide an interesting coda on Bowles's journey of a year earlier.

14. In 1868 Henry C. Brown (1820–1906), builder of Denver's famous Brown Palace Hotel, deeded to Colorado two city blocks, consisting of ten acres of his original ranch, as the site of the future capitol building. That building was not completed and occupied, however, until 1894. In the meantime, many of Denver's wealthy built mansions on the high land near the capitol site, turning "Capitol Hill," as it came to be known, into one of the exclusive and fashionable areas of the city.

15. These new bridges were the result of the Cherry Creek flood of 1864. See note 22 below.

16. Episcopal bishop George Maxwell Randall (1810–73), a native of Rhode Island who arrived in Denver from Boston on June 11, 1866, as bishop of the Missionary District of Colorado "and parts adjacent," almost immediately proposed to build a school for girls, an academy for boys, and a theological school that would also serve as his personal residence. The Episcopal High School for Girls, a fifty-foot-square two-story brick building financed by donations that Randall collected back east, opened in the fall of 1868 with a student body of seventy. It was named Wolfe Hall in honor of its principal benefactor. During the period of Bowles's visit, the school's opening was being regularly advertised in the *Rocky Mountain News*. Randall's contributions to the growth of the Episcopal church in Colorado were considerable. It is said that his career served as the model for the bishop in Owen Wister's famous novel *The Virginian* (1902). On Randall's episcopate, see Allen Du Pont Breck, *The Episcopal Church in Colorado, 1860–1963* (Denver: Big Mountain Press, 1963), pp. 28–66.

17. Bayard Taylor, writing two years earlier, also called attention to the Methodist church as an "edifice with considerable architectural beauty" that helps to "give the place an air of permanence, very surprising to one who has just arrived from the East" (*Colorado,* p. 37). Denver's original Methodist church had been built on the sandy banks of Cherry Creek and did not survive the flood of 1864.

18. The first public school in Colorado opened on October 3, 1859.

19. There were, in fact, at least seven newspapers being published at Denver during the period of Bowles's visit: William Byers's *Rocky Mountain News* (1859–present), the *Daily Denver Gazette* (1865–69), the *Daily Colorado Tribune* (1867–71), the *Colorado Tribune* (1867–71), the *Rocky Mountain Herald* (1868–1946), the *Colorado Democrat* (1868–69), and the *Weekly Denver Gazette* (1865–69) (Donald E. Oehlerts, comp., *Guide to Colorado Newspapers, 1859–1863* [Denver: Bibliographical Center for Research, Rocky Mountain Region, 1964], pp. 27–51).

20. A painting by the Dutchman Henry Van Dyke (1599–1641).

21. Cherry Creek joins the South Platte at Denver.

22. On Thursday, May 19, 1864, following a week of heavy rains, the banks of both Cherry Creek and the South Platte surged over their banks, leaving eight people dead and flooding Denver. As Professor Brewer noted, Denver's "early settlers thought no water ever ran there, and with marvellous foolishness built a part of the town directly on

this wide, dry, sandy creek-bed. Many houses were built there, some even of brick and settlers were lawing about town lots located there. For eight years they were in immunity, no water flowed in the stream. Then suddenly the stream rose . . . in a night, and swept away everything—houses, people, bridges, etc. The jail was there, and neither it nor the prisoners in it have been heard of since. Not a trace of even brick buildings was left. The town building [City Hall?] went; the city records were in an iron safe, which has never been heard of since" (Rogers, ed., *Rocky Mountain Letters*, p. 15).

23. Bowles had seen the Cordilleras of Colombia in September 1865 as he returned from California by steamship at the end of his trip across the continent with Colfax. As noted above, he had visited Switzerland during the summer of 1862.

24. The Smoky Hill road was the famous emigrant trail and stage road between Kansas City and Denver. It roughly followed the Smoky Hill River, which originates at Cheyenne Wells in eastern Colorado, flows into Kansas past Salina and Abilene, and then joins the Republican River to form the Kansas.

25. The population of Denver in 1870, according to the U.S. Census, was 4,579. Bayard Taylor had estimated the population in 1866 as about 6,000.

26. On August 15, 1870, the first train of the Union Pacific's Eastern Division reached Denver from Kansas City.

27. Although chartered by the territorial legislature as early as 1864, the railroad's coming was delayed. The South Clear Creek and Colorado Central Railroad, which provided direct access to the mines and mills of the Clear Creek valley, did not arrive at Black Hawk until December 15, 1872. Until May 1878, Black Hawk remained the end of the line. By 1880, F. V. Hayden could proclaim that "the ride by rail up Clear Creek Canon must be made by all who visit the State, or they miss one of its greatest attractions" (*The Great West: Its Attractions and Resources* [Bloomington, Ill.: Charles R. Brodix, 1880], p. 106).

3. THE GEOGRAPHY OF COLORADO

1. At 14,433 feet, Mount Elbert, in the Sawatch Range, is the highest mountain in Colorado.

2. Timbered and lofty North Park is rimmed on three sides by mountains: by the Medicine Bow Mountains on the east, the Rabbit Ear Range and the Never Summer Mountains on the south, and the

Park Range to the west. On the north, as Bowles suggests below, it opens on Wyoming. Then, as now, North Park was the remotest of Colorado's major mountain parks.

3. San Luis Park, located in south central Colorado at an elevation of some seven thousand feet, is bordered on the east by the Sangre de Cristo Mountains and on the west by the San Juans. The park is 125 miles long and 50 miles wide; covering some 5,000 square miles, it is one of the largest mountain valleys in the world.

4. As Bowles suggests, Longs Peak (14,256 feet), Grays Peak (14,270 feet), and Mount Lincoln (14,286 feet) are prominent features of the Front, or Snowy, Range. Longs Peak is named after its discover, Major Stephen H. Long (1784–1864), who, at the head of a scientific party in search of the sources of the Red River, entered Colorado in late June 1820 and on the morning of June 30 made the first recorded sighting of the mountain that would come to bear his name. Grays Peak (14,270 feet) and its neighbor Torreys Peak (14,267 feet) were named in 1861 after two famous botanists, Asa Gray (1810–98), Fisher professor of natural history at Harvard, and his colleague, John Torrey (1796–1873), who taught botany for many years at Princeton and then served for two decades as an assayer in New York City. The two coauthored *Flora of North America* in 1838. Gray climbed Grays Peaks with Charles C. Parry (see below) in 1872. For a time both Grays and Torreys peaks were considered part of the same mountain, hence the allusion here in the plural to "Gray's Peaks."

5. Placer gold was discovered in the streams north of present-day Como in July 1859, touching off a boom. It has been estimated that by the end of 1860 some eleven thousand miners and prospectors had entered South Park to search for gold, founding the towns through which Bowles and party passed. By the time of his visit, however, as his comments and descriptions plainly suggest, the South Park mining boom had played out.

6. Presumably Bowles is referring to the Indian activity, punctuated by incidents of looting and murder, that took place along the Front Range of Colorado during the summer of 1868. Such activity in turn precipitated the Indian scare that overtook them during the final days of August. See the first paragraph of chapter 9 below.

7. Pikes Peak (14,109 feet) was named after Lieutenant Zebulon Pike (1779–1813), the first official American explorer to enter Colorado. Pike and his twenty-three-man party sighted Pikes Peak on November 15, 1806, and made an unsuccessful attempt to scale it. The identification of Pikes Peak with the destination of gold seekers

in 1859 was caused by the fact that the mountain served as the most prominent landmark for those coming west along the Smoky Hill Road, often visible as far as 150 miles.

8. This was true until Ferdinand V. Hayden (1829–87), head of the U.S. Geological and Geographic Survey of the Territories, conducted his geologic mapping and natural-history surveys of Colorado in the summers of 1873 through 1876. The results were reported in a series of annual descriptive reports (one of which is cited below) and produced the *Geological and Geographical Atlas of Colorado* (1877), a pioneering topographical work that filled in many of the blanks that Bowles alludes to.

9. The Grand River (since 1921 the Colorado River) originates in the northwest region of what is now Rocky Mountain National Park and flows through Middle Park, western Colorado, and southeastern Utah before entering northern Arizona.

10. The White River, some 250 miles in length, rises in the high northeastern plateaus of what is now Garfield County, Colorado, and flows westward across the Utah border.

11. The Gunnison River of west central Colorado, rising in the Sawatch Range, is formed by the confluence of the Slate and Taylor rivers and flows 180 miles before emptying into the Colorado River (then known as the Grand River), near the present town of Grand Junction.

12. Bowles is referring to the explorations being conducted that summer in Middle Park and western Colorado by John Wesley Powell and his Colorado Scientific Exploring Expedition. See chapter 6.

4. Travel among the Mountains

1. The Berthoud Pass (11,314 feet), which spans the Continental Divide and provides access to Middle Park, lies in the Front Range (or the Snowy Range, as it was then called), forty miles west of Denver. It was discovered by a party led by Captain Edward L. Berthoud (1828–1908) on May 12, 1861, and opened as toll road in 1874. For a number of years Coloradans promoted the Berthoud Pass as the route for the transcontinental railroad. Colfax himself added to the enthusiasm about the future prospects of the Berthoud Pass by telling a reporter for the *Rocky Mountain News* on August 21, 1868, that "he saw no greater engineering difficulties in the way of carrying a railroad over either of these routes than had been encountered in carrying it over the Sierra Nevada" (p. 4).

2. Boulder Creek, and its many branches, flows out of the Continental Divide near Rollins Pass (11,680 feet) (or Boulder Pass, as it was then called) and through the town of Boulder. Boulder, in the rock-strewn foothills of the Front Range north of Denver, was founded in 1858, following a gold strike at nearby Gold Hill earlier the same year. The "City" was added to its name in expectation of future growth.

3. Clear Creek rises along the Continental Divide and flows eastward to Golden. It was among the ribbed canyons and ravines of Clear Creek and its tributaries that John H. Gregory made his gold discovery in May 1859. Here are located many of the great mining towns of Colorado: Georgetown, Silver Plume, Empire, Mill City, Idaho Springs, Black Hawk, and Central City.

4. Golden City (Golden) on Clear Creek, east of the Front Range and ten miles west of Denver, was founded as a mining town in 1859 and later served briefly as territorial capital.

5. Black Hawk and Central City are the two Gilpin County towns, a mile apart, created almost overnight by John H. Gregory's discovery in the spring of 1859. By the next year both towns had become important mining, milling, and supply centers for what came to be called the richest square mile on earth.

6. Idaho (or Idaho Springs, as it became) is located in Clear Creek County, thirty-four miles west of Denver. It was initially settled as a placer mining camp in 1859 and by the early 1860s had become a mining center and county seat. Though during his visit of 1866 Bayard Taylor pronounced it "a straggling village of log huts . . . [a] queer, almost aboriginal, village," redeemed only by the presence of "the best hotel in Colorado" (*Colorado,* p. 72), Idaho Springs subsequently became a substantial Victorian community, noted for the hot and cold mineral springs from which it took its name. Idaho's reputation for hot springs and hot baths developed early. "There are two baths, the Mammoth Bath and the Ocean Bath, between which there is a fierce rivalry," Yale's Professor Brewer noted in 1869. "After supper we went up and enjoyed one of the most luxurious baths I have ever had. The water comes in at a temperature of 104½ F. and cools in the bath, where it has a temperature of 70 to 80, mostly about 75. The water is somewhat mineral, has a slight smell of sulphur and deposits a tufa of carbonate of lime and iron" (*Rocky Mountain Letters,* p. 51).

7. Fall River (or Spanish Bar, as it had originally been called) was another early Colorado mining town. Located three miles above Idaho Springs, it was named for the Fall River, which rises to the south of James Peak and flows southwest to Clear Creek. In 1866 it consisted

of "a post office, hotel, and stores" (Ovando J. Hollister, *The Mines of Colorado* [Springfield, Mass.: Samuel Bowles & Company, 1867], p. 230).

8. Mill City, five miles northwest of Idaho Springs, was a mining camp laid out by a party of Californians in 1859 or 1860. It was renamed Dumont about 1880, after a local mine owner who tried to revive the town.

9. Empire, located nine miles west of Idaho Springs, was founded as a mining camp in 1860 but soon went into rapid decline. By the mid-1860s few residents were left. The "only sign of a city," a visitor of 1864 noted, "existed in about a dozen mean log-huts and a few brace of frame houses." Nevertheless, according to Ovando Hollister, visiting two years later, "Of all the towns brought into existence by the fame of Cherry Creek sand, Empire bears away the palm for a pretty location and picturesque surroundings" (*Mines of Colorado,* p. 230).

10. Though founded as a gold town, Georgetown became the site of rich silver discoveries in 1864. Once the third largest town in Colorado, more silver was produced there than in any area of the world until the discoveries at Leadville in 1878. Georgetown prospered until the silver crash of 1893 closed the mines and brought the boom to an end. In May 1868, just months before Bowles's visit, the telegraph had reached Georgetown.

11. One of the early wagon roads linking Denver to Idaho Springs and the Clear Creek gold region.

12. The main source of Bear Creek lies on the eastern slopes of Mount Evans (14,264 feet). Turkey Creek rises nearby on an extension of Mount Evans. Both creeks eventually join, before making their way to the South Platte. Along Turkey Creek was the wagon road from Denver to Fairplay.

13. "A good many of the roads [of early Colorado] were built by toll companies, whose proprietors saw an opportunity to cash in on the gold rush, but since these projects often were financed by bankers in Denver and other commercial towns, local businessmen were deeply interested in them" (Athearn, *Coloradans,* p. 71).

14. As noted in the Introduction, these "appointments" had been made in advance by Daniel Witter (1827–1906), Colfax's brother-in-law.

15. Alexander Cameron Hunt (1825–94), who from 1867 to 1869 served as Colorado's fourth territorial governor, made a fortune in the goldfields of California, only to lose it all in the crash of 1857.

Determined to try again, Hunt was attracted to Colorado by the Pikes Peak rush of 1858. Once in Denver, Hunt prospered as both a businessman and a skillful politician. President Andrew Johnson appointed him governor of the territory in 1867 and at the same time made him ex officio superintendent of Indian affairs. It was in the latter capacity that Hunt succeeded in 1868, with the help of D. C. Oakes (see below), in negotiating the treaty in which the Utes ceded to the United States all lands east of the 107th meridian. Hunt had also helped to negotiate the Middle Park treaty with the Utes two years earlier. He subsequently turned his attention and talents to railroading.

16. Sue Matthews recalled that under the guidance of Governor Hunt, "we went first to Idaho Springs and had lunch at the Beebee House, and then went on up to Empire and camped. That was a great novelty for us; and we stayed, I think, one or two nights. We came back to Central City and stayed with the Briggs', the people who owned the old Gregory diggings. . . . They were from South Bend" (Mrs. Hall, "Seventy Years Ago," p. 164). The *Rocky Mountain News* reported that on August 14 "they took saddle horses from Black Hawk and rode to the top of Bald Mountain, head of Nevada gulch, which affords as fine a view as any place we know of" (August 15, 1868, p. 4).

17. John Pierce (1829–1900), a native of Harwinton, Connecticut, and a graduate of Western Reserve College, class of 1850, studied engineering at Harvard with Louis Agassiz before beginning his career as a surveyor. Following his arrival in Denver in 1861, Pierce was engaged to make the first public surveys in Colorado. In 1863 he was appointed by Lincoln as surveyor general of Colorado and Utah. By the time of Bowles's visit, Pierce had turned his professional attention to the construction of Colorado's first railroads. He served the Denver Pacific as consulting engineer, vice president, and president. Surviving correspondence between the two suggests that Pierce and Bowles were friends of some standing. On September 8, 1867, Bowles wrote Pierce that "the Indians and Mrs. Bowles's health broke up my hopes of the mountains this season. I keep them, however, as bright anticipation for next year" (Merriam, *Samuel Bowles* 2:55).

18. Chief (11,709 feet), Squaw (11,468 feet), and Papoose (11,174 feet) mountains lie east and west at about one-mile intervals some four miles south of Idaho Springs. According to Ovando Hollister, "These hills are covered with the finest turf and in the right season are one bed of flowers" (*Mines of Colorado,* p. 230).

19. The Chicago Lakes lie on the northern slope of Mount Evans.

20. Mount Evans, together with Mount Bierstadt, Mount Rosalie, Mount Epaulet, Mount Warren, Mount Rogers, and Mount Goliath, were originally called the Chicago Mountains. The highest of the group, Mount Evans, was originally named Rosalie, by German-born landscape painter Albert Bierstadt (1830–1902) or his traveling companion, the journalist-author Fitz Hugh Ludlow (1836–70), who visited the area in June 1863 in the company of William Byers. While there Bierstadt started the 12 × 7 canvas titled *Storm in the Rocky Mountains—Mount Rosalie*. (This picture, one of Bierstadt's most celebrated, is now lost and is known only by the chromolithographed copy made in London.) Rosalie was the name of Bierstadt's wife, Rosalie Osborne.

21. Daniel C. Oakes (1825–87), who became one of Colorado's most respected pioneers, was a sawmill operator who later served both as agent to the Ute Indians and as deputy U.S. land surveyor. Born at Carthage, Maine, Oakes lived in Ohio, Indiana, and Iowa before going west to California in 1849 to mine for gold on the American River. Returning to Glenwood, Iowa, Oakes married and took up the career of a contractor-builder before joining the Pikes Peak rush of 1858 for a month of prospecting.

When he came home to Iowa, he brought with him the manuscript of a guidebook written by Luke D. Tierney, one of the original members of William Green Russell's party of Georgians who had participated in the Cherry Creek gold strike of June 1858. Oakes and a Stephen W. Smith proceeded to publish and offer for sale Tierney's book, adding their own guide to the best routes to the goldfields. Oakes and Smith's book—*History of the Gold Discoveries on the South Platte River. By Luke Tierney. To Which Is Appended a Guide of the Route, by Smith & Oaks* [*sic*] (Pacific City, Iowa: A. Thomson, 1859)—was widely circulated in the eastern states and caused thousands to leave their homes to seek their fortunes in the West, an impetuosity that many came to regret. In retribution, Oakes was subsequently buried in effigy on the banks of the Platte near Julesburg by a party of disappointed gold seekers, who bestowed upon him the epitaph:

> Here lies the remains of D. C. Oakes,
> Who was the starter of this damned hoax!

In 1865 Oakes succeeded Simeon Whiteley as Grand River agent for the Northern Utes and four years later was made a deputy U.S. land surveyor, a career he pursued until his death. See D. C. Oakes, "The Man Who Wrote the Guide Book," *The Trail* 2 (December 1909): 7–15 (a sustained excerpt from Oakes's diary, covering his early years in Colorado).

22. The colorful Charley Utter (b. 1838) has left only a brief record of his activities in Colorado between the time of his arrival with the gold rush of 1859 and his disappearance in 1877. Born, apparently, near Niagara Falls, New York, Utter was raised on an Illinois farm, where his immediate neighbor was William Bross. Following his arrival in Colorado, Utter became a friend of the Utes, mastered their language, and as a result was hired in 1864 by Uriah M. Curtis as an interpreter. Summers were spent with the Indians, winters in Empire, where Utter operated a billiard hall and bar. In 1866 Utter married and shortly thereafter built a stable in Georgetown from which he operated a freighting and packing business. Given his abilities as an interpreter, it was hardly surprising that, when Oakes sought to round up the Indians to negotiate the Treaty of Middle Park on August 29, 1866, it was Charley Utter to whom he turned. That treaty, a "Treaty of Amity and Friendship between the United States and the Chiefs and Warriors of the Uinta and Yampa or Grand River Bands of the Utah Indians," signed by Territorial Governor Alexander Cummings (1810–79), Alexander Hunt, and Agent Oakes, marked by ten of the Utes, and sealed by exchange of gifts and the promise of a Federal subsidy, was subsequently rejected by the Senate in February 1869 because it failed to remove the Utes to a reservation.

In the summer of 1873, the well-known author and lecturer Anna E. Dickinson (1842–1932), who, as a member of the Hayden party, on September 13, 1873, become the first woman to climb Longs Peak, met Charley Utter and his "beautiful dark" twenty-two-year-old wife in Georgetown and engaged him for a moonlight climb of Grays Peak. For her, Utter was the epitome of the western hunter and mountain guide.

> Short and slight, with long blonde curling hair, blue eyes that look at you fearlessly and through you searchingly, a wide-brimmed slouch hat, moccasins, and Indian leggins, a red flannel shirt with embroidered collar and cuffs, a short loose coat, a broad belt with bowie knife, pistols, a tomahawk stuck into it.
>
> There he is.
>
> Chary of speech, soft-voiced, abstemious of habit, gentle-mannered, thoughtful of every one, tender-hearted, his eyes filled

> with nature, his soul feeling it, and showing itself through quaint broken sentences, delighting in talk that touches the heart of things, or that concerns the lives of the great ones of the earth, over which he has pored and dreamed by his camp fires. (Anna E. Dickinson, *A Ragged Register (of People[,] Places and Opinions)* [New York: Harper & Brothers, Publishers, 1879], pp. 263–64)

There is one more known chapter to the Charley Utter story. Following the end of his marriage in 1876, Utter led a party of Georgetown men toward the Black Hills goldfields, only to be set upon by Indians. Though several of his companions were killed, Utter escaped to Deadwood, where, described as "a natty, handsome, courageous little man," he became the partner of the famous Wild Bill Hickock. See Louise C. Harrison, *Empire and the Berthoud Pass* (Denver: Big Mountain Press, 1964), pp. 125–27; Robert C. Black III, *Island in the Rockies: The History of Grand County, Colorado, to 1930* (Boulder: Pruett Publishing, 1969), pp. 34, 55–57; and Agnes Wright Spring, *Colorado Charley, Wild Bill's Pard* (Boulder: Pruett Publishing, 1968).

23. Ashley Franklin (Bowles has transposed his name), a Middle Park rancher, is referred to in the August 31, 1868, edition of the *Rocky Mountain News* as an "experienced mountaineer and guide . . . than whom no better could be had" (p. 4). It was Franklin, the *News* reported, who had accompanied Bowles, Bross, and R. F. Lord, a Georgetown mine owner, on their ascent of Grays Peak the previous Saturday (see below). Several days later, with news that Arapahos had been seen in South Park, Governor Hunt called upon Franklin to go to the Ute camp in Middle Park and enlist their support. See *Rocky Mountain News*, September 2, 1868, p. 4.

24. The allusion is probably to the reconnaissance made in June 1862 by a party led by William Byers and John Evans (1814–97), Colorado's territorial governor, to study the possibility of building a wagon road and railroad route over the Berthoud Pass. Governor Evans raised funds in Denver for a feasibility study, but when the report of Francis M. Case, the surveyor general of Colorado and Utah, proved disappointing, the project was dropped.

5. The Middle Park

1. On their descent into Middle Park, Bayard Taylor's party, which included William Byers, lost the trail and became immersed in snow so deep that "I frequently found myself buried nearly to the hips and

thrown upon my face, with the horse's head resting on my back. . . . My boots were completely sodden, and my feet and legs soon became so icy cold that I was forced to walk a good part of the way, although the exercise seemed to rack every joint in the body" (Taylor, *Colorado,* pp. 85–87).

2. Les Trois Frères Provençaux, a fashionable Paris restaurant of the day. Bowles presumably dined there during his European sojourn of 1862. See Lately Thomas (Robert V. P. Steele), *Delmonico's: A Century of Splendor* (Boston: Houghton Mifflin, 1967), p. 66.

3. Bowles's allusion is probably to the U.S. Spring Bed Company, founded at Springfield in 1868 by a J. F. Peck. Peck's new spring bed is advertised in the *Springfield City Directory* for 1869–70 as "a spring bed entirely of iron, which is lighter, cleaner, easier handled than any other bed ever offered."

4. Mr. Hawkins of Mill City and Springfield remains unidentified.

5. Middle Park was one of the traditional summer rendezvous places of the mountain Utes, and Byers reported from Hot Sulphur Springs on August 12 that "about eighty lodges of Utes are camped here now, along the opposite bank of the river; their village presenting a novel and animated appearance. The number is daily increasing and is said will reach three thousand persons by the middle of next week, when Gov. Hunt and Maj. Oakes are expected to hold a talk with them" (*Rocky Mountain News*, August 20, 1868, p. 1).

6. The natural sulphur springs beside the Grand River in Middle Park came to have special significance for William Byers, who apparently first visited there in August 1863. By the end of that year he began to acquire the springs and their immediate vicinity for himself through a series of intricate transactions. In October 1868, only months after Bowles's visit, Byers surveyed and platted the area, put up buildings and a small log "hotel," and attempted (with only modest success) to attract wealthy tourists to his spa-resort (Black, *Island in the Rockies,* pp. 61–73, 77–79; Robert L. Perkins, *The First Hundred Years: An Informal History of Denver and the Rocky Mountain News* [Garden City, N.Y.: Doubleday, 1959], pp. 303–4).

7. Bayard Taylor devotes chapters 12–14 to his experiences in Middle Park, including the one referred to here.

8. The allusion is unclear.

9. Sharon Springs in New York's Schoharie County, west northwest of Amsterdam, was a health resort noted for its sulphur springs.

10. As Bowles notes, Williams Fork joins the Grand River a short distance southwest of Hot Sulphur Springs.

11. The allusion is to Victorian poet Elizabeth Barrett Browning (1806–61). See another reference to Browning in chapter 7 below. The precise source of her "observation," however, is not clear.

12. The Ute Indians, who occupied central and western Colorado as well as northeastern Utah, made the parks of Colorado, including Middle Park, their summer home. The discovery of horses gave the Utes mobility and allowed them to descend onto the plains to hunt buffalo and to make war on the Apaches of eastern New Mexico. Although the Utes and Commanches were originally allies, by the middle of the eighteenth century they had become enemies, which forced the Utes to leave the plains for the mountains. As Bowles notes, there were seven different divisions or bands of Utes. In southern Colorado were the Weminuche, the Mouache, and the Capote. In west central Colorado were the Tebegauche, or Uncompahgre. In the north were the Grand River, the Yampa, and the Uintah. In 1875 the Commission of Indian Affairs estimated the number of Utes at 9,625. On the whole the Utes initially got along well with the invading whites. Because they tended to remain in the interior of Colorado, the Utes were tolerated or overlooked by prospectors and miners who swarmed into and across the Colorado Territory, and as a result they were the last tribe to retain any claim to land in Colorado. Peaceful if uneasy relations lasted until Ute lands too became desirable for settlement. In the end it was their presence in places like Middle Park that led to conflict, culminating in the rallying cry, "The Utes must go!" The years between 1858 and 1882 were marked by a succession of treaties that attempted, unsuccessfully, to broker a modus vivendi. Manifest Destiny, in the end, proved irresistible, and in 1882 Congress opened the Ute lands to public settlement.

13. Brandreth was an apparently well-known brand name of the day.

14. The Arapaho (meaning "Our People"), who made their home to the east of the Continental Divide, were the other major Colorado Indian tribe of the nineteenth century. They were nomadic latecomers, having arrived from the Northeast about 1790 from their traditional home in Minnesota, pushed west toward the Front Range by the fierce Sioux. Almost immediately they became the enemy of the Utes, with whom they engaged in intermittent fighting. The Arapaho too hunted in the mountains, which led them into pitched battles with the Utes in places like Middle Park as late as the 1860s. In number the Arapaho were considerably fewer than the Utes, probably never more than

2,500. The largest group of Arapaho occupied the Arkansas River area of eastern Colorado in the vicinity of Bent's Fort.

15. The Comanches, like the Arapaho, were traditional enemies of the Utes. The name "Comanche," in fact, comes from a Ute word meaning "anyone who wants to fight me all the time." By the late eighteenth century the Comanches migrated from the mountains of Wyoming to the southern plains.

16. The Cheyennes, one of the best known of the plains tribes, were allied by common origin with the Arapahos and thus were also enemies of the Utes. The Cheyennes fell into two divisions. The Northern Cheyenne inhabited the area near the headwaters of the Platte and the Yellowstone River in Montana and Wyoming, while the Southern Cheyenne, between 1832 and 1850, settled on the upper Arkansas River at Bent's Fort. The presence of the Southern Cheyennes helped force the Utes back into the mountains. In 1864 Colonel J. M. Chivington's Colorado volunteers attacked a band of peaceful Cheyennes and Arapahos camped on Sand Creek (mostly women and children), killing three hundred.

17. The Treaty of 1868, negotiated at Washington on March 2, 1868, between representatives of the seven bands of Utes and U.S. Commissioner of Indian Affairs Nathaniel G. Taylor, Colorado territorial governor Alexander Hunt, Indian Agent D. C. Oakes, and ex officio Superintendent of Indian Affairs Kit Carson, was (by contemporary standards at least) a liberal one. In return for the surrender of Middle Park, South Park, and the San Luis Valley, the Utes were given a well-watered and fertile reservation in southwestern Colorado, extending north from the southern border of the Colorado Territory along the 107th meridian (and composing one-third of the Colorado Territory) "set apart for the absolute and undisturbed use and occupation of the Indians herein named." Two years later, in 1870, a series of mineral discoveries in the San Juan Mountains led to the Brunot Agreement (named after Indian Commissioner Felix R. Brunot), under which the Utes ceded a big rectangular chunk of reservation lands back to the whites, paving the way for the next wave of mining booms at Ouray, Telluride, Red Mountain, Silverton, Lake City, and Creede. See Wilson Rockwell, *The Utes, a Forgotten People* (Denver: Sage Books, 1956), pp. 64–105.

Unfortunately, as Black notes, the terms and conditions of the Treaty of 1868 had little immediate impact on many Utes, and friction between the races continued. "A special guarantee of friction was the

Indians' inability to grasp the reality of a boundary line, in particular of a reservation. For years following the Treaty of 1868, sizable bands continued to wander eastward through the mountains and onto the plains, a habit which was granted a kind of official sanction by the retention until 1875 of a special agency for the 'roving' Utes" (*Island in the Rockies,* p. 116).

6. FROM MIDDLE PARK BY BOULDER PASS

1. Grand Lake is the largest natural lake in Colorado.
2. The Blue River rises in an amphitheater south and beneath Quandary Peak (14,264 feet) in the Mosquito Range near Hoosier Pass and flows north past Breckenridge until it is joined by the Snake and Ten Mile rivers at Three River Junction. It finally empties into the Colorado (Grand) River near present-day Kremmling.
3. Boulder Pass (11,680 feet), or Rollins Pass, as it is now called, crosses the Continental Divide several miles north of Berthoud Pass and leads down to Nederland and Boulder.
4. The *Rocky Mountain News* for August 20, 1868, noted that "it was a comparatively unimportant [amendment], making, we understand, some of the original provisions of the treaty less favorable for the Indians" (p. 4). The amendment, in fact, had to do with article 13 and the livestock to be appropriated the Utes—an amendment which, from the Indian point of view, was anything but unimportant. The failure of the Senate to ratify the treaty immediately contributed directly to the problems Governor Hunt faced that summer in trying to maintain peace with the Utes. He reached agreement with the Grand River Utes and the Uintah Utes in Middle Park on August 15, 1868, but it took four more meetings between September 1 and September 25 to reach agreement with the other Ute bands.
5. Major John Wesley Powell (1834–1902), who had lost his right arm at Shiloh, was a professor of geology and natural science at Illinois State Normal University. He was in Colorado with the Colorado Scientific Exploring Expedition to spend a summer in mountain investigations before proceeding to explore the Grand Canyon of the Colorado the following year. Powell's party of twenty-one persons, though representing different branches of natural science, especially geology, botany, ornithology, and entomology, was made up largely of amateur scientists and students from Illinois State Normal and Illinois Wesleyan.

6. A congressional bill, signed by President Andrew Johnson on June 11, 1868, authorized the secretary of war to furnish supplies for Powell's expedition. As Bowles notes, Powell had persuaded his own university and the Board of the Illinois Natural History Society in Bloomington to furnish "small sums of money" (the latter gave $750). To this the Smithsonian Institution contributed some instruments and the Board of Education of the State of Illinois gave $400. All personal expenses, however, were the responsibility of the participants.

7. The Powell expedition left Normal for Chicago on June 29, 1868, where they boarded a special car on the Chicago and Northwestern bound for Omaha. From Omaha they traveled the Union Pacific to Cheyenne, where they remained until July 7 to outfit themselves. It took six days to get the party to Denver. From there they proceeded through Bear Creek Canyon to Empire, where they were joined by Byers and Jack Sumner, a trader and knowledgeable mountain guide who also happened to be Byers's brother-in-law. Byers and Sumner accompanied the party on a leisurely reconnaissance across Berthoud Pass into Middle Park. From their base camp at Hot Sulphur Springs on the banks of the Grand River, where Sumner had a trading post, the Powell party spent three months exploring the mountains, taking measurements, sketching geologic formations, and collecting specimens documenting the natural history of the region. They kept themselves supplied by crossing and recrossing the Berthoud Pass to Empire.

8. The party that made the first recorded ascent of 14,256-foot Longs Peak on August 23, 1868, consisted of Major Powell, Walter H. Powell (Powell's brother-in-law), William Byers, Jack Sumner, and three of Powell's students from Illinois—L. W. Keplinger, Samuel M. Garman, and Ned E. Farrell. Byers reported their five-day journey in a series of stories published in the *Rocky Mountain News* between August 19 and September 1, 1868. For Byers, their success was not without its irony, for in failing in a similar attempt four years earlier, in August 1864, he had assured his readers that "we have been almost all around the Peak and we are quite sure that no living creature, unless it had wings to fly, was ever upon its summit. We believe we run no risk in predicting that no man will ever be, though it is barely possible that the ascent can be made" (*Rocky Mountain News*, September 2, 1864, p. 2). See Perkins, *First Hundred Years,* pp. 299–303; L. W. Keplinger, "The First Ascent of Long's Peak," *Collections of the Kansas State Historical Society* 14 (1918): 340–53. Bowles was not

in Middle Park, as he suggests, to greet Powell and Byers on their return. He had left on August 17, the same day that Powell and Byers had departed for Grand Lake.

9. "The view," Byers wrote, "is very extensive in all directions; including Pike's Peak south, the Sahwatch range southwest, Gore's range and the Elkhorn Mountains west, the Medicine Bow and Sweetwater ranges north, and a vast extent of the plains east. Denver is plainly distinguishable to the naked eye; also the Hot Springs in Middle Park" (*Rocky Mountain News,* September 1, 1868, p. 1).

10. Though the journey to the mouth of the White River proved more difficult and hazardous than expected, Powell successfully completed the preliminary expeditions that left him poised for his great feat of conquering the Colorado the following year. Powell's 1868 explorations are recounted in William Culp Darrah, *Powell of the Colorado* (Princeton, N.J.: Princeton University Press, 1951), pp. 91–107; and Wallace Stegner, *Beyond the Hundredth Meridian: John Wesley Powell and the Second Opening of the West* (Boston: Houghton Mifflin, 1954), pp. 21–39.

11. As Stegner notes, it was about this "great and final object" that Powell "had apparently said least when lining up his backing among the universities and museums. Collecting was never a major aim, but an excuse" (*Beyond the Hundredth Meridian,* p. 32).

12. The story of James White, a miner, and his reputed descent of September 1867 down the Colorado River to the small Mormon settlement of Callville, Arizona, was, according to Wallace Stegner, published twice in 1868. "There is plenty of evidence," Stegner continues, "that Powell as well as Bowles knew the story; there is also evidence that Powell did not believe it, even after he had hunted up White and talked to him" (ibid., p. 33). Historians who have studied White's story generally agree with Powell. See, for example, Frank Waters, *The Colorado* (New York: Rinehart, 1946), pp. 251–52.

13. See note 23 in chapter 4 above.

14. Bowles's party proceeded over Boulder Pass, following the Bear Canyon road along South Boulder Creek toward Boulder Mountain. At Rollinsville they turned south to Central City, where, as noted below, the party separated. Colfax and his brother-in-law, Daniel Witter, returned to Denver on the evening of August 19 to prepare for the expedition to South Park.

15. This was the morning of August 18.

16. The "two lovely lakes" were undoubtedly Yankee Doodle Lake and Jenny Lake.

17. According to Colorado journalist Ovando Hollister, the town site of South Boulder on South Boulder Creek was laid out by J. Q. A. Rollins (1816–94), the general director of the Rollins Gold Company, another of Colorado's able promoters. Hollister describes South Boulder as he visited it in 1866: "The main street curves regularly with the creek, and along its lower side a race has been located, five thousand feet long, calculated to carry the entire Boulder, and furnishing 15 water-lots of 300 feet front each with power for mills. On the other side of the street, which is 60 feet wide, a tier of building lots, each 40 by 80 feet, has been surveyed. Beyond this is another street parallel with the first with its double tier of building lots the same as the above. The spot is 25 miles from Golden Gate over an excellent wagon-road; 20 from Boulder City over old Gordon Road, ten north from Central City; and on any road that shall ever enter the Middle Park via. the Boulder Pass. The town-site covers a beautiful, natural park, about half or three-fourths of a mile wide by a mile and a half long, the north side of it, along which are the surveyed streets, most delightfully turned to the kiss of the sun" (*Mines of Colorado,* p. 220). The road to the summit of Boulder Pass and across into Middle Park, to which Hollister alludes, was not built until 1873.

7. Over Gray's Peak to South Park

1. The South Park excursion party, which left Denver on Saturday, August 22, was indeed a large one. As the *Rocky Mountain News* reported the following Monday, it consisted of "the Hon. Speaker, Mr. and Mrs. Mathews [*sic*], Sallie Bowles, and Nellie Wade; Mrs. Daniel Witter, Mrs. Hiram Witter, Mrs. Gov. Hunt, Mrs. R. L. Hatten, Miss Alice Hatten, Miss Issa [*sic*] Hunt, and little Cora Witter [a baby of six weeks]; Wm. Todd, the Speaker's private secretary, Mr. E. G. Mathews [*sic*], Gov. Hunt, Hiram Witter, Maj. Oakes and the necessary help, teamsters, cooks, servants. . . . They are well provided with conveyance, carriages and saddle horses and with provisions and camp conveniences, tents, blankets, &c., Mr. Witter and Governor Hunt having outdone themselves in the Quartermaster and Commissary line. Governor Hunt and Major Oakes have along a load of Indian goods and mean to meet the Southern Utes, and get their assent to the treaty as amended by the Senate. With the politics, the Indian business, traveling, sight-seeing, fishing, camping, riding, &c., the party is not likely to suffer from ennui at least" (August 24, 1868, p. 4). Territorial Secretary Frank Hall and reporter W. R. Thomas of

the *Rocky Mountain News* accompanied the party the first day; Daniel Witter, former governor John Evans and his family, Bross, and Bowles joined this main group in South Park. Also on the trip was Ovando Hollister, associate editor of the *News*.

2. August 22, 1868.

3. The allusion is to John Loudon McAdam (1756–1836), "the macadamizer of roads," a Scotsman who perfected the process of building roads with broken stones and then in 1815, as surveyor general of Bristol roads, was given the opportunity to put his theories into practice on local highways.

4. As the *Rocky Mountain News* reported on Wednesday, September 2, 1868, "The Snowy Range is catching the grasshoppers this year. In its western slope clear up to the summit the air is alive with them, but nearly all alight and soon become chilled off and cannot rise again. On the great snow fields the dead can be scooped up by the wagon load, and the bears, which infest that country, are fattening upon them" (p. 4). Professor Brewer encountered the same phenomenon the next summer (see *Rocky Mountain Letters,* p. 32).

5. Latin: "At one's pleasure."

6. Dr. Charles C. Parry, (1823–90), an English-born botanical explorer, visited Colorado in 1861 and made the most accurate barometric measurements to date of a number of peaks in the Front Range. As noted above, he named Grays and Torreys peaks for his fellow botanists Asa Gray and John Torrey. Four years later, in 1864, Parry was a member of the party led by William Byers that made an unsuccessful attempt to scale Longs Peak.

7. According to William Buehler, this is "perhaps the first published, clearly identifiable reference to the 14,005-foot Mount of the Holy Cross" (*Roof of the Rockies: A History of Colorado Mountaineering* [Evergreen, Colo.: Cordillera Press, 1986], p. 48). As Bowles notes, however, its existence was then widely known.

8. Buehler notes that Bowles is mistaken in his identification of Mount Sopris: "Actually, 12,823-foot Mount Sopris could not possibly have appeared to an observer on Grays Peak as higher than the Mount of the Holy Cross. What Bowles described was Capitol Peak, the most westerly of the six 14,000-foot peaks of the Elk Range" (ibid.).

9. Mount Sopris was apparently first climbed by members of the Hayden Survey in 1873. It was named about 1865 for Captain Richard Sopris (1813–93), a native of Pennsylvania and a carpenter by trade, who came to Cherry Creek in February 1859, made money prospecting, and almost immediately began to participate in Colorado's public

affairs as the first president of the Agricultural Society in 1863, a captain in Colorado's first volunteer infantry, sheriff of Arapaho County, 1864–66, a railroad pioneer, and Denver's mayor, 1878–81.

10. The source of these lines is Elizabeth Barrett Browning's long "novel poem" of 1857, *Aura Leigh* 9:951–57.

11. The names Colfax Park and Colfax Lake do not appear on contemporary or more recent Colorado maps. Bowles is probably accurate when he notes that both were "so named by an enthusiastic and appreciative miner in the lower valley" in honor of the occasion.

12. The road from Georgetown leads across Argentine Pass (13,132 feet) and down into Snake River Valley. Three miles down from the head of the valley the Snake meets its tributaries; the group camped that night at Irving's Fork. The following day Bowles and his party moved on down the Snake and camped at its junction with the Blue River.

13. Stephen Decatur (d. 1888), reportedly the brother of none other than William Bross, was born in Sussex, New Jersey, attended Williams College, and briefly taught school in Orange County, New York, before up and leaving his family to fight with Stephen Kearney in the Mexican War. He came to Colorado about 1859 and, it was said, accumulated at least one more family en route. Decatur was a resident and popular figure of Georgetown for many years, from where he edited the *Colorado Miner* between 1869 and 1873. He was, writes John Horner, "as colorful a figure as Colorado exhibited. He was editor of one of the two newspapers in the community, a statewide politician and an irrepressible Fourth of July spellbinder. He founded some towns over the Divide and because he editorialized so often and so fluently about a certain silver mineral, he was called 'Old Sulphurets' by his cronies. Mountains are named for him. He died in poverty as an alcoholic under the roof of an elderly sporting woman [at the town of Rosita] in far off Wet Mountain Valley. There his tomb reads only 'Stephen Decatur'. . . . His real name was Stephen Decatur Bross, but he never acknowledged it even to his own brother, the founder of the *Chicago Tribune* and one of a distinguished family" (*Silver Town* [Caldwell, Idaho: Caxton Printers, 1950], p. 11; see also pp. 264–67). One of the towns that he founded (in 1868) was the Summit County mining community of Decatur, located at the foot of Argentine Pass, over which he was instrumental in building the first wagon road. Decatur subsequently represented Summit County in the Colorado territorial legislature and the new state as commissioner to the 1876 Centennial Exposition in Philadelphia. The best reconstruction of

the known details of Decatur's life is found in Mary Ellen Gilliland, *Summit: A Gold Rush History of Summit County, Colorado* (Silverthorne, Colo.: Alpenrose Press, 1980), pp. 274–80.

14. The story Bowles refers to, one that in context seems strangely gratuitous, concludes chapter 33 of Albert D. Richardson's book: "A sarcastic resident was rallying one of my traveling companions on his inability to drink buttermilk, declaring that no man can be quite civilized who does not relish that beverage. Mr. Bowles quickly replied: 'In my section we give the buttermilk to our pigs!' " (*Across the Mississippi,* p. 406).

15. The year before, in 1867, William H. Seward (1801–72), secretary of state under both Lincoln and Johnson, had completed the purchase of Alaska from Russia, a transaction that some referred to as Seward's Folly.

16. Owen J. Goldrick (1829–82), a schoolteacher turned newspaperman, was known for his pedantry and long-windedness. Allegedly born in Sligo County, Ireland, and educated at the University of Dublin and at New York's Columbia University, Goldrick immigrated to America, taught school for a time in Ohio and Missouri, and then, succumbing to the Pikes Peak gold fever, came west to Denver in 1859. His entrance into Denver, clad in a Prince Albert coat, striped trousers, high-crowned hat, and kid gloves, became legendary. "Probably no entry of that or any other year," recalled contemporary historian Frank Hall, "attracted so much attention, or elicited more diverse comment. But the Professor was not born to blush unseen, nor to live in a community, whatever its character, without making his influence felt" (*History of the State of Colorado* 1:218).

Goldrick founded the first school in Colorado (with thirteen pupils in attendance) at Auraria on October 3, 1859. He subsequently served as the first reporter, and then as city editor and associate editor, for William Byers's newly established *Rocky Mountain News* before moving on to Salt Lake City, where he became managing editor of the *Daily Vidette*. When his paper ran afoul of the Mormon establishment and he was asked to leave in 1866, Goldrick returned to Denver and for a brief period coedited the *Daily Colorado Times* at Black Hawk. At the time of Bowles's visit Goldrick was back in Denver as editor and publisher of the weekly *Rocky Mountain Herald,* a position he held for the rest of his life. See Owen J. Goldrick, "The First School in Denver," *Colorado Magazine* 6 (March 1929): 72–74; Levette Jay Davidson, "O. J. Goldrick, Pioneer Journalist," ibid. 8 (January 1936):

26–37; and Nolie Mumey, *Prof. Oscar* [*sic*] *J. Goldrick and His Denver, Together with His Address Delivered on the Early History of Denver, July 4, 1876* (Denver: Sage Books, 1959).

17. On G. R. Bechler's "Outline Map of the South Park and Adjoining Regions" in Hayden's *Ninth Annual Report . . . of the Territories* (Washington: Government Printing Office, 1877), the name "Georgia" is plainly visible, attached to a cluster of buildings some five miles northeast of Breckenridge on the west side of the Swan River. This, however, is Georgia Gulch, where placer gold was discovered in June 1860. It may or may not be Bowles's "Georgia Ranch."

18. At Three River Junction.

19. Bowles arrived in Breckenridge a little after noon on Monday, August 24. Breckenridge was one of the mining towns founded as a consequence of the discovery of gold on the Blue River on August 10, 1859. The town was organized in early 1860 and named for John C. Breckinridge (1821–75), sitting vice president. (When Breckinridge joined the Confederate Army, residents changed the spelling.) Unfortunately, the placer deposits lasted only three years, so that by the time of Bowles's visit, the town's first heyday was clearly past. The discovery of gold in the early 1880s led to a second boom, and by 1885 the town had two thousand residents and a new look of prosperity.

20. Hayden concurs with Bowles in his assessment of the valley of the Blue River: "As we look up the Valley of the Blue, our eyes meet on the horizon the sharp peaks about Hamilton Pass, and several miles east of them we see Mount Guyot dominating over lesser peaks and rugged mountains, while, when we look down the valley of the Blue, our eyes are arrested by huge mountain-masses of the Gores [*sic*] Range, with its countless lofty peaks and its sharp spurs" (*Ninth Annual Report,* p. 401).

21. Bowles and Bross arrived on August 24, 1868.

22. Undoubtedly the family of Judge Marshall Silverthorn (1811–87). Bayard Taylor had much the same experience in 1866: "We discovered a hotel—or its equivalent—kept by Mr. and Mrs. Silverthorn, who welcomed us like old friends. The walls of their large cabin were covered with newspapers, and presented a variety of advertisements and local news, from New Hampshire to Salt Lake. If the colored lithographs on the wall were doubtful specimens of art, there were good indications of literature on the table. The kind hostess promised us beds,—real beds, with sheets and pillows,—and the good

host would have taken me to any number of lodes and gulch-washings, if I had not been almost too sore to bend a joint" (*Colorado,* pp. 113–14).

In contrast, Professor Brewer, who arrived in 1869, was not so fortunate. He recalled for his wife that "as I reined up to the first 'hotel,' we saw a fat, good-natured woman come to the door, and with her such a troop of women and girls (some of the latter decidedly pretty), that I feared the room was too little in that house for all of them and my troop of young men, so I went on to the next. Alas, I had not read what Bowles had said of Judge Silverthorn and his pretty daughters. I went on to the other hotel, where we had no cause of complaint, but I was sorry on some accounts I had not stopped at the first place. But we had a quieter time, for there was a big party on hand that evening. I, however, went up and made the acquaintance of the 'Judge'—also several other notables of the place—from whom I got much information relative to the geography of the region" (*Rocky Mountain Letters,* p. 45).

The diminutive Marshall Silverthorn was a native of Pennsylvania, who came to Denver in 1859 and to Breckenridge a year later, where he was, by turns, a hotel keeper, storekeeper, postmaster, blacksmith, landlord, judge of the local miner's court, and justice of the peace. The Silverthorn Hotel on Main Street, which he established in 1861 and enlarged in 1862, survived until 1957, when it was torn down. His "pretty" daughters were Matilda and Martha. See also Gilliland, *Summit,* pp. 264–73.

23. Breckenridge Pass (now Boreas Pass), which spans the Continental Divide at an altitude of 11,053 feet, connects Summit and Park counties.

24. Hamilton and its near neighbor Tarryall owed their existence to the discovery of gold in the waters of Tarryall Creek at Deadwood Gulch (north of the present-day town of Como) in July 1859, which brought a stampede of prospectors into the northwest part of South Park. By the end of 1860 the new town of Tarryall boasted some three hundred log houses. So promising was the outlook that in 1861 William Byers brought in a press and began to publish a newspaper, the *Miner's Record*. The town struggled through decline in the 1860s and by 1872 was dead.

Hamilton, on the south side of the creek, was started at almost the same time as Tarryall by a dissident faction led by Earl Hamilton, one of Tarryall's original founders. In its heyday Hamilton consisted of a single long narrow street running parallel to the creek, so that contemporaries often spoke of Tarryall-Hamilton in a single breath, though the two towns refused to merge. Hamilton's history was much the same as Tarryall's, and by 1867, in fact, one visitor pronounced the town "dead to the waist, its seeming early promise having been broken by hope" (Hollister, *Mines of Colorado,* p. 290). See also LeRoy H. Hafen, "Ghost Towns—Tarryall and Hamilton," *Colorado Magazine* 4 (July 1933): 137–43.

8. THE SOUTH PARK AND MOUNT LINCOLN

1. Tuesday, August 25.

2. Sue Matthews recalled that they came by way of the Turkey Creek road, which followed the North Fork of the South Platte River through the small hamlet of Bailey and into South Park by way of Kenosha Pass (Mrs. Hall, "Seventy Years Ago," pp. 164–65).

3. Undoubtedly Bowles is looking toward Red Hill, thc last obstacle before Fairplay on the road from Kenosha Pass (9,950 feet). This road generally followed present U.S. Highway 285.

4. Shortly after their rendezvous, Colfax returned to Breckenridge over Breckenridge Pass to honor a speaking engagement with Bross, arriving at six o'clock the evening of August 25. "After a rest of two hours," the *Rocky Mountain News* reported, he "was ready for the evening's effort. The room in which the meeting was held was not large, but it was crowded to overflowing" (August 31, 1868, p. 4). Early the next morning, Colfax and Bross went over the Hoosier Pass to Montgomery to rejoin the rest of the party.

5. Fairplay, like Hamilton, was founded in 1859 by disgruntled placer miners from Tarryall, who discovered upon their arrival that all the best claims had already been taken up. When they moved to their new camp on the Main or Middle Fork of the South Platte River, they named it "Fair Play" to rebuke their "grab-all" colleagues at Tarryall. In 1866 the county seat was moved there from Buckskin Joe. That same year Bayard Taylor noted that "Fairplay is a quiet little place, with perhaps two hundred inhabitants, at the foot of a wooded slope, looking to the south, with a charming view far down the Park" (*Colorado,* p. 141). The *Rocky Mountain News* reported in its July 14, 1868, edition that "the Land Office, Court House, and several handsome residences, are among the new buildings. A Masonic Hall is contemplated, and we were told is to be gone on with at once. There are two public houses, flourishing stores, smith and carpenter shops, saloons, etc" (p. 4).

6. Montgomery, located near the place where the Middle Fork of the South Platte enters South Park, owed its existence to a gold discovery of 1859. By July 1862 the town contained more than 150 cabins. Four years later Bayard Taylor noted that the population, once three thousand, "now numbers three or four hundred. But as the cabins of those who left speedily became the firewood of those who remained, there are no apparent signs of decay" (*Colorado,* p. 119). Decay or not, by the time that Bowles and his party arrived, Montgomery had become just another of the many deserted mining towns of Colorado. The town was temporarily resurrected in 1881, when silver was discovered on the slopes of Mount Lincoln and nearby Mount Bross. The opera house to which Bowles alludes was completed in 1862. A reservoir built by the city of Colorado Springs now covers the site.

7. Mount Lincoln (14,297 feet), in the Mosquito Range, rises close behind Montgomery. Thought at one time to be the highest peak in the Colorado, it was named by the town fathers of Montgomery at a meeting in 1861 in honor of the president who had granted Colorado its territorial status.

8. Their camp on August 26 was located some three miles below Montgomery at the base of Mount Lincoln. Colfax and Bross "found less romantic, but more comfortable quarters at the house of Mr. Joseph H. Myers, in the town." W. R. Thomas, covering the event for the *News,* painted a vivid picture of the encampment. "Sloping gradually toward the creek, its background was a dark forest of pine, while opposite rose the rugged sides of Mount Lincoln, which on the coming morning we were to climb. White tents dotted the ground, and as the sun sank behind the western mountains, and the evening shadows began to gather, eight fires cast a glow of warmth and light around the camp. From tent to tent, from fire to fire, passed the cheerful members of the camping party" (September 3, 1868, p. 4).

9. Thomas of the *News* noted that "including Mr. Myers and Mr. Mullen, who had kindly volunteered as guides, there were thirteen who in Indian file wound their way up the trail, and after nearly three hours of steep and difficult climbing the whole party stood upon the summit of the mountain" (ibid.). The climb took place on Thursday, August 27.

10. While Bowles and his party gazed out at the scene described below, Schuyler Colfax, according to tradition, proposed to Ellen (Nellie) Wade. According to a another story picked up by David Lavender, "The view from the top . . . exhilarated William Bross to such an extent that he pulled the shivering group together and led

them in singing the Doxology. Caught up in their turn, the chorus spontaneously declared that the big (14,170 feet) hump to the south should evermore be known as Mount Bross, as it still is" (*The Rockies* [New York: Harper & Row, Publishers, 1968], p. 250). Though Lavender cites no source, such an action was very much in keeping with Bross's religious disposition; back home in Chicago he was known as Deacon Bross for his support of the Second Presbyterian Church.

11. The view from Mount Lincoln was a favorite of early visitors to Colorado. In 1873 Hayden noted that "the view from the summit of Mount Lincoln is wonderful in its extent. To the east, far distant, is distinctly seen Pike's Peak, with the contiguous ranges which border the east side of the park and extend northward toward Long's Peak. . . . Probably there is no portion of the world, accessible to the traveling public, where such a wilderness of lofty peaks can be seen within a single scope of the vision" (*Annual Report of the United States Geological and Geographical Survey of the Territories, Embracing Colorado, Being a Report of Progress of the Exploration for the Year 1873* [Washington: Government Printing Office, 1874], p. 40).

12. Mount Whitney, in the southern Sierras of California, has an elevation of 14,495 feet.

13. The single occupants were Joseph H. Myers and family, with whom Colfax and Bross spent the night of August 26.

14. Founded in 1859, Buckskin Joe was among Colorado's first mining camps. (Just how it came to be called Buckskin Joe has never been authoritatively established, though Professor Brewer claimed that it had been "named for an old mountaineer and explorer of that name, but the town dropped the last part of the name, and [it] is known simply as Buckskin" [*Rocky Mountain Letters,* p. 42].) By 1861 there were two hotels, fourteen stores, a bank building, and the first courthouse in Park County. By 1865 the mines began to give out, and by late 1866 the town was virtually empty. The county seat then passed to Fairplay. Brewer noted its desolation in 1869: "At present, the entire population is about twenty-five or thirty, not a single family, but only a few men who get a living by 'prospecting' for others or digging gold from the abandoned leads. The place is more nearly destroyed than Montgomery. There are perhaps forty or fifty houses and cabins standing—in various degrees of dilapidation—not counting the piles of logs which tell where houses once were. Gay signs tell of former billiard halls, barrooms, saloons, etc.—more modest ones enumerate more necessary articles kept for sale. The bank is in ruins, its books are kept

as a curiosity by one of those who remain" (ibid., p. 43). The town was renamed Laurette in 1860 (for two sisters, Laura and Jeanette Dodge), but the new name never took hold.

15. The *Rocky Mountain News*, September 3, 1868, p. 4, identifies Joseph Myers as the host.

16. The audience, the *Rocky Mountain News* reported, was "large and enthusiastic. . . . Mr. Colfax was never more eloquent, and was often interrupted by applause. . . . Gov. Bross, as he always does, gave the Democracy [*sic*] some facts on which to meditate, and by his fun, humor, and eloquence, often brought down the house" (ibid.).

17. The Bowles party crossed the Mosquito Range, presumably by way of Weston Pass (11,945 feet). From there, Colfax and Bross turned north to keep a speaking date at Oro City, a mining camp located in California Gulch near Leadville. The rest of the party moved on southeast to the Twin Lakes.

9. An Indian Scare—the Twin Lakes

1. On the morning of Thursday, August 27, with news of Indian depredations running wild in Denver, Frank Hall, as acting governor, decided that the Colfax party must be warned not to come home via Colorado City. Just where Bowles and party were encamped when they first received the news alluded to here is unclear, though presumably it was above Twin Lakes and on August 28. It is also unclear just who brought them the news. But the unfolding story, which Bowles narrates below, can be reconstructed from various accounts in the *Rocky Mountain News*.

At eight o'clock on the evening of August 28, W. R. Thomas reported that Ashley Franklin arrived in Breckenridge from Fairplay with news that "he had met the messenger sent by Secretary Hall, that the messenger brought news of terrible outrages near Denver, and that he had been fired into by Indians near Tarryall creek. Franklin himself saw the bullet hole in the saddle" (*Rocky Mountain News*, September 2, 1868, p. 4). That same night, about midnight, the mail arrived confirming Franklin's story.

Colfax and Bross were scheduled to speak that evening in Granite, a mining town southwest of Twin Lakes. "The first news of Indian troubles came in here . . . just before the speaking commenced and created for the time some excitement, but it was decided to let the speaking go on and talk of Indian scare afterwards" (ibid., September 12, 1868, p. 1).

2. During the summer of 1868, the coming of the railroad and all that it implied about the Indian's way of life occasioned increasing restlessness among the plains Indians. A series of incidents between Indians and settlers ensued that resulted in widespread calls for military protection. One such incident took place along the Front Range of Colorado, where a band of two hundred Arapahos were reported to be out raiding and stealing cattle. With Governor Hunt off in the mountains with Bowles and Colfax, Frank Hall was in charge as acting governor. His response, prompted by a rising tide of panic, was to send off a series of telegrams to General Philip Sheridan at Fort Leavenworth and to other senior officers informing them that the Indians were looting and killing in all directions and demanding the intervention of the military. Among his messages was one indicating that Speaker Colfax and his party were in imminent danger. Sheridan and his superior, William Tecumseh Sherman, who had command of the plains, wisely (as it turned out) expressed their skepticism. This did not deter Hall, who by August 31 was openly stating that the territory and the Indians were openly at war. Though the military remained unimpressed, other voices joined in the confusion. "To arms! To arms," trumpeted the *Colorado Chieftan,* published at Pueblo. "The red fiends are again on the warpath. The bloody scenes that have been witnessed for years past in our Territory are being re-enacted. Whole families are being murdered and scalped by these devils incarnate. The temporizing policy of the Government is felt to be inadequate to our protection."

It was at the height of this panic, with its calls to arm the local citizens, that Colfax and party, escorted by a band of friendly Utes, rode boldly into Denver. Still the scare went on, now with Colfax joining in the demand for the deployment of U.S. cavalry. Sheridan and Sherman continued to resist, for there were Indian problems in Kansas and on the plains to be dealt with, and their forces were already overextended. By mid-September 1868, three weeks after it had begun, the Indian scare of 1868 was over. See Athearn, "Colorado and the Indian War of 1868," pp. 42–51.

3. The messenger dispatched to warn the Colfax party by Frank Hall—the man seen by Ashley Franklin—was named Bonser. As Hall points out in his history of Colorado, "The messenger . . . to achieve some personal glory for himself, fabricated an account of his having encountered the hostiles en route, and been fired upon by them, but that he escaped without further harm than a bullet hole through his saddle, which he exhibited, though it turned out that he had not seen

an Indian on the way, but found a bottle of whiskey, the most of which had entered his person, and was then taking effect" (*History of the State of Colorado* 1:457).

4. Sue Matthews remembered that night vividly as well. "The night the message came about the Indians we were pretty scared. There were so many women in the party and scarcely any firearms. And some of the men didn't know how to fire anything except a match. But guards were set. D. C. Oakes was one of the guards. He was an Indian Agent and knew what to do and all about it. But in the night one of the guards got hungry and came to the mess chest to get something to eat. The lid to the chest dropped and made a noise like a pistol shot. You should have seen us all shell out, scantily clothed, with our hair hanging down our backs. We huddled together, thinking the Indians were upon us, expecting every minute to see them creeping from behind the trees. But there was no attack and we soon settled down again" (Hall, "Seventy Years Ago," p. 166).

5. Bowles was correct. Part of the Indian unrest may be attributed to the fact that Congress, preoccupied with the impeachment of Andrew Johnson, neglected to appropriate the funds called for to meet the government's obligations under the 1867 Treaty of Medicine Lodge, which established reservations in the Indian Territory for the Cheyennes, Arapahos, Kiowas, Commanches, and Kiowa-Commanches.

6. This particular comment, though unidentified, probably came in the fall of 1868, at a time when treaty violations, which included raids by bands of Cheyennes and Arapahos on isolated farms, persuaded Sherman that the Indians would have to be dealt with harshly. "Spite of Indian Peace Commissions, and all our efforts to keep the rascals quiet," he wrote on September 25, 1868, "they have broke out simply because they can make more by war than Peace. We must not let up this time, but keep it going till they are killed or humbled" (quoted in Robert G. Athearn, *William Tecumseh Sherman and the Settlement of the West* [Norman: University of Oklahoma Press, 1956], p. 224).

7. As noted above in note 1 of chapter 7, these Indian goods, under the control of Governor Hunt and Major Oakes, were intended for the Southern Utes.

8. The Twin Lakes are located twelve miles southwest of Leadville at the foot of Independence Pass (12,095 feet). Near at hand are Mount Elbert (14,433 feet) and Mount La Plata (14,336 feet), two of the highest mountains in the state. The lower lake covers some 1,525 acres, the upper 475.

9. The Sawatch Mountains of central Colorado are bordered on the

east by the Arkansas River. The name (which means "water of blue earth") has been variously spelled Sahwatch, Saguache, Sahawaych, and Sogoochi.

10. As noted above, Colfax and Bross had been speaking in California Gulch at Oro City. They brought with them an escort of Oro miners, the "Lake County boys," who would escort the party back to Fairplay in South Park.

11. Saturday and Sunday, August 29 and 30.

12. Bayard Taylor was ever mindful of the needs of his stomach; his Colorado narrative is filled with culinary references.

13. Though Dayton (as Twin Lakes was then called) was simply another collection of vacant cabins in 1868, it would become by the 1880s what George A. Crofutt, a subsequent visitor, described as "the most charming summer resort in Colorado."

10. From the Twin Lakes to Denver

1. Canyon City, settled in 1859, is located where the Arkansas River leaves the mountains. To the west lies the Grand Canyon of the Arkansas, which gave the town its name.

2. Colorado City on Fountain Creek, just west of the future site of Colorado Springs, was settled in August 1859. The present Colorado Springs was not laid out until July 1871. In 1917 Colorado Springs absorbed Colorado City.

3. Granite, seventeen miles south of Leadville, was the site of a short-lived placer discovery in 1860 and a second discovery in 1867. Shortly thereafter the *Rocky Mountain News* noted that "it's pleasantly situated, and with stores, hotels, and saloons, bears quite a business, sir." In 1872 the same paper reported that "Granite looks a little rusty, and most of the houses are for let." While at Granite, Sue Matthews recalled, the miners "took us to their sluice boxes and showed us how placer mining was done" (Mrs. Hall, "Seventy Years Ago," p. 165).

4. The town is Cache Creek, not Cash Creek. Bayard Taylor records that in 1866 it contained "three taverns, a store, a saloon, and some gulch mining" (*Colorado,* p. 133).

5. According to the *Rocky Mountain News*, September 5, 1868, p. 4, it was "a band of ten Utes."

6. Their encampment that evening (Monday, August 31) was at the head of Trout Creek. From there, the next day, the party crossed into South Park over Trout Creek Pass (9,346 feet), passed by the alkali

and salt deposits in the vicinity of Salt Creek, then turned north toward Fairplay.

7. Their noon encampment was at Buffalo Springs.

8. Sue Matthews recalled this particular event and its aftermath vividly.

> Just after we stopped for lunch, after entering South Park, we saw Indians circling around. The men said, "There are the Indians now," and they had all the wagons backed in together, so that in case of attack they could put the women within the circle for protection. Mr. Colfax said, "If the Indians do come, I'm going to kill you girls." But I knew he couldn't shoot and I said, "I think I would rather take my chances with the Indians." He was no shot—didn't know one end of a gun from the other. However, the Indians turned out to be friendly Utes who had come to take the place of the miners and escort us back to Denver. They all sat around and smoked the pipe of peace. We were glad we were not men, because they had to take that old dirty pipe in their mouths.
>
> That night Governor Hunt bought a beef for the Indians and they barbequed it right there. He also gave them sugar, which they liked very much. The worst of it, he got them to sing—you know they chant—and we couldn't get them to stop. They wanted to entertain us. . . .
>
> Part of the Indians came all the way back with us to Denver. I think there were twenty-five in all. Of course, Governor Hunt had to feed them. They would eat as long as they could hold it—they never saved anything. They were especially fond of biscuits and sugar." (Hall, "Seventy Years Ago," pp. 166–67)

9. Appropriately enough, they christened their encampment Camp Ute.

10. Daniel S. Witter had married Clara V. Matthews (1836–1914), the half sister of Schuyler Colfax, at South Bend, Indiana, on March 29, 1855. Four years later, Witter left wife, home, and friends to come to Colorado, where he purchased property in the Tarryall Mining District of South Park and for two years engaged in mining with tolerable success. He served in the first territorial legislature and as postmaster at Hamilton and in 1862 was appointed U.S. assessor of internal revenue by President Abraham Lincoln. That same year he brought his wife and two children (there would ultimately be eleven)

to Colorado. At the time of the Colfax visit, the Witters and their growing family made their home in Denver, in a house at Seventh and Larimer streets. Witter was also a major factor in Republican politics, serving as president of both the Denver Republican Club and the Grant and Colfax Club. Clara Witter recalled the 1868 journey in a 1910 sketch written for her children and later published as "Pioneer Life," *Colorado Magazine* 4 (December 1927): 172–73.

11. The Witters's baby was only six weeks old. On the trip her parents renamed her Nell in honor of Ellen Wade.

12. Following the death of her husband in the fall of 1822, Speaker Colfax's mother, the former Hannah Stryker (1805–72), married George Matthews (1809–74).

13. William Russell Thomas (1843–1914), a young reporter from Chicago and the nephew of William Bross (who introduced him to William Byers), became associate editor of the *Rocky Mountain News* in May 1867. Thomas, who had helped entertain Bayard Taylor during his visit of 1866, shortly thereafter married Byers's sister Elizabeth. The last ten years of his life were spent as a professor of history and economics at Colorado Agricultural College (now Colorado State University) (Perkins, *First Hundred Years,* pp. 294–95).

14. Uriah Martin Curtis (born c. 1837) was born in Illinois and raised in Missouri. As a teenager Curtis had run away from home and lived with the Utes, in whose language he soon became fluent enough to be sought after as an interpreter. When the agency for the Northern Ute bands opened at Hot Sulphur Springs in April 1863, Indian agent Simeon Whiteley appointed Curtis as his interpreter and sent him out to locate the Indians. Curtis helped negotiate a formal agreement (the Conejos treaty) with the Tebegauche Utes in October 1863, which in effect ceded Middle Park to the whites and put an end to Ute claims on the area. Unfortunately, the other Ute bands had not been consulted, and the Indian problem in Middle Park was left unresolved (Black, *Island in the Rockies,* pp. 44–47).

15. Henry Bergh (1811–88) was the founder and first president of the Society for the Prevention of Cruelty to Animals (1866) and a founder of the Society for the Prevention of Cruelty to Children (1875).

16. Sue Matthews, too, recalled that "Governor Hunt was a great hand at making flapjacks. He would put them on the skillet and turn them over by just flipping them up in the air. They dared me to try to do it. Of course I took the dare. But mine came down in a sand pile and nobody wanted to eat it" (Hall, "Seventy Years Ago," p. 165).

17. A similar account of the evening was recorded by William R.

Thomas for readers of the *News*. See *Rocky Mountain News*, September 5, 1868, p. 4.

18. Presumably this was near the hamlet of Grant on the North Fork of the South Platte.

19. The Via Mala is a narrow gorge of the Hinterrhein River in the Alps of eastern Switzerland with vertical cliffs of sixteen hundred feet.

20. The Garden of the Gods, a series of fantastically shaped reddish sandstone formations, are located just northwest of what is today Colorado Springs.

21. Bear Creek flows out of the mountains immediately west of Denver, through Bear Creek Canyon, and enters the plains near the present town of Morrison before flowing due east to the South Platte.

22. Sue Matthews Hall remembered the scene in precisely the same way. "On arriving back in Denver we must have looked a sight. One of the wheels of ex-Governor Evans' carriage had broken and they substituted a pole dragging on the ground. We had been two weeks without conveniences. I thought we would never get cleaned up" (Hall, "Seventy Years Ago," p. 167).

23. John Evans served as governor of the Colorado Territory from 1862 to 1865. He, along with William Byers, was largely responsible for the growth of Denver during the 1860s.

24. The allusion is to the Cherry Creek flood of May 19, 1864.

11. Mines, Mining and Miners

1. When Nathaniel P. Hill (1832–1900), a professor of chemistry at Brown University, arrived in Central City in 1864 at the invitation of a group of eastern capitalists who were considering purchasing mining properties in Gilpin County, he found most of the easily extracted surface gold had been removed and the town largely deserted. He made two additional trips in 1865, during which he again saw at firsthand the difficulty of reducing Colorado's "refractory" ores with the mining technology then available. Hill's pioneering contribution, the search for which took him to the smelting mills at Swansea in South Wales and to Germany, was a new and efficient process for extracting gold and silver. It led him to establish his own matting furnace, the Boston and Colorado Smelting Works, at the foot of Gregory Gulch at Black Hawk in 1867. Hill's success revived mining throughout the Gilpin area.

Hill's process can be described as follows: "First the new ores or mill tailings were roasted to drive off most of the sulfur in great noxious clouds of sulfur dioxide that clogged the narrow valley. Then the mineral was smelted in a reverberatory furnace, whose curvature distributed and focused heat to 1400 centigrade. Gold, silver, and copper sank to the bottom along with iron and copper sulfides, while the slag floated on the surface. The slag was skimmed and discarded, the rich copper 'matte' was tapped, cooled, and shipped to Swansea [in Wales] for additional refining into its constituent metals" (Abbott, Leonard, and McComb, *Colorado,* p. 85). Hill later turned to politics. He served as Black Hawk's mayor in 1871 and as senator from Colorado from 1879 to 1885. See also Taylor, *Colorado,* pp. 61–69; and "Nathaniel P. Hill Inspects Colorado: Letters Written in 1864," *Colorado Magazine* 33 (October 1956): 241–76.

2. The Equator Mine is located near Georgetown. According to Fossett's guidebook of 1879, "The Equator is a wonderfully large and rich vein, but has not been worked as steadily or extensively as its value warrants. This was the leading producer of Clear Creek county for a time in 1868. Up to 1869 the yield was $68,600. The ore sold at one to five hundred dollars a ton. The main shaft was carried down some 400 feet, but for reasons best known to its Chicago and Colorado owners, mining was not continued for years after 1870 except by tributors" (Frank Fossett, *Colorado: Its Gold and Silver Mines, Farms and Stock Ranges, and Health and Pleasure Resorts. Tourist's Guide to the Rocky Mountains* [New York: C. G. Crawford, 1879], p. 403).

3. The Hoosac Tunnel is the 4.7-mile railroad tunnel that penetrates the Hoosac Mountains of northwestern Massachusetts to connect the state to Williamstown and eastern New York. The Burleigh drill, the first successful pneumatic drill, was named after Charles Burleigh of Fitchburg, Massachusetts, who adapted the idea from a patent he purchased. Burleigh introduced his drill to the tunnel on November 1, 1866, where it was used successfully to complete the construction. The water-cooled drill reportedly weighed more than five hundred pounds and advanced a two-inch-diameter hole at two inches per minute to depths of up to thirteen feet, cutting drilling time by half. The Hoosac Tunnel, begun in 1854, took twenty-two years to complete and remained for half a century the longest railroad tunnel in the United States. Interestingly enough, Burleigh preceded Bowles to Denver that summer, arriving on July 18, the *Rocky Mountain News* reported, "with a view, perhaps, of introducing his machines to our Territory" (*News,* July 20, 1868, p. 4). He left again for the East on August 4, four days before Bowles and Colfax arrived.

4. Placer gold had been discovered on the Blue River in Summit

County on August 10, 1859, leading to the organization of Breckenridge the next year.

5. The quotation is from the *Rocky Mountain News,* September 22, 1868, p. 4. That summer Thomas authored a series of columns entitled "Among the Miners."

6. The series of camps and the town that composed the Granite District sprung into being in the early 1860s with the discovery of gold along the bed and bars of the Arkansas River.

7. Bowles is undoubtedly referring to two mines (Elizabethtown and Baldy) near Cimmaron, New Mexico, which began operation in 1867. Expectations were exaggerated, and after a few years both mines had petered out. Cimmaron is located "just over the southern border" of Colorado in Colfax County, New Mexico.

12. The Agriculture of Colorado: Conclusion

1. At 6,228 feet, Mount Washington is the highest elevation in New Hampshire's White Mountains.

2. The Arkansas River makes its way across the plains toward Kansas through bottomland, which produces one of Colorado's richest agriculture areas.

3. The Fontaine Qui Bouille (the "Boiling Fountain"), which originally received its name from the hot springs at what would later become Manitou Springs, just west of Colorado Springs, originates near Pikes Peak and flows south to meet the Arkansas at Pueblo.

4. In late August 1860, Oliver Loving (1812–67) and his partner, the legendary Charles Goodnight (1836–1929), who accompanied him partway, drove a herd of cattle from northern Texas to the new goldfields at the mouth of Cherry Creek (the site of Denver), where Loving sold the herd in the spring of 1861. Some seven years later, in 1866, Goodnight and Loving blazed the first major cattle trail through Colorado (a route later known as the Western Trail), when they drove some two thousand steers through Comanche and Kiowa country and over the Raton Range to Denver. Texas cattle often carried with them a type of tick-induced bovine typhoid (known as Texas Fever or Spanish Fever) to which they were immune but which caused devastation among local herds. Colorado and a number of other states eventually passed laws banning or restricting the introduction of Texas cattle. Kansas banned Texas cattle in 1859. Nevertheless, the Colorado cattle industry was subsequently begun with Texas longhorns. See Sue

Flanagan, "Charles Goodnight in Colorado," *Colorado Magazine* 43 (Winter 1966): 1–21.

5. Bayard Taylor had noted that Golden City, which served as territorial capital from 1864 to 1867, before losing that honor to Denver, possesses "several substantial stores, a school-house, two flour-mills (Clear Creek furnishing excellent water-power), and a manufactory of fire-brick. . . . I visited the veins of fire-clay and coal, which are found in conjunction, within half a mile of Golden City. The clay is found in large beds of a chocolate color and greasy texture." Like Bowles, Taylor predicted that "from this time forward it will rise in importance" (*Colorado,* p. 49).

6. Louis Agassiz (1807–73), Swiss-born zoologist and geologist and perhaps the single most important figure in contemporary American science, had joined Harvard's new Lawrence Scientific School as a professor of zoology in 1848, having already established a major reputation for zoological and glacial research in Europe. In the summer of 1868, Agassiz, who had never before been west of Burlington, Iowa, journeyed to the Rocky Mountains to study glaciation and to observe the progress of the Union Pacific Railroad. He arrived in Denver on September 6, in the company of New York senator Roscoe Conkling and Massachusetts congressman Samuel Hooper. Agassiz's visit to Wyoming, on which he was accompanied by General William Tecumseh Sherman, was cut short by poor health. Agassiz had visited Brazil in the spring of 1865. The result of that trip was *A Journey in Brazil* (1868), written mainly by his wife.

7. Those eastern notables included Roscoe Conkling (1829–88), the senator from New York; Samuel Hooper (1808–75), the congressman from Massachusetts; and Ward Hunt (1810–86), justice on the New York court of appeals.

BIBLIOGRAPHY

Primary Sources

Bowles, Samuel. *Across the Continent: A Summer's Journey to the Rocky Mountains, the Mormons, and the Pacific States, with Speaker Colfax*. Springfield, Mass.: Samuel Bowles & Company, 1865.

——— *Our New West: Records of Travel Between the Mississippi River and the Pacific Ocean*. Hartford, Conn.: Hartford Publishing, 1869.

——— *The Pacific Railroad—Open. How to Go: What to See*. Boston: Fields, Osgood, 1869

——— *The Switzerland of America: A Summer Vacation in the Parks and Mountains of Colorado*. Springfield, Mass.: Samuel Bowles & Company, 1869

Brewer, William H. *Rocky Mountain Letters, 1869*. Edited by Edmund B. Rogers. Denver: Colorado Mountain Club, 1930.

Bross, William. *Address of the Hon. William Bross, Lieutenant-Governor of Illinois, on the Resources of the Far West, and the Pacific Railway*. New York: J. W. Amerman, 1866

Byers, William N. Unpublished diary for 1868. Western History Department, Denver Public Library.

Dodge, Grenville H. *How We Built the Union Pacific and Other Railway Papers and Addresses*. [New York?: 1910?]

Goldrick, Owen J. "The First School in Denver." *Colorado Magazine* (March 1929): 72–74.

Gregg, Isa Stearns. "Reminiscences of Isa Hunt Stearns." *Colorado Magazine* 26 (July 1949): 183–93.

Hall, Mrs. Frank. "Seventy Years Ago—Recollections of a Trip Through the Colorado Mountains with the Colfax Party in 1868. Edited by LeRoy R. Hafen. *Colorado Magazine* 15 (September 1938): 161–68.

Hayden, F. V. *Annual Report of the United States Geological and Geographical Survey of the Territories, Embracing Colorado, Be-*

ing a Report of Progress of the Exploration for the Year 1873. Washington: Government Printing Office, 1974.

——— *Ninth Annual Report . . . of the Terrorities*. Washington: Government Printing Office, 1877.

Hill, Nathaniel P. "Nathaniel P. Hill Inspects Colorado: Letters Written in 1864." *Colorado Magazine* 33 (October 1956): 241–76.

Keplinger, L. W. "The First Ascent of Long's Peak." *Collections of the Kansas State Historical Society* 14 (1918): 340–53.

Oakes, D. C. "The Man Who Wrote the Guide Book." *The Trail* 2 (December 1909): 7–15.

Oakes, Daniel C., and Stephen W. Smith. *History of the Gold Discoveries on the South Platte River. By Luke Tierney. To Which Is Appended a Guide of the Route, by Smith and Oaks. [sic]* Pacific City, Iowa: A. Thomson, 1859.

Rocky Mountain News 9–10 (July 4–September 23, 1868).

Sheridan, Philip. *Personal Memoirs of P. H. Sheridan*. 2 vols. New York: Charles L. Webster, 1888.

Taylor, Bayard. *Colorado: A Summer Trip*. New York: G. P. Putnam and Son, 1867.

Willard, James F., and Colin B. Goodykoontz, eds. *Experiments in Colorado Colonization, 1869–1872: Selected Documents Relating to the German Colonization Company and Chicago-Colorado, St. Louis-Western, and Southwestern Colonies*. Boulder: University of Colorado, 1926.

Witter, Mrs. Daniel. "Pioneer Life." *Colorado Magazine* 4 (December 1927): 165–74.

SECONDARY SOURCES

Abbott, Carl. "Boom State and Boom City: Stages in Denver's Growth." *Colorado Magazine* 50 (Summer 1973): 207–30.

Abbott, Carl, Stephen J. Leonard, and David McComb. *Colorado: A History of the Centennial State*. Boulder: Colorado Associated University Press, 1982.

Athearn, Robert G. *The Coloradans*. Albuquerque: University of New Mexico Press, 1976.

——— "Colorado and the Indian War of 1868." *Colorado Magazine* 33 (January 1956): 42–51.

——— *William Tecumseh Sherman and the Settlement of the West*. Norman: University of Oklahoma Press, 1956.

Black, Robert C., III. *Island in the Rockies: The History of Grand County, Colorado to 1930*. Boulder: Pruett Publishing, 1969.

Breck, Allen Du Pont. *The Episcopal Church in Colorado, 1860–1963*. Denver: Big Mountain Press, 1963.

Buehler, William. *Roof of the Rockies: A History of Colorado Mountaineering*. Evergreen, Colo.: Cordillera Press, 1986.

Castro, Jess Augustin. "Alexander Cameron Hunt: Colorado Territorial Governor, 1867–1869." Master's thesis, University of Denver, 1957.

Collins, George W. "Colorado's Territorial Secretaries." *Colorado Magazine* 42 (Summer 1966): 185–208.

Covington, James Warren. "Federal Relations with the Colorado Utes, 1861–1865." *Colorado Magazine* 23 (October 1951): 257–66.

Darrah, William Culp. *Powell of the Colorado* Princeton, N.J.: Princeton University Press, 1951.

Davidson, Levette Jay. "O. J. Goldrick, Pioneer Journalist." *Colorado Magazine* 8 (January 1936).

Dayton, Abraham C. *Last Days of Knickerbocker Life in New York*. New York: G. P. Putnam's Sons, 1897.

Dempsey, Stanley, and James E. Fell, Jr. *Mining the Summit: Colorado's Ten Mile District, 1869–1960*. Norman: University of Oklahoma Press, 1986.

Dickinson, Anna E. *A Ragged Register (of People[,] Places and Opinions)*. New York: Harper & Brothers, Publishers, 1879.

Eberhart, Perry. *Guide to the Colorado Ghost Towns and Mining Camps*. Denver: Sage Books, 1959.

Fell, James E., Jr. *Ores to Metals: the Rocky Mountain Smelting Industry*. Lincoln: University of Nebraska Press, 1979.

Flanagan, Sue. "Charles Goodnight in Colorado." *Colorado Magazine* 43 (Winter 1966): 1–21.

Fossett, Frank. *Colorado: Its Gold and Silver Mines, Farms and Stock Ranges, and Health and Pleasure Resorts. Tourist's Guide to the Rocky Mountains*. New York: C. G. Crawford, 1879.

Gerber, Richard A. "Liberal Republicanism, Reconstruction, and Social Order: Samuel Bowles as a Test Case." *New England Quarterly* 4 (September 1972): 393–407.

Gilliland, Mary Ellen. *Summit: A Gold Rush History of Summit County, Colorado* Silverthorne, Colo.: Alpenrose Press, 1980.

Greever, William S. *The Bonanza West: The Story of the Western Mining Rushes, 1848–1900*. Norman: University of Oklahoma Press, 1963.

Hafen, LeRoy H. "Ghost Town—Tarryall and Hamilton." *Colorado Magazine* 4 (July 1933): 137–43.

Halaas, David F. "Frontier Journalism in Colorado." *Colorado Magazine* 44 (Summer 1967): 185–203.

Hall, Frank. *History of the State of Colorado*. 4 vols. Chicago: Blakely Printing, 1889–95.

Harrison, Louise C. *Empire and the Berthoud Pass*. Denver: Big Mountain Press, 1964.

Hayden, F. V. *The Great West: Its Attractions and Resources*. Bloomington, Ill.: Charles R. Brodix, 1880.

History of the City of Denver, Arapahoe County, and Colorado. Chicago: O. L. Baskin, 1880.

Hollister, Ovando J. *Life of Schuyler Colfax*. New York: Funk & Wagnalls, 1886.

——— *The Mines of Colorado*. Springfield, Mass.: Samuel Bowles & Company, 1867.

Hooker, Richard. *The Story of an Independent Newspaper: One Hundred Years of the Springfield Republican*. New York: Macmillan, 1924.

Horner, John W. *Silver Town*. Caldwell, Idaho: Caxton Printers, 1950.

Hutton, Paul Andrew. "Phil Sheridan's Frontier." *Montana: The Magazine of Western History*. 38 (Winter 1988): 17–31.

Larson, T. A. *History of Wyoming*. Lincoln: University of Nebraska Press, 1965.

Lavender, David. *The Rockies*. New York: Harper & Row, Publishers, 1968.

Lipsey, Julia. *Governor Hunt of Colorado Territory: His Life and His Family*. Colorado Springs: J. J. Lipsey, Western Books, 1960.

McConnell, Virginia. *Bayou Salado: The Story of South Park*. Denver: Sage Books, 1966.

McIlvanie, Mabel, ed. *Reminiscences of Chicago during the Forties and Fifties*. Chicago: Lakeside Press, 1913.

——— *Reminiscences of Chicago during the Great Fire*. Chicago: Lakeside Press, 1915.

Merriam, George S. *The Life and Times of Samuel Bowles*. 2 vols. New York: Century 1885.

Mumey, Nolie. *Prof Oscar* [sic] *J. Goldrick and His Denver, Together with His Address Delivered on the Early History of Denver, July 4, 1876*. Denver: Sage Books, 1959.

Noel, Thomas J. "All Hail the Denver Pacific: Denver's First Railroad." *Colorado Magazine* 50 (Spring 1973): 91–116.

Perkins, Robert L. *The First Hundred Years: An Informal History of Denver and the Rocky Mountain News*. Garden City, N.Y.: Doubleday, 1959.

Richardson, Albert D. *Across the Mississippi: From the Great River to the Great Ocean*. Hartford, Conn.: American Publishing, 1867.

Rockwell, Wilson. *The Utes, a Forgotten People*. Denver: Sage Books, 1956.

Shinn, Marie M. "Sidelights on Nineteenth Century Colorado History as Revealed by the Letters of Frank Hall." Master thesis, University of Denver, 1960.

Smith, Willard H. *Schuyler Colfax: The Changing Fortunes of a Political Idol*. Indianapolis: Indiana Historical Bureau, 1952.

Sprague, Marshall. *The Great Gates: The Story of the Rocky Mountain Passes*. Boston: Little, Brown, 1964.

Spring, Agnes Wright. *Colorado Charley, Wild Bill's Pard*. Boulder: Pruett Publishing, 1968.

Stegner, Wallace. *Beyond the Hundredth Meridian: John Wesley Powell and the Second Opening of the West*. Boston: Houghton Mifflin, 1954.

Thomas, Lately. *Delmonico's: A Century of Splendor*. Boston: Houghton Mifflin, 1967.

Turner, Wallace B. "Frank Hall: Colorado Journalist, Public Servant, and Historian." *Colorado Magazine* 53 (Fall 1976): 328–51.

Utley, Robert M. *The Indian Frontier of the American West, 1846–1890*. Albuquerque: University of New Mexico Press, 1984.

Waters, Frank. *The Colorado*. New York: Rinehart, 1946.

Watson, Elmo Scott. "The Indian Wars and the Press, 1866–1867." *Journalism Quarterly* 17 (December 1940): 301–12.

Weisner, Stephen G. *Embattled Editor: The Life of Samuel Bowles*. Lanham, Md.: University Press of America, 1986.

Wendt, Lloyd. *Chicago Tribune: The Rise of a Great American Newspaper*. Chicago: Rand McNally, 1979.

Yount, Charles A. *William Bross, 1813–1890*. Lake Forest, Ill.: Lake Forest College, 1940.

INDEX